T0328933

Managing Public Services

This book explores innovations in public management, including establishing a corporate vision, strategizing an organization and change management.

Chapters provide a valuable frame of reference for the 21st-century manager of public services by assessing the renewal of existing practices such as strategic costing, performance management, digitization and procurement and innovations in management practices, including branding, Lean Management, resilience and risk management. The book suggests that, as the management of public services is imbued with financial, social, economic and political uncertainties, management needs to be flexible and responsive to new ideas and practices to fulfil its purpose. This book ultimately supports the reflective manager, those who think about their job and are open to new ideas on how their job can be done better, by revisiting existing practices and examining innovations in public management.

Enriched with real-life cases and thought-provoking discussion questions, this is the ideal textbook for reflective, open-minded advanced students of public management and actual, or aspiring, reflective managers in public services.

Irvine Lapsley is director of IPSAR at the University of Edinburgh Business School, UK. He is editor of *Financial Accountability and Management* and chair of the EIASM Public Sector Conference.

Ola Mattisson is senior lecturer in strategy and public management at the School of Economics and Management at Lund University, Sweden.

Managing Public Services

Making Informed Choices

Edited by
Irvine Lapsley and Ola Mattisson

Routledge
Taylor & Francis Group

LONDON AND NEW YORK

First published 2022
by Routledge
2 Park Square, Milton Park, Abingdon, Oxon OX14 4RN

and by Routledge
605 Third Avenue, New York, NY 10158

Routledge is an imprint of the Taylor & Francis Group, an informa business

British Library Cataloguing-in-Publication Data
A catalogue record for this book is available from the British Library

Library of Congress Cataloging-in-Publication Data
Names: Lapsley, Irvine, editor. | Mattisson, Ola, editor.
Title: Managing public services : making informed choices / edited by Irvine Lapsley and Ola Mattisson.
Description: Abingdon, Oxon ; New York, NY : Routledge, 2022. |
Includes bibliographical references and index.
Identifiers: LCCN 2021024314
Subjects: LCSH: Public administration--Decision making. |
Public administration--Evaluation.
Classification: LCC JF1525.D4 M354 2022 | DDC 352.3--dc23
LC record available at https://lccn.loc.gov/2021024314

ISBN: 978-0-367-72325-5 (hbk)
ISBN: 978-0-367-72324-8 (pbk)
ISBN: 978-1-003-15438-9 (ebk)

DOI: 10.4324/9781003154389

Typeset in Times New Roman
by Taylor & Francis Books

Contents

vi   *Contents*

Figures

Tables

Boxes

Contributors

Deborah Agostino is Associate Professor of Management Accounting at Politecnico di Milano. She is a core faculty member of MIP – Graduate School of Business, where she teaches financial and management accounting in executive and post-graduate courses. She is a member of the scientific committee of the EIASM Public Sector Conference. She published over 50 contributions in academic journals and conference proceedings on the subject of performance measurement and management in public sector and cultural institutions.

Anders Anell is professor in Business Administration at Lund University School of Economics and Management. Anell's research focus on governance and management in health care services, with a particular interest in incentives and motivation, payment systems, performance measurement and management, person-centeredness and primary care. He has published several books, reports and articles in scientific journals. He has worked as a consultant and advisor for a number of Swedish and international organizations.

Michela Arnaboldi, Ph.D., is Full Professor of Accounting Finance and Control at Politecnico di Milano. She is Director of the PhD Programme in Management Economics and Industrial Engineering. She is coordinator of Urbanscope, the interdepartmental Lab of Politecnico di Milano on the use of analytics for decision making. She is author of over 70 papers published on national and international journals and conference proceedings.

Jon Bertilsson, Ph.D. and senior lecturer in marketing, is a brand and consumer researcher at the Department of Business Administration, Lund University, Sweden. He conducts consumer cultural research of consumption practices, with a particular focus on brands. With Katie Sullivan and Jens Rennstam, he is working in a project on brand orientation in public sector organizations.

Mikael Hellström is Senior Lecturer at Department of Business Administration, Lund University School of Economics and Management. As a member of a local research unit at the School (KEFU), he is engaged in and has completed many different research projects and is the author of many books and articles on management. He specializes in organization, leadership and management control in public organizations.

Jörgen Hettne is Professor of Business Law and Head of Department at the Department of Business Law, Lund University School of Economics and Management. He is also Director of the Centre for European Studies at Lund University. His research interests are mainly in the field of European Union's constitutional law and issues relating to the internal market and competition policy, in particular state monopolies, public procurement and state aid law.

Stein Kleppestø is Senior Lecturer at Department of Business Administration, Lund University School of Economics and Management. He is currently focusing on exploring what Strategic thinking might mean in an increasingly more complex and uncertain world and how the ability to deal with complexity can be developed in management students and managers.

Hans Knutsson is a senior lecturer at the School of Economics and Management, Lund University. He has published articles on strategic management, benchmarking and competitive tendering, all relating to the public sector. Empirical issues of interest span social welfare reforms and public procurement with a special focus on local government and municipalities.

Irvine Lapsley is Professor of Accounting Emeritus and Director of the Institute of Public Sector Accounting Research at the University of Edinburgh Business School. He is an Honorary Professor at Queen's University Belfast and a Visiting Professor at NTNU Trondheim. He is a Joint Editor of Financial Accountability & Management and Chair of the EIASM Public Sector Conference.

Jonas Ledendal is a senior lecturer in business law at the School of Economics and Management at Lund University. The main focus of his research is law and digital transformation, especially automated decision-making, and access to data and privacy in the public sector.

Ola Mattisson is a senior lecturer at the School of Economics and Management, Lund University. He is the author of several books and articles on strategy and public management. His research interest is directed towards strategy and management control in both public and private contexts with a special focus on competition and cooperation.

Ulf Ramberg is Associate Professor at Department of Business Administration, Lund University School of Economics and Management. He is engaged in many research projects as research director for a local government research unit at the School (KEFU) and the author of several books and articles on management. He specializes in public management, local government cooperation, strategy in local government, public leadership, and performance measurement.

Jens Rennstam is Associate Professor at the Department of Business Administration, Lund University, Sweden. His research interests include organizational control, materiality in organizations, practice theory, gender and sexuality in organizations and branding in public organizations.

Katie Sullivan, Ph.D. University of Utah, is an assistant professor in the Department of Communication at the University of Colorado, Colorado Springs. Katie's research concerns the role of branding in contemporary professional life and diversity and inclusion, particularly the intersections between professionalization, gender and embodiment.

Anna Thomasson is a senior lecturer in Business Administration at the School of Economics and Management and Lund University. In her research Anna mainly focuses on issues related to governance and organization of public sector services, among them innovation, digitalization, collaboration and corporatization.

Section one

Introduction

1 Introduction

Irvine Lapsley and Ola Mattisson

Managing public services

Managing Public Services: Making Informed Choices stems from the perception that public organizations and public managers are facing increasing challenges and growing complexities. Effective public organizations and competent public managers are crucial in such a period of transition, both to fulfil the ambitions of public policy and to maintain public trust in the governance of public institutions. Still, even if they do not function perfectly, or lack potential for improvement, public institutions generally do function and deliver a wide range of services. However, such functioning receives little attention from external stakeholders and the media. An ordinary day at the office simply does not trigger public interest in the same way as mistakes or examples of the mismanagement of public resources do. The daily activities of the government at all levels are performed with competence by officials committed to providing public services for society.

At a time when support is strongly needed, this book aims to support those with an interest in public-service organizations in their endeavours to develop services and improve public governance. Effective management within a system of separated powers and infinite needs entails intellectual and practical challenges that are extraordinary among modern industrial democracies. The purpose of this book is to educate and support managers in dealing with these challenges and scholars who undertake research in effective public services.

Within an organization, managers in different positions at different levels are involved in leading activities. They are the management of the organization. In general, the management of an organization is accountable for meeting at least three different demands: efficiency, legitimacy and the ability to innovate and change.

The demand for *efficiency* comes from the fact that an organization never exists for its own purposes. An organization is created for a reason, and it has a purpose that specifies what should be achieved and what type of values should be created, both for the principals (people or organizations) that have created it and for other stakeholders that support or depend upon it. Ultimately, an organization is efficient when it meets its purpose and delivers the expected values to its principals and other stakeholders, within the current circumstances. It is worth noting that efficiency should not be perceived in a single-dimensional (i.e. monetary) way. In commercial settings, efficiency is normally defined in monetary terms as a return on investment or as low costs. However, efficiency is a broader concept that includes delivering all the values that are expected from an organization, for all the stakeholders involved. Therefore, in public-sector organizations, an

DOI: 10.4324/9781003154389-2

evaluation of efficiency is multifaceted and complex in terms of the resources used and the results of activities. Regardless of the type of organization, it is a crucial task for management to manage resources and ensure the desired outcome of the organization's activities – that is, to seek efficiency.

The second demand of management is *legitimacy*. Organizations need trust and support from their principals as well as from all the other stakeholders involved. People do not only seek the delivery of products or services; they also seek a relationship with a counterpart they trust and respect. Building this kind of relationship is normally a demanding and time-consuming process, and one that can easily be ruined due to scandal or mismanaged relations with an important stakeholder. In recent decades, stakeholder relations have become more complicated as increased attention has been given to stakeholders positioned further "away" from an organization. Considerations about procurement and supply are becoming more complex due to the increased public attention and focus on issues that stretch far outside the organization, such as issues about environmental and social sustainability.

The third management task is to maintain and develop the *ability to innovate, adapt and change*. No organization operates in a vacuum, as all of an organization's activities are based on interactions with others. These interactions can be influenced by global trends or events, as well as by strictly local, limited occurrences. In both cases, inter- actions constitute the conditions for an organization. Therefore, it is a vital task for management to develop and maintain the organization's ability to innovate and change in order to adapt to external changes. Without this process continually occurring, there is a risk of misalignment between what is expected of the organization and what it is actually doing.

All three demands are relevant for managers and aspiring managers of public organi- zations who are facing practical challenges in their daily activities. The literature contains a great variety of tools and concepts that offer help and solutions for managers in solving the most complicated problems. However, reality is seldom so nicely organised. Real challenges do not usually align with book descriptions, and the tools provided often do not have the intended effects. Therefore, dealing with the three demands of management requires analytical, critical thinking and an ability to refine these thoughts into convincing argumentation for well-balanced managerial actions. This book offers help in under- standing and reviewing the applicability of certain convincing managerial concepts, espe- cially for public-sector services. Managers today face a growing challenge. A multitude of promising concepts are available on the general level but need to be applied for a specific purpose in a specific organizational setting. This tension brings greater complexity to managerial processes and causes extensive uncertainty for decision-makers. In effect, the complexity of decision-making requires a reflective manager capable of expert judgement. This needs the ability to be decisive. This, in turn, depends on the manager being analytical and critical, with a nuanced understanding and awareness of the situational context for the decision. This is the essence of "reflection-in-action" as discussed below.

An uncertain environment brings challenges into supplying public services

In order to be – or aspire to be – the manager of an organization that delivers public services, an individual must comply with the requirements set forth previously. It is necessary to create structures and systems that enable the organization to meet the requirements for efficiency; legitimacy and an ability to innovate, adapt and change.

Next, concerns with uncertainty arise due to the continual evolution of and changes in external factors. The faster and more extensive these changes are, the more complicated it becomes for a manager to make decisions and act in the interests of the organization. An individual decision-maker must take a stance on several uncertainties that may affect other dimensions of the decision, which is a demanding task. A fundamental idea within this book is that a public organization's situation undergoes extensive changes at high speed, which creates a high degree of uncertainty. The signals that an organization must act on are increasingly ambiguous and variable. Managers' situations encompass increasingly complex uncertainties due to several different factors, which are discussed below.

Being part of a political structure always results in uncertainties. The politicians who direct an organization's activities must conform with the needs and currents that exist at different levels in society. Long-term political decision-making is dependent on (planned) terms of office. Although these can be stable, the development over the last two decades indicates a changed political landscape with increased fragmentation, greater attention to single issues and increased short-term settlements within limited parts of activities. Thus, the basis for governing and leading public organizations is constantly changing. Global trends, as well as more individual local events, can occur suddenly and clearly characterise the governing policy that is implemented. Furthermore, these uncertainties can occur in both the interaction between political levels and the interaction between politics and execution. Disruptions of this kind can create room for opportunism on the part of individual actors to create temporary benefits, at the expense of long-term development. What was a sure factor in the foreground yesterday can be an eventuality in the background today. For public managers, this kind of change creates an extremely uncertain situation in which to make decisions and initiate executive measures. In addition to the risk of contributing to slower processes, swings of this kind can create ambiguities about influence, and thus about accountability issues as well.

Another noticeable uncertainty facing public managers is the balance between a public organization's mission and the resources that are available for the execution of this mission. Public assignments are determined based on what are perceived to be the general needs in society, whereas available financial resources can vary greatly. Uncertainty about financial resources introduces difficulty into planning for capacity, programmes and investments. Public managers must then make decisions to operate, implement and deliver professionally in an environment with uncertain access to resources. We have seen that international financial crises have had significant consequences for the scope of public services. Perhaps the most obvious of these is the financial crisis of 2008, which resulted in extensive austerity programmes in many countries, in acute forms. In addition to reducing financial commitments, such programmes reduce public organizations themselves in the form of, for example, personnel and physical resources. Today, the public sector is still characterised by savings and restraint. Managers in public organizations are in a situation in which the needs always exceed the available resources, and the needs are constantly growing to meet both political and public expectations. For all managers, this prioritization situation creates uncertainty about the extent to which there is room to develop capacities and what the priorities should be.

In addition to the need to comply with the political agenda and the resources available, managers of public organizations have been faced with a separate set of challenges in the form of the climate crisis. These challenges have a profound impact, as they affect everyone on a global level, far beyond what an individual or organization can influence or affect at any level. At the same time, there is an imperative for sustainability, which requires attention and compliance from public organizations. There are requirements (expectations) for public organizations to act as role models and to lead the development towards increased sustainability. However, the execution of sustainability requires difficult trade-offs. On the one hand, it can be difficult to know what the right decision is in such a complex environment. On the other hand, each decision is associated with prioritization, and it can be difficult to obtain support from other stakeholders for an effort towards sustainability. Overall, public managers act in uncertain circumstances in which their professional decisions are largely dependent on arenas within which they have neither influence nor transparency, while they are simultaneously forced to act and to relate to what is happening.

Thus, a public manager must deal with several structural uncertainties. Moreover, certain unexpected events and crises have an extensive impact on society, at all levels. We have seen how the migration crisis arose in Europe, with consequences that will continue to be felt for several years to come. We have also heard how forest fires have paralyzed communities in the United States and Australia. Furthermore, the current global pandemic has and will continue to have far-reaching effects. Crises of this kind place great strain on public organizations. These events have direct consequences that must be handled by public organizations when people need support urgently. However, there are also indirect consequences, such as unemployment, lack of access to public transport, lack of availability of healthcare and more. In general, public managers carry extensive responsibilities and must act within a context of great uncertainty, with no obvious tools or quick fixes to turn to. Instead, every situation must be assessed on its own grounds and be dealt with accordingly. This task calls for a public manager with an analytical mind who is willing to experiment and seek new ways of acting.

The reflective manager is needed

There is a relentless need for public-sector bodies to become more efficient and to demonstrate this efficiency to external stakeholders. The focus on "more with less" has become a mantra in the contemporary operating environment of public services. In this uncertain environment, public-sector management needs to be responsive and flexible towards new ideas in order to fulfil its purpose. Even a manager with the ability to adapt quickly to unpredictable changes in circumstances may be side-tracked by the complexity of the latest managerial fads.

The *reflective approach* to decision-making emerged in the works of Dewey (1933) in his book *How We Think*. This work on the 'reflective mind' in education was followed by a series of studies on the reflective mind in education (this includes Korthagen, 1985; Mezirow, 1998; Taggart and Wilson, 2005), in psychology (Boyd and Fales, 1983; Thiele, 2000; Tiberius, 2008; Fischhoff, 2013) and to all professions (Schön, 1983). But, for this book, we add to and enhance the stream of management literature on 'reflection-in-action' (Gosling and Mintzberg, 2003; Dane and Pratt, 2007; Yanow and Tsoukas, 2009; Nannaka et al., 2014; Shotter and Tsoukas, 2014).

The general management literature contains a vast flow of concepts, models and tools recommended to managers facing problems (Brunsson, 2017). Many of these concepts are generic, in the sense that it is claimed that they are applicable in any type of context, regardless of the original source. This book discusses several examples of such concepts, including vision, strategizing, change management, Lean Management and performance management. All of these concepts represent management ideas with the seductive power of providing benefits and solutions to deal with practical problems. In some cases, such designs are specific to or have been adapted for public-sector organizations. Although such concepts seldom originate from public-sector organizations, it may be claimed that versions of these concepts have been adapted to and are suitable for this sector (Agger Nielsen, Wæraas and Dahl, 2020). Public-sector managers have a long list of potential tools they need to decide upon when selecting the appropriate means to achieve a given end. Brunsson (2006) describes this process as one of problems and solutions seeking each other out within organizational reforms. One source of problems is the ongoing tension between the way an organization is presented and the way in which it actually operates. An organization may be described as (or a situation wished to be) working consistently towards a definite set of goals under the control of the management. However, this is seldom the case in real-life practice, and it is known that organizations are characterised by a higher degree of ambiguity, difficulty in mobilising resources and processes that are less controlled by management (Brunsson, 2006).

This gap triggers management to call for a diverse set of techniques in order to develop the ability to plan, steer and control. Such requirements constitute a set of problems that must be met by many solutions. In recent decades, various managerial concepts and techniques have been proposed as unique tools to support leadership and management in directing activities within the organization. Such concepts have also been strongly proposed by consultants offering their services based on these techniques (Wright, 2019). Fads based on the latest management trends have also been promoted. For public organizations that are facing difficult decisions, aligning with the current trend can be a strategy to avoid opposition and critique. By following what is standard in the sector, a decision-maker can gain a shield against mismanagement complaints. The problem is that these techniques often do not live up to their promise, causing new problems and triggering new management initiatives. Nevertheless, by constantly following what is considered to be the latest knowledge, management is perceived as modern, updated and successful (or, at least, not making unique mistakes). This ongoing implementation of new management ideas represents a continuous search for algorithms or recipes that provide a complete solution. However, this kind of repetitive mechanical implementation of management ideas is caused by a general urge to take action, rather than the actual applicability of the solution. Without proper analysis and planning, there is a risk that the implementation will be harmful, and the intended outcome will not be achieved. The managers in such a case might appear to be knowledgeable, both individually and as a team, but their actions will result in potentially severe consequences for the organization.

Critical voices have been raised against the constant application of new management ideas as a replacement for seriously considering the fundamental assumptions behind their implementation of managerial concepts. Implementing these concepts is never as simple, rational or safe as it may seem at first glance. Such techniques cannot be used as rationally as the theories behind them may stipulate, resulting in tension between the ideal situation and what is possible in practice. To counteract ill-considered repetitions of mistakes, continuous learning and development are required on both the individual and collective level.

This need for development requires "reflective practitioners", that is, people performing reflection-in-action on an individual level. Reflection-in-action involves:

on-the-spot surfacing, criticising, restructuring, and testing of initiative understanding of experienced phenomena; often it takes the form of reflective conversion
with the situation.

(Schön, 1983: 241–2)

Instead of optimising what is seen on the surface, managers need to take a step back
and flexibly and intuitively draw on their practical knowledge without mechanistically
applying given models. Reflection may help managers to analyse their actions critically
in order to improve their management practice. In Latin, the word *reflect* means "turn
back" and suggests that attention first be turned inward in order to subsequently be
turned outward to see things differently. Gosling and Mintzberg (2003) differentiate
between 'window people' and 'mirror people'. Window people see an image as it is and
see nothing beyond. Mirror people, on the other hand, focus on reality as a reflection
of their own behaviour. Organizations need managers who have mastered being both
window and mirror people: reflective managers who can see both ways and who hold
to facts while being able to review them in a new light.

The reflective manager approaches work in terms of continuous learning, possessing
the skills to reflect on actions and outcomes and to critically assess how personal performance can be enhanced. In practice, being a reflective manager means that, regardless
of whether reflection occurs individually or in work teams, the process of thoughtfully
examining one's experience is informed by ideas that can help us make sense of social,
political and technical processes. A retrospective focus can be replaced by a practice of
reflection as an integral part of day-to-day activities. Management action will generate
knowledge about current tools and circumstances, and this knowledge will provide
learning opportunities in subsequent activities and decisions (Gray, 2007).

This book is for reflective managers who are interested in experiencing management
tools and concepts from various fields in order to put them into well-balanced use within
their own context. The material presented in this book includes work on challenging
managerial judgements. It demonstrates analytical and critical evaluations of specific
management tools by the authors. It shows how situational context can shape and
influence interpretations and actions. This is a book about reflective thinking in action, as
the authors appraise each of the management practices discussed in each chapter.

The plan of this book

This book is targeted at actual – or aspiring – reflective managers in public services and
scholars who share our enthusiasm for studying the challenges of public services. As
described earlier, the term "reflective" refers to managers who think about their job
and are open to new ideas on how their job can be done better. This book supports the
reflective manager by revisiting existing practices and examining innovations in public
management. In section one the topics of the book was outlined. In the following, the
book is organised in four sections.

Section two deals with *strategic positioning* and contains three chapters covering
three different dimensions of this phenomenon. An organization that supplies public
services requires a strategic orientation in order to clarify what it should do, what to
direct its attention towards and what resources to aim in the right directions. Furthermore, strategic positioning is not something an organization does just once; rather,
there is an ongoing need to adapt to the changing conditions that characterise public

services. The first dimension, addressed in Chapter 2, discusses the role and use of a corporate vision in a public organization. It is a vital task to define what public needs an organization will fulfil and to use an overview to prioritise among wants and among stakeholders. A corporate vision provides guidance in this complex process. The second dimension, addressed in Chapter 3, deals with the phenomenon of strategizing. Public-service managers must have an awareness of possibilities and challenges for strategy and strategic management. Strategizing comprises how, and to what degree, it is possible to translate this awareness into practice. The third dimension, addressed in Chapter 4, is about the management of change. This chapter presents a reflective approach to change management and recognises the human elements in change programmes.

In section three, the focus shifts to the *renewal of core practices*. This section comprises four chapters addressing four different management practices in a reflective manner. Potential benefits are discussed by addressing the complexity involved in applying these practices. In Chapter 5, cost management is repositioned at the strategic level, and we investigate whether and how cost data are a source of reflection enabling top management to set and pursue a strategy. Chapter 5 offers a reflection on how cost data can play a strategic role within an organization. Next, Chapter 6 provides a rethinking of performance management. Through a discussion of the traditional approach, in which performance management is a tool for central control, this chapter paves the way for a more modern approach that focuses on the use of performance measurement for learning and development. Chapter 6 presents guidance on several design questions that arise when performance measurement is used for such a purpose, and discusses what might realistically be expected from such use. Chapter 7 then explores public procurement. Reviewing the challenges of public procurement makes it possible to see a potential to use these processes as a vehicle for change. By turning to the market, public-sector organizations can stimulate innovation and the development of new and improved products and services. Chapter 8 examines the challenges of governing in a digitalized era and discusses the belief that digitalization can free up resources and make public-service provision more efficient. This chapter explores the consequences of digitalization on public services provision, based on the claim that such consequences are far from unproblematic.

Section four examines *innovations in management practices* in public-sector services. New management techniques and ideas are continuously being introduced to the market. Some of these are genuinely new, while others are newly developed approaches to known concepts. The four chapters in this section build on established concepts while reflecting on and applying them in a new way. Chapter 9 addresses the effects that result from public institutions engaging in branding and adopting a brand orientation. Although such orientation aims at positive effects, it is important to understand the actual consequences. A value-based framework can be used to encourage an analysis of branding in public services. Chapter 10 discusses Lean Management by asking whether this is a natural order for public-service transformation. The chapter comments on the emergence of Lean Management in public organizations and offers guidance to public-service managers on what they might realistically expect from the adoption of Lean Management. The focus of Chapter 11 is on resilient management. By discussing the two interrelated concepts of resilience and sensemaking, this chapter elaborates on how resilient management may be constituted and understood in the context of small municipalities facing extraordinary challenges. Chapter 12 calls for a discussion that reasserts the merit of risk management in the face of the fundamental uncertainties that challenge public-sector institutions.

It examines the risks of risk management: the drawback of a risk management that is primarily ceremonial and holds little instrumental value and the potential for a risk management approach to be used to address significant challenges facing public services. This chapter discusses risk management as a tool in addressing climate change and the Covid-19 pandemic as illustrations of the potential of rigorous risk management.

In section five, Chapter 13 elaborates on the need, forms of and potential for *reflective managers* in public services. Reflective managers are open to reviewing existing knowledge and solutions and are open to new ideas on how their job can be done better. This reflection involves viewing work in terms of continuous learning and critically assessing how personal performance can be enhanced. Such actions will lead to learning about current tools and will provide learning opportunities in further decisions. Thus, the contributions offered herein provide a valuable frame of reference for the public-service manager in the 21st century.

References

Agger Nielsen, J., Wæraas, A. and Dahl, K. (2020) When management concepts enter the public sector: A dual-level translation perspective. *Public Management Review*, 22 (2): 234–254.
Boyd, E. and Fales, A. (1983) Reflective learning: Key to learning from experience. *Journal of Humanistic Psychology*, 23 (2): 99–117.
Brunsson, N. (2006) Administrative reforms as routines. *Scandinavian Journal of Management*, 22 (3): 243–252.
Brunsson, K. (2017) *The Teachings of Management: Perceptions in a Society or Organization.* Springer International Publishing.
Dane, E. and Pratt, M. (2007) Exploring intuition and its role in intuition managerial decision-making. *Academy of Management Review*, 32 (1): 33–54.
Dewey, J. (1933) *How We Think: A Restatement of the Relation of Reflective Thinking to the Educative Process* (revised edition). Buffalo NY, Prometheus Books.
Fischhoff, B. (2013) *Judgment and Decision Making*. Routledge, New York.
Gosling, J. and Mintzberg, H. (2003) The five minds of a manager. *Harvard Business Review*, 81 (11): 54–63.
Gray, D. (2007) Facilitating management learning: Developing critical reflection through reflective tools. *Management Learning*, 38 (5): 495–517.
Korthagen, F. (1985) Reflective teaching and preservice teacher education in the Netherlands. *Journal of Teacher Education*, 36 (5): 11–15.
Mezirow, J. (1998) On critical reflection. *Adult Education Quarterly*, 48 (3): 185–198.
Nannaka, I., Chia, R., Holt, R., and Peltokorpi, V. (2014) Wisdom, management and organization. *Management Learning*, 54 (4): 365–376.
Schön, D. (1983) *The Reflective Practitioner: How Professionals Think in Action*. Basic Books, Routledge, New York, USA.
Shotter, J. and Tsoukas, H. (2014) In search of phronesis: Leadership and the art of judgment. *Academy of Management Learning and Education*, 13 (2): 224–243.
Taggart, G. and Wilson, A. (2005) *Promoting Reflective Thinking in Teachers: 50 Action Strategies.* Cowin Press, Thousand Oaks, CA, USA.
Thiele, L. (2000) *The Heart of Judgment: Practical Wisdom, Neuroscience and Narrative.* Cambridge University Press, Cambridge.
Tiberius, V. (2008) *The Reflective Life: Living Wisely With Our Limits.* Oxford University Press, Oxford.

Wright, C. (2019) Thought Leaders and Followers: The Impact of Consultants and Advisers on Management Ideas, in A. Sturdy, S. Heusinkveld, T. Reay and D. Strang (eds.), *The Oxford Handbook of Management Ideas*. Oxford University Press, Oxford.

Yanow, D. and Tsoukas, H. (2009) What is reflection-in-action? A phenomenological account. *Journal of Management Studies*, 46 (8): 1339–1364.

Section two
Strategic positioning

2 Managing with a vision

Ola Mattisson

Introduction

When we find ourselves involved in a situation with other people, it is necessary for us to come together in a collective form and to make decisions and take action to address joint issues. However, acting together is difficult. The problems we experience in such circumstances originate from an inability to make individuals systematically act together while using their best individual abilities. Activities that lack a systematic structure and coherence will not produce the desired outcome, and the desired results will be weak. Therefore, despite the difficulties of acting together, we want and need structure in order to become organized. We are aware that organizations can be shaped by alternative concepts of how the organisation is structured (like the classic Weberian bureaucracy, the General Motors Head Office and divisional structure or the Nokia flat structure), but here we use organization in the generic sense as a mechanism for gathering people together within defined boundaries to achieve a common purpose. In this respect, the precise nature of an organization`s structure is not critical to our discussion. The question is then, how can organizations bring individuals together and cause the actions of individuals to function together as a collective whole?

Apart from a need for coordination, scholars have noticed that organizations have many goals and that this variety of goals introduces inconsistencies or conflicting ambitions (Desmidt, 2016). For management, goal ambiguities create vague conditions for decision-making and priorities. To counterbalance unclear conditions, organizations search for tools to help them distinctly communicate why the organization exists. The reason and purpose of the organization must be understood in a way that "not only articulate[s] what the organization hopes to accomplish, but also how the organization hopes to accomplish it and why such accomplishments benefit [stakeholders and surrounding society]" (Wright, Moynihan and Pandey, 2012, p. 212). Vision statements are an example of such tools, in both private- and public-sector organizations.

In the academic literature, much attention has been devoted to the role and significance of vision statements over the last thirty years. Visions have been considered to be necessary aspects of the strategic management process in various types of organizations, including private and public, profit and non-profit. A vision requires an integrated overview of the situation and the stakeholders involved, and should provide and communicate a clear image of what is to be accomplished. It also adds to the organizational identity (Özdem, 2011) and provides a foundation for all types of strategic decision-making by identifying what is expected in terms of the organization's performance (Khalifa, 2012).

DOI: 10.4324/9781003154389-4

In public-sector organizations, these concepts are complicated. Different groups of the public have different needs and, since the available resources are always limited, priorities are necessary. These priorities must deal with conflicting needs and prioritize between them as well as between stakeholders and their interests. In one sense, a public organization exists to realize political visions about contemporary and future society. In another sense, it exists to solve individual and joint problems for the people living in that area. Thus, a public organization must clearly understand the public needs it plans to fulfil, define those needs, and have a grasp of the available resources to be used in this endeavour.

A mission statement can illustrate and communicate what the organization stands for and create a shared interpretation of the organization's essence by raising employee awareness of organizational values and goals (Ryu, 2015). In comparison, a vision is a projection of the organization into an undefined future, when it reaches a mature and successful position. The vision describes a preferred end state for the organization in the future. It is an idealistic projection of what the organization could be and could achieve, and is the base for policy-making and a reference point for making management decisions within the organization (Ciampa and Watkins, 1999; Lansdell, 2002). The goals of different stakeholders can be brought together by a vision, while clarifying what the stakeholders consider to be important and urgent (Desmidt, 2016). Political visions form a basis for decisions, actions, and priorities in public-sector organizations. For managers in public-sector organizations, the vision statement should be a crucial starting point for policy execution.

This chapter focuses on the role and importance of visions in the management of public-sector organizations. Taking the organization's mission as its starting point, a vision is a frame that describes and discusses the organization's aims and the future state it will act towards. In turn, the vision acts as a starting point for choices of what means to use to realize the organization's objectives.

The first part of this chapter focuses on where an organization begins and examines the characteristics of a public organization's mission. The second part discusses the characteristics of a vision and gives examples, while the third part presents examples of the use of visions in public-sector organizations. Finally, the last part discusses some managerial implications of the discussion.

The mission: a starting point for public organizations

When an organization is formed, there is always a rationale; that is, someone wants to fulfil some kind of purpose and organizes resources and activities accordingly. The management literature generally defines this rationale as the "mission" of the organization. Mission statements answer the question of why the organization exists and what the organization must do (Ciampa and Watkins, 1999). More fundamentally, mission statements are supposed to capture the overriding purpose of an organization, in line with the values and expectations of its stakeholders (Nanus, 1992). Starting from the shareholders, a mission statement will typically provide answers to the questions of "What business are we in?" and "What is our business for?" (Darbi, 2012).

It is important for most, if not all, members of an organization to share these joint beliefs about why the organization exists. There is a need for an overall order – a foundation – of guidelines expressing what is, and what is not, a priority within the organization. It is only once these factors are in place that the members of the organization can make more detailed decisions and take action. The mission statement creates an identity for the organization as it tells the world about the organization's purpose and its present activities; that is, it says "who we are", "what we do" and "why we are here". In this way, it collects various components or parts of an organization around a common cause. Overall, a mission statement is a broad overarching framework around which other strategic concerns can be developed, such as the vision, strategic intent and capabilities, goals, objectives and core values. The mission provides "the necessary guidance for developing strategy, defining critical success factors, searching out key opportunities, making resource allocation choices and pleasing stakeholders" (Bratianu, 2008, p. 22).

Mission statements that define an organization are widely believed to be antecedents to the strategic development process. In general, this effort starts from a summary of the organizational goals and objectives, described in terms of mission and vision. These two statements serve different purposes. According to Bartkus et al. (2004), the mission focuses on the present by describing the client's major processes and informing the organization about the desired level of performance. A mission statement is useful, as it provides day-to-day guidance in decision-making and priorities within a particular organization in a particular competitive setting. This is in contrast to the vision, which aims to envisage the future, show direction, create motivation and stimulate change.

To be useful, a mission needs to be specific and adapted to the situation at hand. A well-written mission statement identifies the specific purpose of the organization and its field of activities that cover the needs of the people and organizations it intends to serve. The mission reflects active choices, should be unique and should differentiate the organization from others. A too-broad mission statement would apply to most organizations, and would thus be of little value in establishing the identity and focus of any given organization.

The literature provides a multiplicity of definitions and characteristics of mission statements. In an overview of the field, Khalifa (2011) notes that there is a flourishing inconsistency in definitions, creating confusion in both theoretical and practical settings. Apart from minor variances in definitions and views, he identifies two different approaches to the mission concept: compilation logic and framework logic.

The most extensive literature on mission statements is based on the compilation logic, which focuses on a "checklist of items" (Khalifa, 2012). Based on a large collection of mission statements from different organizations, this approach analyses and classifies components into comprehensive lists, thereby defining the "ideal" mission statement (e.g. Akeem, Alani and Edwin, 2016). However, the results of these lists are rarely seen in practice, as organizations seldom manage to include all, or even most of, the items in their statements. This is not surprising, however. The normative advice from the same literature is to formulate a mission from the unique circumstances in every specific case. Thus, it would be rather surprising to find clear common features and characteristics in different missions. The concept of a mission statement emphasizes being different; that is, every organization has its own purpose.

Although they are difficult to apply in practice, these ideal lists are still useful. David and David (2003) suggest using this method to evaluate the quality and precision of mission statements, inventorying to what extent these issues are covered (or not covered). However, there is no conclusive evidence that the items on such a checklist are the requirements for an ideal mission statement. The list has an internal focus, and does not consider potential external factors explaining deviations from the list. Using this kind of list sets up a broad definition of the mission concept that covers a variety of aspects, such as core values, goals, creed, strategies and (sometimes) vision. Overall, this type of list is helpful for inspiration, ideas and reviewing the situation. However, such a loosely defined concept is less useable for analysing and giving normative directions.

The alternative approach is a framework logic, which emphasizes the necessity and coherence of the items that constitute a model or a framework. One such example, frequently referred to, is the work of Collins and Porras (1997), who build a framework from two components. Core ideologies are the first component, working as the glue that keeps the organization together. The second component is the envisioned future, representing what the organization wants to become or achieve. Another example, presented by Campell and Yeung (1991), uses purpose, strategy, values and standards of behaviour as central components. A common characteristic of these and other model frameworks is that they are constructed from logic with coherence in the foreground, rather than being generated from practical examples.

To summarize, the concept of an organization's mission is defined and used in a variety of ways, and is more or less explicitly related to other concepts. Khalifa (2012, p. 242) suggests a combination of the two approaches. The mission is a "resolute commitment to create a significant value or outcome in service of a worthy cause – a cause that the members of the organization admire and be willing to exert their attention and energy in its pursuit". He summarizes mission definitions into three pillars (Box 2.1).

Box 2.1 Three pillars of a mission statement

A mission statement expresses:

- Commitment (authenticity to the situation)
- A significant value or significant output (inspiration)
- A worthy cause (creating meaning to the organization's members)

Source: Khalifa (2012, p. 242)

This definition appears to be useful in practice. It does not contradict any other major model or definition, and it is consistent with initial definitions of the concept. It focuses solely on purpose and choice. The first pillar is the organization's commitment to bring authenticity into the situation. The second pillar is the presence of a significant value or outcome that signals a challenge to bring inspiration. The third and last pillar is a worthy cause, which creates meaning for the organization's members. One company that uses these pillars in its mission statement is Spotify (Box 2.2). Spotify commits to unlocking the potential of human creativity. As such, its existence carries value for both artists and fans, and will result in a greater good in terms of better dynamics between creative artists and their fans.

Box 2.2 Spotify's mission

Spotify's corporate mission is "to unlock the potential of human creativity – by giving a million creative artists the opportunity to live off their art and billions of fans the opportunity to enjoy and be inspired by it".

Source: Spotify (2021)

Another important aspect is where the mission focuses attention. Where are the effects from the organization to be found: inwards or outwards? An outward mission statement "creates a sense of contribution – that something good is being done for the world" (Engel, 2018, p. 8). Engel (2018) found both charitable organizations and Fortune 100 companies describing effects that benefit stakeholders outside the organization, such as veterans, homeless pets or customers. However, she also found examples of internally focused statements that described what they do for the target group rather than what they do for society. Other combinations, such as Spotify, have mission statements that focus both inwards and outwards.

The distinction between inwards and outwards attention is particularly relevant in public organizations or public-sector services. Such organizations exist to serve a public interest, which explicitly directs attention outwards from the organization. Certain goods or services are needed in society and certain groups have special needs, which are covered by public bodies and often financed by public funds. Political bodies perceive needs and give organizations legitimacy and financial funding. However, as soon as the politicians find other areas of higher importance, they may switch their support to other priorities.

Defining the mission is, therefore, a highly political process, and receiving attention from political arenas is important. For example, mission statements for public hospitals in Australia were found to focus on communicating their purpose and enhancing the legitimacy of their operations. The mission statements of private hospitals, on the other hand, show a greater focus on competitive advantage and encouraging staff (Leggart and Holmes, 2015).

Many public organizations have the same or similar obligations to execute, due to generic needs in society (e.g. pre-school, public transport) or legal regulations (e.g. social services, health care, waste management). Regional or local governments usually have a set of obligations and duties to fulfil. Often, these duties are "given" to a public-sector organization from the outside in terms of legislation or by instructions from other public bodies (providing funding). The focus that is displayed by how these instructions are articulated varies greatly in different countries and contexts. As a result, such instructions have a major standardizing impact on mission definitions in public services (i.e. the outward attention). Still, the instructions contain space for deciding on a particular situation, which provides regional or local governments room to independently define (and thereby differentiate themselves from others) characteristics in mission statements. In many countries, there is extensive use of publicly financed private suppliers acting independently, which opens a path for a variety of missions in different organizations (Allen et al., 2018).

However, despite the promising reports of using mission statements it is important to notice that it is a delicate task to use it successfully. Conditions in the specific situation require adjustments from standard approaches and the concepts need to be applied with care. The characteristics of public sector organization implies some difficult challenges. Chaston (2012) notes that the public setting contains a larger number of stakeholders and a higher degree of complexity. This complexity brings potential problems. One such problem is lengthy complex mission statements that are difficult to understand and relate to. Another one is that varieties in opinions cause broad unspecific missions or, alternatively, missions containing contradictions. A third problem stems from a tendency to exaggerate aims and ambitions in complicated formulations, reducing the potential use of the mission statement as a device for policy implementation (Chaston, 2012) due to an incoherence between the mission statement and the actual practice (Rey and Bastons, 2018). Not being observant of these problems and focusing on mission as a tool without reflections will run the risk of occupying a great deal of organizational resources with confusion as the main outcome.

In conclusion, mission statements in public services are highly dependent on the specific setting – that is, on legal regulations and the administrative structure in terms of authorities and responsibilities. Some aspects are regulated legally, while others are left open and can be created within the organization. In public services, however, much of this creativity occurs in the political arena rather than in the managerial one.

The vision: where the organization is going

In addition to knowing why an organization exists, its members need to look forward. A vision can be used to describe what they see when looking into the future. An organization's vision is a guide to what that organization should become, rather than a description of what it is. A vision can represent an idealized future state for the organization; that is, it can include ideas, descriptions and mental images of the future for the organization (James and Lahti, 2011). By describing future achievements or a future state that the organization will accomplish or realize, a vision can inspire the organization's members and enable them to focus on work activities. An early example of a short vision is Henry Ford's declaration of his organization's focus on "a car that families could afford". Engel (2018, p. 10) summarizes the concept of a vision by claiming that "your mission describes what you do for the world. Your vision describes what the world looks like once you've done it".

Formulating a vision of how things will evolve in the future is a natural starting point. Through an organization's vision, its members can agree on what direction to go in and what steps may be required to get there. Each organization wants a separate vision that makes it unique and distinguishes it from other organizations. Since the 1980s, considerable research attention has been devoted to the possibilities of designing and using visions to prepare for action in the future (Helm, 2009). In practice, extensive attention and energy are devoted to the concept of vision creating. A survey of business conditions in Britain showed that more than 90% of organizations claimed that they had a vision for the organization (O'Brien and Meadows, 2000).

Research has provided different definitions of a vision, which vary in complexity. There is also considerable flexibility in when and how the vision is realised, if at all. Despite this variation, the consensus claims that a vision describes a future state that an organization is aiming for. However, the interpretation of what a "future state" may be varies greatly. Some scholars suggest focusing on a timeframe not too far into the future, in order to make the vision concrete and enable people to relate to it (Khiew, Chen and Shia, 2017). Other scholars suggest a longer timeframe. If appropriate, a vision can be a description of what will occur at a remote point of time that individuals today might (but will not necessarily) experience (Rahimnia et al., 2011). Ciampa and Watkins (1999, p. 168) claim that a vision should describe what a preferred future state will look like and how people will act when it arrives.

Regardless of when this future state occurs, there are different views regarding the extent to which a vision should be realistic, likely and achievable. Collins and Porras (1997) emphasize creative aspects, and suggest that a vision is about creating a future, not predicting it; that is, a vision is not about right or wrong, but is about ambitions.

This is a most important observation. Other authors view the vision as a key component for core values, strategy and planning (Darbi, 2012) and discuss a vision as something that is concrete and can be used as a benchmark to discuss performance. Lansdell (2002, p. 8) offers a very useful summary of a vision as follows:

- A description of the organization's guiding philosophy or aspirations
- A statement of purpose
- A picture of where and how the organization wants to be in the future
- A promise or a goal

What, then, are the attributes of a vision? A great deal of the literature uses a compilation approach to define a vision. Based on a study of examples, this approach seeks to derive common characteristics of visions and compile them into lists of attributes (Akeem et al., 2016; Kantabutra, 2009; Kantabutra and Avery, 2002; Kirkpatrick, 2017). In a recent extensive review of the literature, Rahimnia et al. (2011) found nine attributes of a vision (Box 2.3). What these examples do not offer is a set of milestones at which elements of the visions are enacted. The vision is much more a means of projecting identity and reaffirming the practices of the organization.

Box 2.3 Attributes of a vision

Brevity – Most organization use shorter slogans stating the ambition of the organization.

Clarity – The statement of the vision should point out a distinct goal in a given time frame.

Future orientation – The vision should centre around a long-term perspective of the organization and the environment in which it functions.

Realistic – It should be realistic about the conditions under which the organization operates, to establish direction in uncertain times.

Challenging – It motivates people to make an extra effort to get the desired outcome.

Ambitious – A vision can set ambition targets for the strategy, to be pursued over many years.

Provide a general sense of direction – A vision provides a focus and converges all actions into a desired direction for the organization.

Broad – A vision should be broad enough to cover all aspects of the organization's activities, reaching both inside and outside the organization.

Motivating – A vision statement promotes optimism and confidence in future activities.

Source: Rahimnia et al. (2011)

The list contains attributes or factors that studies have found to be featured in numerous organizations' visions, with the distinct exception of the introduction of "clarity" which is interpreted as a time frame for implementation. However, this list should be considered as a gross list of potential attributes presented in random order (i.e. no ranking importance), and it is not claimed that all the attributes on the list are necessary. Thus, ticking off all the items on this list in a vision statement will not guarantee success, and leaving some items out will not be a vital weakness. Rather, this type of compilation provides a source for inspiration and a benchmark for potential factors of importance.

Another approach is to discuss a vision within a framework of concepts. The concept of a vision is closely related to several other concepts and phenomena about leading an organization. Terms like strategy, core values, philosophy and policy, which may be present in a vision, are all used in different contexts and have varying meanings. A vision guides an organization in what core to preserve and what future to stimulate. The term "vision", however, is claimed to be one of the most overused and least understood words in the English language; it conjures up different images for different people – of deeply held values, outstanding achievement, societal bonds, exhilarating goals, motivating forces or raisons d'étre (Collins and Porras, 1997). Visions may be interpreted as ambiguous unless they have a short, sharp message which has meaning for employees and users of the organization's outputs.

To grasp the term "vision" better, it is important to distinguish it from other terms that are used as exchangeable synonyms. One such distinction is the separation between vision and strategy. Vision is about a future state the organization is aiming for, rather than how to get there or what means to use to get there. "Strategy is the path that an organization chooses to pursue its future", while a vision should describe a future in which "goals and strategy are being successfully achieved in lockstep with the organization's guiding philosophy and values" (Rahimnia et al., 2011, p. 34f). James and Lahti (2011) also point out that there is a distinct difference between visions and related concepts such as strategy, goals or values. Visions typically have a longer lifespan than strategies and focus on innovation and change to a greater extent. Nutt and Backoff (1997, p. 309) identify four important properties that distinguish a vision from other forms of direction setting. A vision:

- Has clear and compelling imagery;
- Offers an innovative way to improve;
- Recognizes and draws on traditions; and
- Connects to actions people can take to realize change.

Box 2.4 illustrates two practical examples of visions. The first is that of Spotify, whose preferred future state (i.e. vision) is that professional creators can act without medium constraints and that everyone can enjoy this opportunity or its results and can feel like a part of a greater whole. There is no time limit, and the formulation of this vision is open in terms of breaking free from constraints and being relevant for everyone.

Box 2.4 The visions of Spotify (music) and IKEA (Swedish furniture)

Spotify's corporate vision is to be:

> a cultural platform where professional creators can break free of their medium's constraints and where everyone can enjoy an immersive artistic experience that enables us to empathize with each other and to feel part of a greater whole.

Source: Business Strategy Hub (2021)

Ikea's corporate vision is:

At IKEA our vision is to create a better everyday life for the many people ...
[The business idea] supports the vision by offering "a wide range of well-designed, functional home furnishing products at prices so low that as many people as possible will be able to afford them.

Source: IKEA (2021)

The IKEA vision statement has remained the same for decades and is very well spread throughout the company. This sheer longevity underpins how successful IKEA have been. It is an illustration of success. There is no formal mission statement; instead, the company elaborates on the topic within the vision statement under the heading of a "business idea". The concept of the "business idea" is both simple and powerful – it has immediate appeal. It also has an enduring strength. Also, the IKEA vision is ambitious, as it focuses on "the many people" receiving a "better" life – meaning that there is no end to reach in the endeavours. Nevertheless, the vision statement directs attention and provides guidance about the organization's priorities and what actions it should take.

Based on a management perspective, it is crucial to look forward and act for the future. In themselves, vision documents are proactive and aim to achieve something in the future. Future performance and expectations of the future are crucial when individuals or organizations act in the short and long term. Those who lead a business must try to understand and anticipate the future in order to make decisions about future actions, often in terms of deciding on and prioritizing goals. People try to link their experiences and knowledge to make decisions about the future (O'Brien and Meadows, 2001). Regardless of whether it is an individual or an organization, an image of the future is needed in order for that individual or organization to be able to orient themselves and respond to changes in conditions. A clear and working vision can be vital in initiating and driving strategic change.

A vision can help people to bring their energy and emotion into play at the workplace, sometimes at levels resembling their behaviour during their leisure time. Other means of steering people's behaviour do not seem to achieve this quality. A shared vision can give the members of an organization a clearer perception of purpose and direction, while simultaneously allowing individual entities, parts and resources to be coordinated or integrated into the organization. In times of emerging opportunities with limited resources, this coordination is of particular importance. Without an accepted and shared belief, members of an organization risk pointing their enthusiasm in any direction. A shared vision can channel these efforts in the same direction and increase the possibility that the efforts will be fully effective.

However, strong visions might also be a problem. When working to implement and create support for the vision, too much success might hinder diversity and development. By being too conformed in thinking and acting the organization faces huge risks, either by over-emphasizing non-important factors, or by disregarding important factors. Regardless of which, the consequences are difficult. One example is the scandal around the energy company Enron Corporation that had a powerful vision presenting something new, bringing success by redefining the whole industry (Spector, 2004). The company was formed in 1985 and by the year of 2000, it had grown substantially, and was listed by Fortune as "the most innovative company" for the fifth year in a row. The company were receiving praise from everywhere. But the strong vision also required support and loyalty. It was not to be questioned and dissenting thinking was not encouraged or accepted. It was either in or out. When the company collapsed during a turbulent month in 2001, it revealed a great number of top management actions that were either illegal or morally wrong. However, before the total collapse, among the people within the company there were never any openings for questioning the vision or the values of the company.

Another example is the website Boo.Com, a global e-tailer offering fashion clothing to customers in their local languages. The company vision stated, "bringing beautiful clothes to the world" (Stockport, Kunnath and Sedick, 2001, p. 56). From this vision the founders managed to both raise and spend some US$125 million between 1997 and 2000. In hindsight, one of the founders claimed that the technology wasn't ready yet, and that their vision and ideas were so powerful that they raised expectations above what was possible to fulfil. After starting the project, the only way to go was forward, and there was no room for questioning the ideas, or the approach. The best approach was to believe in the concept and go on. Therefore, both the fall and the financial losses got bigger. CNET networks has listed Boo.com as one of the ten biggest IT failures ever.

Visions might be powerful tools to bring about actions but there are also risks in terms of streamlining views about what is right and what is wrong, and what is important. Both Enron and Boo.com are examples of very powerful visions bringing devastating consequences from the absence of critical reflections.

Use of vision in public-sector organizations

Most of the literature on vision statements stems from commercial profit-seeking companies. Concept development and examples often focus on choosing clients and surviving competition – that is, in private market conditions. Vision statements are mainly regarded as a task for senior management (Lansdell, 2002). They are a tool to express and communicate views and priorities to stakeholders, both inside and outside the organization. The majority of organizations (companies) use vision statements, and the concept is believed to work well in that context (Collins and Porras, 1997; Ciampa and Watkins, 1999).

However, this concept also appears in public-sector or non-profit organizations. Several studies have reported on the endeavours of such organizations. The use of vision statements is also found within the university sector (Özdem, 2011), the school sector (Allen et al., 2018) and the hospital sector (Leggart and Holmes, 2015). Khiew et al. (2017) conclude that a careful process may turn the somewhat abstract vision into something that is concrete and helpful to support performance in daily activities within the hospital sector. Similarly, Liao and Huang (2016) report that several empirical studies support the conclusion that working with a vision increases service performance and stimulates a positive perception of the public services by users or customers.

Two examples of Swedish organizations whose visions are considered to be important and to have a high degree of impact are presented below. Both organizations focus on prevention (Box 2.5), and both visions suggest that good work and a good outcome involves the elimination of something harmful. The Swedish Transport Agency was among the first of such agencies in the world to have a "vision zero" (i.e. a vision of there being no lifelong injuries or casualties in traffic accidents) as a guiding principle, and thus received international attention. Its vision is also known to be vitally important to the agency itself, both in terms of politics and within the agency's operations. Statistics are published periodically to review performance and to discuss to what extent that actions that have been taken bring the agency closer to its vision. Any leadership within the agency must relate to this vision and present the priorities and actions that should be taken to move towards it.

Box 2.5 Two public organizations' visions about elimination

The Swedish Transport Agency: road safety

> Vision Zero is the ethical standpoint that no-one should be killed or suffer lifelong injury in road traffic. This means that the view of safety in the road transport system concurs with those values that apply for safety in society as a whole. In working life, and within the rail, shipping and air transport sectors, it goes without saying that no deaths should occur as a consequence of accidents.
>
> Source: Trafikverket (2021)

Swedish Public Dental Service (Folktandvården), Region Norbotten

> "En frisk mun i alla åldrar"
> "A healthy mouth in all ages"
>
> Source: Folktandvården i Norrbotten (2021)

The Public Dental Service in Region Norbotten took inspiration from the zero vision and created one for its own situation by writing a short vision statement stating the aim of its work: the organization will keep its clients' mouths healthy. The statement contains a short and powerful description of what the Public Dental Service wants to achieve (vision), which is frequently communicated both internally and externally.

Both examples are organizations operating within a single supply, meaning it is possible for them to formulate a vision within a distinct set of activities, making the vision powerful. However, many public organizations have a wider purpose with a greater variety of activities and/or supplies to account for. Local governments and municipalities are examples of organizations that have another set of characteristics. They are fundamentally heavily diversified and serve within a wide array of activities that require a wide set of differing capacities. Operating within a limited geographical area, such organizations have relations with a large portion of the people living there. Defining just one mission and one vision in such a setting is a challenge, as the statements must relate to a diverse set of activities, some of which lie outside of the control of that municipality.

Boxes 2.6 and 2.7 present the mission and vision statements of two North American municipalities: Phoenix and Powassan.

Box 2.6 Mission and vision of the city of Phoenix, AZ, USA

Mission statement
To improve the quality of life in Phoenix through efficient delivery of outstanding public services.

Vision statement
We will make Phoenix a great place to live, work and visit by fostering a dynamic and sustainable environment with exceptional public services.

Source: City of Phoenix (2021)

Box 2.7 Mission and vision of the municipality of Powassan, ON, Canada

Mission statement
Through efficient and effective leadership, Powassan supports a high quality of life for all of its citizens. Its citizens have a strong sense of pride and ownership in the community.

Vision statement
Powassan is a community that embraces change while respecting the rich heritage of the area. It is a municipality based on strong fiscal government with a durable economy that recognizes the rights of all citizens, respects the environment and the amenities that it affords and offers to citizens a healthy, active lifestyle.

Source: Municipality of Powassan (2021)

It is interesting to note how similarly these two municipalities present themselves in their statements. In their mission statements, both support their citizens' quality of life (outbound) and both want to achieve this through well-functioning public bodies (inbound). Powassan also adds the role of citizens. Judging by their mission statements, these municipalities have similar obligations (i.e. being municipalities), which make it difficult for them to show uniqueness. They have similar roles to fulfil.

In its vision statement, Phoenix briefly presents more of an aim or promise than a vision. The vision statement alone shows little focus and few priorities. The vision statement of Powassan contains more details about vital components in the municipality's vision. It also refers to the specific setting, describing priorities and what is unique about Powassan more than Phoenix does. However, both municipalities focus on happy citizens sustainably living a good life, in a municipality that embraces change. To conclude, organizations with similar obligations tend to focus on similar things, making it difficult for each organization to genuinely appear different from other organizations. Somehow, it is still fundamental for organizations to formulate what is significant and why this is important, and to drive performance and change in the organization's operations. Still, these visions are open and apply to a very general level. In a regional or local government setting, such overall statements stem from the political arenas that set the structure and conditions for public services and public-sector organizations.

Despite the good examples of helpful visions, it is still an uncertain path to take when initiating change. Apart from problems of conformed thinking, or reducing criticism, there is also the problem of creating a weak force for change (or actions). One main challenge in public sector services is to develop a vision strong enough to raise enthusiasm. Too broad or weak mission and vision statements risk ending up in a file in a bookshelf, but never put to practice. Then the vision work will only be using resources and energy for development. Then there will be costs but without any positive effects.

Managerial implications

What is the managerial role, and what are the managerial implications of this discussion? The specific legal and administrative structure will decide the arena for the manager. Legal and political decisions will specify the arena for actions, direct the mission and set important input factors for vision work. The role of the manager is to develop a supply/ supplies or an organizational unit, and this is where the vision can be useful.

The process of managing with a vision can be based on at least two different approaches (Wang and Rafiq, 2009). The classical approach defines vision work as a task for top management, typical of a Weberian bureaucracy. The vision is the starting point for strategic planning and decision-making using a top-down approach. By deciding on a focus and priorities, the leadership designs a vision and strategy and then secures their implementation using planning, reporting and incentives. Ciampa and Watkins (1997) describe this approach as "using push tools". Ideally, strategic planning will encourage the organization to align its systems and resources behind a particular set of goals that are important for success. The idea is that a systematic design will take full advantage of opportunities and minimize organizational exposure to threats.

A second approach is presented in the literature on organizational learning, more typical of a flatter organization structure. It focuses on consensus building, using the shared visions as a transformational factor for organizational learning (Nutt and Backoff, 1997; Collins and Porras, 1997). Since the conditions for operations are changing more and more rapidly, it is becoming increasingly difficult to design alignment between the different components of an organization (e.g. mission, vision and strategy). Therefore, the so-called "push tools" (top-down approach) are not enough. People need to be inspired as well; that is, "pull tools" are also necessary (consensual approach) (Ciampa and Watkins, 1997). Pull tools come in different shapes but are generally based on relationship-building skills. A shared vision about a future attractive state to work towards will be enhanced by other pull tools within a culture of active listening and team-building skills. This approach seems to favour organizations that view themselves as proactively contributing to the common good and that are willing to adjust their ambitions to meet the challenges identified in the vision, based on a diverse set of values brought forward from stakeholders (Moxley, 2004). Ciampa and Watkins (1997) draw the conclusion that push (top-down) and pull (consensual) tools are complementary. On their own, neither is sufficient; both are necessary to create sufficient force for change in an organization.

The vision is a starting point for making things happen and initiating activities in a coordinated and adequate way. In the setting of a public organization, the vision is a way for members to create direction together. Different people from different parts of the organization can share the same future ambitions. For public managers, it is a crucial task to facilitate the process of jointly defining the vision and bringing it into action. The vision must be painted stroke by stroke in a reflective process that uses experiences from the past (Gosling and Mintzberg, 2003). Involving organization members in vision creation increases their participation and facilitates translating the vision into action (Lansdell, 2002). This approach can be described as a creative process that focuses on creating a future and elaborating on what to aim for, rather than analysing what is most likely to happen (Collins and Porras, 1997). Therefore, it makes no sense to analyse whether a vision is the "right one" (i.e. predicting the organization's future); instead, the question is whether the vision is stimulating enough. Does it motivate people to act in order to create the envisioned future?

When sharing a vision, different actors can contribute to bringing reality closer to the ideal future state. Furthermore, a vision may spread well outside the single setting and form connections between organizational borders. Stakeholders from different organizational settings may join forces in the pursuit of bringing reality closer to the ideal future state. Thus, a vision may direct attention and form a basis for decision-making. An organization with a shared vision is more likely to relate to multiple perspectives within the existing body of knowledge that are in line with the organizational goals. Hence, a shared vision facilitates adaptive approaches towards a desired future state.

Actively balancing a diverse set of stakeholders and values is a demanding process, but a rewarding one that allows a vision to be accepted and consequently to influence actions in the organization and the collective performance. The managerial challenge is to manage this process in an environment with growing complexity in which ambiguity is increasing. In a context of such pluralism, it is a vital task for the public managers to ensure the organizational vision is broadly shared and inspiring within that organization. Once in place, a vision statement is a good start for working with strategies – that is, for strategizing, which is further described in the next chapter.

References

Akeem, T., Alani, L. and Edwin, A. (2016) Vision and Mission in Organization: Myth or Heuristic Device? *International Journal of Business & Management*, 4 (3): 127–134.

Allen, K.-A., Kern, M., Vella-Broderick, D. and Waters, L. (2018) Understanding the Priorities of Australian Secondary Schools Through an Analysis of Their Mission and Vision Statements. *Educational Administration Quarterly*, 54 (2): 249–274.

Bartkus, B., Glassman, M. and Mcafee, B. (2004) A Comparison of the Quality of European, Japanese and U.S. Mission Statements: A Content Analysis. *European Management Journal*, 22(4): 393–401.

Bratianu, K. (2008) Vision, Mission and Corporate Values: A Comparative Analysis of the Top 50 U.S Companies. *Management & Marketing*, 3 (3): 19–38.

Business Strategy Hub (2021) Spotify: Mission, Vision and Core Values. Available at: https://bstrategyhub.com/spotify-vision-mission-core-values-a-complete-analysis/. Accessed 10 July 2021.

Campell, A. and Yeung, S. (1991) Creating a Sense of Mission. *Long Range Planning*, 24 (4): 10–20.

Chaston, I. (2012) *Public Sector Reformation: Values-driven Solutions to Fiscal Constraint*. Palgrave Macmillan.

Ciampa, D. and Watkins, M. (1999) *Right from the Start: Taking Charge in a New Leadership Role*. Harvard Business School Press.

City of Phoenix (2021) City of Phoenix Mission, Vision and Values. Available at: https://www.phoenix.gov/citymanager/vision-and-values. Accessed 10 July 2021.

Collins, J. and Porras, J.I. (1997) *Built to Last: Successful Habits of Visionary Companies*. Harper Press, New York.

Darbi, W. (2012) Of Mission and Vision Statements and Their Potential on Employee Behaviour and Attitudes: The Case of a Public but Profit-Oriented Tertiary Institution. *International Journal of Business and Social Science*, 3 (14): 95–109.

David, F.R. and David, F.R. (2003) It is Time to Redraft Your Mission Statement. *Journal of Business Strategy*, 4 (1): 25–43.

Desmidt, S. (2016) The Relevance of Mission Statements: Analysing the Antecedents of Perceived Message Quality and Its Relationship to Employee Mission Engagement. *Public Management Review*, 18 (6): 894–917.

Engel, M. (2018) Crafting the Ideal Mission Statement for Your Organization. *Hesselbein & Company*, Winter: 7–12.

Folktandvården Norrbotten (2021) Folktandvårdens vision och mål. Retrieved from: https://vis.nll.se/process/administrativ/Dokument/divtv/Styrande/M%C3%A5ldokument/Folktandv%C3%A5rdens%20vision%20och%20m%C3%A5l.pdf. Accessed 10 July 2021.

Gosling, J. and Mintzberg, H. (2003) The Five Minds of a Manager. *Harvard Business Review*, 81 (11): 54–63.

Helm, R.V. (2009) The Visions Phenomenon: Towards a Theoretical Underpinning of Visions of the Future and the Process of Envisioning. *Futures*, 41 (2): 96–104.

IKEA (2021) Vision and Business Idea. Available at: https://www.ikea.com/gb/en/this-is-ikea/about-us/vision-and-business-idea-pub9cd02291. Accessed 10 July 2021.

James, K. and Lahti, K. (2011) Organizational Vision and System Influences on Employee Inspiration and Organizational Performance. *Creativity and Innovation Management*, 20 (2): 108–120.

Kantabutra, S. and Avery, G. (2002) *A Critical Review of the "Vision" Literature*. 7th Asia-Pacific Decision Sciences Institute Conference: 1–9.

Kantabutra, S. (2009) Toward a Behavioral Theory of Vision in Organizational Settings. *Leadership & Organization Development Journal*, 30 (4): 319–337.

Khalifa, A. (2011) Three Fs for the Mission Statement: What's Next. *Journal of Strategy and Management*, 4 (1): 25–43.

Khalifa, A. (2012) Mission, Purpose, and Ambition: Redefining the Mission Statement. *Journal of Strategy and Management*, 5 (3): 236–251.

Khiew, K.-F., Chen, M.-C. and Shia, B.-C. (2017) Derivation Process of Vision That Bind the Overall Business Performance. *Journal of Management and Strategy*, 8 (1): 10–17.

Kirkpatrick, S. (2017) Toward a Grounded Theory: A Qualitative Study of Vision Statement Development. *Journal of Management Policy and Practice*, 18 (1): 87–101.

Lansdell, S. (2002) *The Vision Thing*. Capstone Publishing, Oxford.

Leggart, S.G. and Holmes, M. (2015) Content Analysis of Mission, Vision and Value Statements in Australian Public and Private Hospitals: Implications for Healthcare Management. *Asia Pacific Journal of Health Management*, 10 (1): 46–55.

Liao, K.-H. and Huang, I.-S. (2016) Impact of Vision, Strategy and Human Resource on Non-Profit Organisation Service Performance. *Procedia – Social and Behavioral Sciences*, 224: 20–27.

Moxley, D. (2004) Factors Influencing the Successful Use of Vision-Based Strategy Planning by Non-Profit Human Service Organizations. *International Journal of Organization Theory & Behavior*, 7 (1): 107–132.

Municipality of Powassan (2021) Mission/Vision Statements. Available at: http://www.powassan.net/content/municipal-services/mission-vision-statements. Accessed 10 July 2021.

Nanus, B. (1992) *Visionary Leadership*. Jossey-Bass, San Francisco.

Nutt, P. and Backoff, R. (1997) Crafting Vision. *Journal of Management Inquiry*, 6 (4): 308–328.

O'Brien, F. and Meadows, M. (2000) Corporate Visioning: A Survey of UK Practice. *Journal of the Operational Research Society*, 51 (1): 36–44.

O'Brien, F. and Meadows, M. (2001) How to Develop Visions: A Literature Review, and a Revised CHOICES Approach for an Uncertain World. *Journal of Systemic Practice and Action Research*, 14(4): 495–515.

Özdem, G. (2011) An Analysis of the Mission and Vision Statements on the Strategic Plan of Higher Education Institutions. *Educational Sciences: Theory and Practice*, 11 (4): 1887–1894.

Rahimnia, F., Moghadasian, M. and Mashreghi, E. (2011) Application of Grey Theory Approach to Evaluation of Organizational Vision. *Grey Systems: Theory and Application*, 1 (1): 33–46.

Region Norbotten (2021) Styrande måldokument, Uppdrag. Folktandvårdens vision och mål. Luleå.

Rey, C. and Bastons, M. (2018) Three Dimensions of Effective Mission Implementation. *Long Range Planning*, 51: 580–585.

Ryu, G. (2015) The Missing Link of Value Congruences: The Mediating Role of Employees' Acceptance of Organizational Vision. *Public, Personnel Management*, 44 (4): 473–495.

Spector, B. (2004) *Enron: What Went Wrong*. Richard Ivey School of Business, Northwestern University.

Spotify (2021) Company Info. Available at: https://newsroom.spotify.com/company-info/. Accessed 10 July 2021.

Stockport, G., Kunnath, G. and Sedick, R. (2001) Boo.com: The Path to Failure. *Journal of Interactive Marketing*, 15 (4): 56–70.

Trafikverket (2021) Vision Zero. Available at: https://www.trafikverket.se/en/startpage/operations/Operations-road/vision-zero-academy/This-is-Vision-Zero/. Accessed 10 July 2021.

Wang, C. and Rafiq, M. (2009) Organizational Diversity and Shared Vision: Resolving the Paradox of Exploratory and Exploitative Learning. *European Journal of Innovation Management*, 12(1): 86–101.

Wright, B., Moynihan, P. and Pandey, S. (2012) Pulling the Levers: Transformational Leadership, Public Service Motivation, and Mission Valence. *Public Administration Review*, 72 (2): 206–215.

3 Strategizing

At a new crossroads?

Mikael Hellström, Stein Kleppestø and Ulf Ramberg

A call for awareness of the fundamental conditions for strategizing

Strategic landscapes and how to navigate within them vary a lot for managers of public services. Two main reasons for this derive from the public service mission and the institutional arrangement of which the service is a part. A mission to operate public transport is very different from a mission to operate a public school, as these are two quite different services with different control conditions, success factors, stakeholders, etc. Institutional arrangements (laws, administrative culture, governance structure, etc.) can differ between countries, within a country, within an organization, etc., and have consequences for both the public service mission and the context in which it operates (Kuhlmann and Wollmann, 2019).

Consequently, how to act and think when navigating strategically as a manager in public services is usually strongly, and specifically, linked to the service's mission and the context in which it operates. With this in mind, we elaborate on different kinds of considerations and issues related to strategy on a more general and conceptual level in this chapter. The ambition is to create managerial awareness of possibilities, limits, and challenges for strategy and strategic management in public services. How, and to what degree, it is possible to translate this awareness into practice, that is, to strategize, is up to each future or already engaged manager to explore.

This chapter begins by recognizing that there is a general shift towards higher complexity in some of the strategic contexts in which public services operate. We argue that this shift in complexity can be interpreted as a new crossroads for public managers to consider. It is therefore increasingly important that public managers be aware of the fundamental conditions for strategizing in the contexts in which they operate. Strategic management ultimately aims to develop strategies and make strategic decisions in which the long-term ambitions of public service are linked to the limited resources available to the organization. The challenges of making these decisions vary considerably depending on the conditions under which they are made.

The strategic management of public services is shaped by several fundamental traits of such organizations. A first fundamental trait is that public services face demands that far exceed the resources available to them. As a consequence, prioritising is essential, that is to say, we need strategies. A second trait is that public services' ambitions are related to changing political ambitions. Hence, strategy needs to be related to policy, political judgements, and decision making. For public managers, it is therefore crucial to understand the underlying logic of assigned political visions, translate them into their organizational setting, and secure their fulfilment. A third trait

DOI: 10.4324/9781003154389-5

is that the visions and objectives of public organizations are multifaceted and related to many and potentially contradicting stakeholder expectations. There are few uncontested objectives or visions. Hence, public organizations must be seen as a nexus of continuous political negotiations with complex consequences for the strategic management of the organization. A fourth trait is that public services are supposed to address shifting public concerns and conditions. Strategic management, consequently, must track, understand and report the short- and long-term changes in public demands and needs, and convey these back to the politicians. And the fifth and final trait is that public services' ambitions are to be achieved in a more or less distant future. For this reason, strategic foresight is important.

Taken together, all these traits of public organizations and the services they offer, in combination with a sometimes much higher level of complexity, require an awareness of various approaches to what we call *strategizing*. Strategizing is a managerial practice and ongoing process of formulating foresight; creating, translating, and understanding political visions; developing strategies and securing the execution of these strategies; and giving continuous, grounded, strategic feedback to the politicians. It is not an easy task for the public manager, but nevertheless an essential responsibility and an ability important to managing their work.

The chapter is divided into four parts. *The context and concept of strategy* describes different contexts and concepts of strategy, how different contexts affect the input and output of the strategizing process, and why it is important to understand public organizations' internal and external conditions in order to wisely strategize the execution of the vision for the organization.

Thinking strategically covers how managers' cognitive abilities affect what role and impact their strategic thinking has on public services' overall performance.

Acting strategically connects strategizing to the "internal life" of managing, leading, organising, and controlling. In this sense, the internal life is about the organizational ability to execute as a part of the strategy formulation. Different perspectives on this "internal life" are covered in depth in the following chapters of the book. This part gives an overview of some important executive approaches and issues to be aware of and consider as managers when executing strategies.

Managerial implications argue for the need for a new approach to strategy and strategizing in the public sector. Managers in public services face several choices every day, both minor and major ones. Some of these choices can be managed routinely or administratively, some need new approaches.

The context and concept of strategy

As a product of multifaceted and varying social desires, the ambitions of public services are always more extensive than the available resources. A strategy is the alignment of these unlimited ambitions with the relevant limited resources (Gaddis, 2018). The lack of resources emphasises the need to prioritise their use against political visions and objectives. The overall purpose of strategizing is to create a strategy to reach the stated vision. A strategy can be used as a guide in a continuous process of decisions. We can also develop an understanding of the required actions and relevant changes needed in the organization, its operations, resource allocation, and so forth. However, how we understand the concept of strategy is intertwined with our understanding of the context of strategy.

We argue that it is valuable to imagine a continuum of strategic contexts. At one end, the contexts could be characterised by a high degree of certainty, predictability, and known and tested linear rationalities (we call this the *rational strategic environment*), and at the other end, strategic contexts could be characterised by uncertainty, high ambiguity, low predictability, high complexity, and a lack of known and tested rationalities (we call this the *systemic strategic environment*).

A rational environment is also characterised by a low rate of change, dilemma-free (or low) shareholder expectations, and a high level of control over the resources needed to execute strategies. These conditions are key assumptions in the rational (and traditional) models of strategic management. The systemic environment is characterised by a high rate of disruptive change, dilemma-ridden shareholder expectations, and a low level of control over the resources needed to execute strategies. Snowden (2002) and Snowden and Boone (2007) developed a framework that outlines four contexts with fundamentally different conditions for decision making and strategizing. The framework can be used to elaborate the Rational-Systemic continuum. Their framework describes four characteristics of a context. In a simple context, the world is known, that is, certainty is high and ambiguity is low. In a complicated context, the world is currently not fully known, but it is knowable, that is, certainty can be developed through effort. The third context – complex – includes a shift from linear to non-linear. Such a world is not fully knowable. Finally, in chaos, the world is unknowable.

For the purpose of this chapter, we choose to simplify the framework into a continuum of decision making stretching from the obvious (sometimes called simple) to the complicated to the complex. In an obvious context, the situation is known, that is, we have previous experience of the situation, and tested and successful solutions exist. In a complicated context, the number of dimensions to consider and the rate of change we experience make understanding the situation harder. Past experience is not fully applicable, and recognising the key features of the situation requires some expertise and effort. The situation is not known, but knowable. In a complex context, the situation is not knowable. The systemic feedback loops make complex situations non-linear; we cannot find clear and stable cause-and-effect relations.

As organizational ambitions are to be achieved in a more or less distant future, of which we have imperfect knowledge, we are forced to make strategic decisions under varying levels of uncertainty. Strategic decision making is about allocating limited resources, often for a long time and under uncertainty. Foresight is consequently a key aspect of strategizing.

McCarthy et al. (2010) developed a methodology for creating a multidimensional conceptualisation of environmental velocity. Velocity is the product of speed and direction. By identifying the key components (determinants) of the strategic context as well as their velocity and relationship, it is possible to get a workable understanding of what challenges the strategy needs to address. It also helps to understand the level of complexity and uncertainty that needs to be addressed when strategizing. A context of low rates of continuous change allows for an obvious (that is, known) strategic context, and foresight is to a large degree unproblematic. The level of predictability is high. In a context of high rates of discontinuous change, foresight is much more challenging and predictability is low.

In a rational strategic environment, foresight can be created in a systematic and deductive way. Based on experience, we know what types of change to expect; we often understand the driving forces for change and the cycles these forces are undergoing.

Even if the future does hold unknown elements, we are for the most part able to identify the areas where we are most vulnerable to changes in the environment and can take measures to increase our ability to handle these changes. The ambition of foresight in this context is to predict what will happen (or most likely happen).

In a systemic strategic environment, foresight is more challenging. We might be able to map strong trends that might shape the future, but our ability to judge what trends are most relevant is low. Also, as a consequence of the non-linear quality of the context, our ability to understand how these trends will shape the future is also low. Foresight is more inductive as we are searching for new models to describe and explore new ideas of the future. Even if we cannot develop a sufficiently clear, distinct, and certain (undisputed) view of our relevant future, we should be able to develop a sufficiently clear conceptualisation of the change regime we are facing. We should be able to develop a broader understanding of what can happen.

The dominant school of strategic thought and practice – historically – is built on the assumption that the environment and the future are known and can be described with a reasonable level of certainty and clarity (Mintzberg et al., 2009). This corresponds to what we call the rational strategic environment. According to this school, the concept of strategy is the outcome of a rational process based on rigorous analysis of available data, usually of high quality. A strategy is, in other words, data-driven. The tools available for analysing the data are known and they are based on a more or less rigorous (research-based) formalisation of past experience. This school is characterised by a strong belief in planning. Strategic management is proposed to be an orderly process in which data collection, analysis, decision making, planning, and execution are conducted in a step-wise and orderly manner. Strategic planning and execution are internal concerns and built on the idea that the organization itself has control.

The other end of our continuum is built on schools of thought that assume that the environment cannot be known or described in such a way that it lends itself to linear, analytical logic. This corresponds to the systemic strategic environment. In these schools, strategy is conceptualised as an ongoing and complex process without a clear step-wise logic. Even though we have access to some data, the process is not data-driven. It is idea-driven. The relevant tools are mostly helping to create ideas of how to relate to uncertainty and complexity in the environment and still be able to make strategic decisions. Whereas operational planning might be meaningful, strategic planning is not. Strategic decisions are not made at a fixed stage in an orderly process, but continually and to some extent ad-hoc as the need or the opportunity arises. A strategy is not an internal matter and cannot be controlled by one organization, it must be created and executed in a relevant (open and varying) system of stakeholders.

Thinking strategically

Following the logic of our continuum, strategic thinking takes different forms depending on the strategic context. Two schools or perspectives can be identified (Sloan, 2006). The first, the Analytical school (or Rational reasoning perspective), is characterised by rigid analyses of vast amounts of data. It is methodical and calculated. This structured, step-by-step process has long been dominant in textbooks on strategy (Andrews, 1971; Porter, 1985; Dixit and Nalebuff, 1991). It emphasises the use of analytical tools, often in the form of "strategic models" or "strategic logic". This school is often associated with words like converging, methodical, formal, structured, conventional, and planned.

The second, the Systemic school (or Generative reasoning perspective), argues that strategic thinking must be shaped by the apparent lack of unambiguous data (about the future) and the unfamiliar aspects of the future (we have not yet been there and have no relevant experience of it). Hence, rigid analyses are meaningless and impossible (there is little relevant data and we do not have obviously relevant analytical tools). Creativity, exploration, synthesis, integration, and divergence are essential elements (Ohmae, 1982; De Wit and Meyer, 2010). This school is often associated with adjectives such as divergent, flexible, informal, and intuitive.

The Analytical school is related to a rational, linear strategic context. In this context, data and experience-based analytical tools are available. The Systemic school is related to a systemic, non-linear strategic context. More data does not necessarily facilitate decision making, and experience-based tools are necessary and fully relevant. The two schools can be connected to the concepts of convergent and divergent thinking. The Analytical school aims to accurately predict the future and identify the best strategy, in other words, converge on a strategy. The Systemic school, on the other hand, argues that the complexity of the strategic context requires us to break the dominant frames, or logic, and open up for divergence. This provides more diversified novel ideas of possible strategies (Schoemaker et al., 2013; Heracleous, 1998; Bonn, 2001; Chevallier, 2016).

On a more general note, strategic thinking can be understood on three levels (De Wit and Meyer, 2010). On one level – application level – the manager as a thinking human being cognitively conducts a process aiming to understand the situation at hand by *identifying, diagnosing, conceiving*, and *realising*. On a second level, the manager has cognitive maps or cognitive schemata. These are previously stored and applied perceptions of the world. The cognitive maps are created through experience, education, and social interaction. The third level is the manager's cognitive abilities and limitations, such as limited ability to concurrently sense and process the strategic situation. A manager deals with this by taking shortcuts and creating frames and simplifications.

Cognitive simplification is an important concept in the discussion of strategic thinking. It is argued that strategic thinkers (like all thinkers) must create simplified mental models to understand and solve the problems at hand (Simon, 1957, 1976). As unavoidable as this is, it is also a source of cognitive flaws. Strategic thinkers can only analyse a limited amount of information and therefore are susceptible to selective cognition and, for that matter, also perception. The risk of biases contaminating the reasoning process and questionable judgement has been described by numerous authors (see e.g. Tversky and Kahneman, 1974). In our attempt to understand the world around us, we create cognitive maps. All sorts of cognitive and perceptual biases are affecting the creation of these maps. Unfortunately, this reinforces the experience of linear rationality – the manager's understanding of rationality shapes the understanding of the world and thereby falsely confirms the same logic.

Kahneman (2011), Acciarini et al. (2020), and others have made us aware of several common human cognitive biases. Several of these are highly relevant in strategic thinking. Cognitive biases, mental models, and mindsets shape the thoughts and actions of individuals and organizations and are therefore shaping the strategic thoughts and actions of public organizations. The seminal work of Argyris and Schön is one example of this strand of thinking (Argyris and Schön, 1978; Argyris, 2004). They argue that human beings have embedded two main mindsets shaping the way they test the validity and effectiveness of their actions: defensive reasoning and productive reasoning. One mindset does not preclude the other, and individuals usually employ a mix of both. Defensive reasoning has as its purpose to avoid change and discomfort and to avoid questioning whether current behaviour is actually right. Defensive reasoning does not encourage the detection and correction of the error, and consequently it prohibits the detection of alternative, potentially better, solutions. This, of course, has negative implications for strategizing and includes escalating misunderstanding, self-fulfilling prophecies, and self-sealing processes. Much of this cover-up happens implicitly and is therefore difficult to detect and avoid.

Productive reasoning, on the other hand, is about acknowledging problems, complexity, and uncertainty, and trying to understand what needs to be improved. It is about seeing the "big picture", being open to new solutions, and questioning the current thinking. This mindset brings other guiding principles characterised by seeking valid information, informed choice, and vigilant monitoring to assess the effectiveness of the implemented actions. Defensive reasoning is associated with single-loop learning, that is, learning that aims to correct errors without questioning the fundamental reasons for the errors, whereas productive reasoning is associated with double-loop learning, which emphasises inquiry and testing. Double-loop learning occurs in the detection and correction of errors/non-conformances that require changes in the overarching strategies and values that govern how organizational members act.

Learning through correcting errors or learning by inquiring whether you are actually doing the right thing are two fundamentally different approaches to both learning and the concept of strategic management. Often, organizational boundaries and responsibilities reward an inward-looking perspective. The managers' perspectives become narrow and the incentives to encourage the use of more external and broader perspectives when acting strategically are sometimes non-existent.

Acting strategically

The efficient execution of strategic intent rests on many auxiliary tools; budgets and performance measurements are two of the most popular tools in public services. However, which tools are needed depends on the nature of the strategic context. In this third part, we will investigate the two endpoints of a continuum from hierarchy to dialogue.

Hierarchy refers to strategic planning that can be executed in a management process. This would be possible when strategic intent is shared, authority or power is succinctly allocated, relevant competencies are present, structural features are basically in line with the plan, etc. In other words, the conditions for rational, linear exploitation of strategy are in place. To execute their strategies, managers in public services have a wide array of resources, both tangible and intangible. However, as mentioned, the traditional approach to managing (such as budgets, reward systems, and responsibility structures) tends to create silos and narrows the focus in terms of space and time. Having a strong focus on the budgets and similar tools is like looking through the little hole from the big opening of a funnel. An alternative approach for managers in public services would be to turn the funnel 180 degrees and see the small opening as their resource base and try to understand how these resources can interact with a broader scope of resources and opportunities at hand, both internally and externally.

This open-minded view of strategic management can, in Simon's (1976) words, be described as a process of searching and satisfying (procedural rationality). As such, the process itself is an art of craftsmanship coloured by the manager's former experiences. To take Vickers' (1965) perspective, this appreciation of the content in the funnel's wider scope of resources involves making judgements, both reality-based judgements (what is or is not the case) and value-based judgements (what ought to be or ought not to be the case), before executing a strategic decision or action (instrumental judgement). To find the best possible solution, given the resources and means available, and reduce the mismatch between the present "is" and what the situation "ought to be" is not a purely analytical or explicit activity for managers. Managers' appreciation and different judgements are tacit and complementary to their analytical and explicit work.

Making reality-based judgements when managing public services is not only about understanding contemporary services, their contexts and specific conditions. To navigate to what "ought to be", managers also need to be aware of how different kinds of institutional arrangements (such as laws, rules, norms, and values) and historically ingrained patterns of problem solving affect their manoeuvring space (Pierson, 2004; Pollitt, 2008). Solutions to new or emerging problems often depend on how problems have been solved in the past. Without a deep understanding of the modus operandi in place, managers may fail in strategizing and, in the worst case, run aground. Obeying the laws is, of course, a must for managers in public services, but to manage a public service they also need to problematise and communicate when and where institutional arrangements and yesterday's problem-solving may hinder the implementation of political visions. Institutional arrangements and path-dependency are both constant companions to public service managers when strategizing. Those companions create stability and predictability within given limits and support a hierarchical approach. What happened in the past is likely to happen again, according to Wildavsky's (1964) incremental approach to budgeting.

Further, aligning subordinates with overarching visions and objectives is not an easy task for managers. The use of hierarchy is by far the most common way to handle this task. With the stated vision in mind, formulating and using objectives, budgets, and measurements as a means of executing political visions is a major issue in public management in the first decade of the 21st century. Organizations are regarded as hierarchies, meaning there are superior levels that control subordinates. The prevailing strand of thinking states that objectives must be broken down into sub-goals for various organizational units, which in turn must break down their sub-goals for subordinate levels, and so it continues until the main objective has become a goal-congruent action that supports the execution of the political vision. Managers, at various levels, have a particular responsibility to understand, organise, and translate political visions and overarching objectives into concrete actions. In turn, subordinates have a particular responsibility to meet the goals.

In the follow-up phase, managers turn to measurements for help. The usually quantifiable targets, such as budget targets, that are meant to support managers in their assessment of whether or not they have attained the objectives are assessed and evaluated. If goals have not been met, the targets may be wrongly formulated or rules may be inadequate (Emmanuel et al. 1990; Simons, 1995). It might also be that the action performed is inconsistent with the main objectives. That goal congruence crack is a common management problem, fundamental and classic. Some explanations can be found in variables that can be regarded as uncontrollable, such as strikes and shifting energy prices. Other explanations can be found in controllable variables. Is there something in the objectives, the formulation of objectives, and measurements and the use of the measurements that resulted in the faulty action? Describing and visualising the organization's vision and objectives is a requisite step in the objectives formulation process, as discussed in Chapter 2. Only then is it possible to relate explicitly to objectives and, for instance, judge whether the objectives are steering in the right or wrong direction.

However, a hierarchical approach is dependent on the predictability of the public organization's resource transformation and outcomes. Research has shown that this kind of predictability, or other forms of control conditions, varies a lot for public services, especially when it comes to outcome measures. For example, control conditions are generally very good for planned orthopaedic procedures but are less favourable for psychiatry treatments and human services (Hofstede, 1981; Speklé and Verbeeten, 2014; Ramberg, 2017).

The hierarchical approach to executing a vision into action is by far the most common management idea in place, both in practice and in textbooks. However, the way to foster and embrace a productive reasoning mind in this approach is not obvious. When and where is it possible to question the chosen strategic pathway? The question to bear in mind is whether those kinds of systems are still adequate for strategizing when public service managers face the dynamics of more diversified needs and wants from users and clients of the services.

The other endpoint to execute a vision is a *dialogue approach*. This approach refers to situations where circumstances supporting a hierarchical view of execution are not in place.

Luke (1998, p. 3) writes:

> Public problems are interconnected, they cross organizational and jurisdictional boundaries and they are inter-organizational. No single agency, organization, jurisdiction, or sector has enough authority, influence, or resources to dictate visionary solutions.

Those conditions differ from what is needed for the hierarchical approach and may also, in some managerial situations, more closely represent the function and challenges of contemporary public services. More and more tasks are done in collaboration or on a contract basis with other public and/or private organizations. The need for coordination and oversight and efforts to achieve these have penetrated the single organizational boundaries and in many cases involves a network of organizations connected to the same vision (e.g. less crime, healthier population, better transit). Also, public services need to involve various stakeholder groups in society. In the search for ways to coordinate many and diverse stakeholders, new forms of meta governance have evolved, not least in many densely populated territories such as metropolitan areas. Problems that were only seeds in one's organization may grow both in form and scope in such contexts, and so do the problems embedded in the seed. Luke (1998, pp. 10–11) describes some of the "new" problems contemporary public services face as nested in a complex of other problems. Maybe there is no absence of information regarding a problem but still, there is limited understanding and knowledge of the multiple causes and effects. Luke argues that a problem's definition has less to do with data and scientific analysis than with values, traditions, and internalised mental models of a multiplicity of stakeholders and affected parties. They see the problem and its best solutions from their own perspective or mental model.

In a highly complex strategic context with multifaceted problems, we cannot expect to accomplish our strategic intent (or for that matter, to create a strategic intent or understand the environment for which we need strategies) by focusing on control. Instead, there is a need to open up for a multiplicity of local initiatives. What is required are new forms of strategizing that are boundaryless and essentially non-hierarchical (Luke, 1998).

This suggested dialogue approach is coloured by a productive reasoning approach and may have the strength to open up policy gridlocks, common features when it comes to making holes in different kinds of organizational silos. The way to act according to Luke (1998, p. xv) is:

1 Focus attention by elevating the issue to the public and policy agendas.
2 Engage people in the effort by convening the diverse set of people, agencies, and interests needed to address the issue.
3 Stimulate multiple strategies and options for action.
4 Sustain action and maintain momentum by managing the interconnections through appropriate institutionalisation and rapid information sharing and feedback.

Growing complexity does not always benefit from thinking in terms of strategic "formulation" and strategic "implementation" or "operational" and "strategic" plans (Whittington et al., 2006). The idea of a smooth sequence where we first do "strategy" and then implement the strategy is an uncommon situation in many practical situations. It is more about duality and simultaneous processes, sometimes intertwined and hard to distinguish. From a management perspective, this can be quite annoying and disturbing, sometimes far from the traditional knowledge about how to understand and implement a strategy. A way to manage this situation and also broaden the strategizing audience is to work in a more dialogue-based way when strategizing (Mack and Szulanski, 2017). The case below illustrates a Swedish municipality's stepwise experience in the process to work in a more dialogue-based way when strategizing:

> For many years, the municipality had had a governance system strongly characterised by the fact that there were 12 departments and thus 12 different ways of governing and aligning political visions to actions. In the planning of the next year's operations, goal chains were created with overall goals that were broken down into sub-goals, which in turn were broken down into goals for different activities. It was a very resource-intensive way of working and there was also no interest in following up on the goals, although the goals were linked to a large number of key performance measures. It was also rare that the goals were met correctly because things happened in the environment or internally in the organization that caused the conditions to change.
>
> Therefore, some years ago, an organizational change was initiated in 10 different areas, of which the strategic management process was one. The aim to change this process was to find a common way for the entire municipality to work with strategic management and thus have a more involving process where continuous work with external reconnaissance and future analyses formed the basis.
>
> Step by step, a change was initiated towards a more dialogue-based approach. The dialogue takes place between the executive politicians, trade unions, the municipality's management team, and the services representatives. Before each dialogue meeting, of which they have several per year, external environmental analyses and future analyses are used as a basis for the dialogues. For the politicians, for example, a simulation model is developed that the different parties can

work with to simulate different outcomes depending on, for example, economic and demographic development. The dialogues contribute to the activities and policies being more up to date on the conditions that apply. This in turn creates a preparedness so that managers responsible for different services know different future scenarios. Therefore, it comes as no surprise when the proposals are presented, as they are well prepared. Through constant dialogues, everyone also becomes more involved and the anchoring becomes greater.

The challenging duality of strategizing is surely a concern for the public manager. However, it is also common that there are competing institutional logics in the organization (Ezzamel et al., 2012; Pache and Santos, 2013). In a public service setting, one obvious example is the difference between bureaucratic/management logic and political logic. The public manager needs to understand different institutional logics inherent in the organization when strategizing. Those logics can surely work for both sides as the example below shows:

> After many years of discussions and investigations, the politicians in two neighbouring municipalities decided to merge their Water and Sewage (WS) organizations, but still with separate WS collectives. A more cost-effective operation, better possibilities to get necessary skills when recruiting (for increasingly strict and comprehensive environmental legislation), and better development capabilities were three main motives. One of the founding organizations was famous for both its progressive thinking about WS operation and how to manage and control the service. They had a performance measurement system (PMS) that was both nationally and internationally recognised as innovative and well-functioning in the industry.
>
> During the merger process and in the following few years, the PMS was seen as a guarantor of creating a resilient and successful WS organization. Further, due to the WS services' control conditions, the use of PMS was judged favourable from a managerial logic. The PMS made it possible to monitor how the new WS organization gradually adapted to its new structure and continuously improved its performance. However, the PMS never got this role. During the four years following the merger years, the professionals drowned in operational concerns about how to secure operations due to the transformational change, such as determining the organization's structure, employees' new tasks, and recruiting new staff, while the politicians were busy sorting out governance and ownership questions, determining principles for WS fees, and connecting more nearby WS services. In these circumstances, the managerial logic attached to the PMS was squeezed and trapped between the political and operational logic.
>
> However, when politicians, in connection to growth in the WS investments, wanted some proof of efficiency and, at the same time, operations wanted explicit political visions and quality standards (when planning for new investments), the PMS regained importance. In other words, four years after the merger there was a match between the three different logics.

Many factors affect the outcome of managers' strategic efforts, such as the degree of complexity, organizational history, relations between colleagues, external factors, politics, and changes in the population's composition. To navigate through all these obstacles, possibilities, pitfalls, and changes to reach a vision about the future is unquestionably a delicate task.

Managerial implications

In the first three parts of this chapter, we have described various aspects of a continuum from a rational to a systemic approach to strategy. Summarising the various aspects into a composite description of the two endpoints would give us the following approach to public strategic management. You may argue that strategizing is always about making decisions and choosing a pathway whenever reaching a crossroads. However, we argue that the crossroads described by the endpoints below are new ones, new in the sense that strategizing is more than choosing a pathway. Strategizing is also about how public service managers view their strategic plans, how they think about different challenges in their services, and how they act according to those challenges due to different contextual conditions.

The rational approach is based on a number of principles. The strategic management process is sequentially separated into blocks ranging from defining (or clarifying for the purpose of planning) the mission and vision to monitoring strategic execution and performance. The Cynefin framework suggests a Sensing-Analysing-Responding process for the obvious and complicated strategic contexts. The various blocks are linked but nevertheless distinct and separate. This means that they can be used to define and assign roles and responsibilities. The rationality of the process can be turned into clear and comprehensive instructions and the process can (and should) be repeated on a regular (annual) basis. The rational model is a planning model with a clear distinction between collecting and analysing data, making and communicating decisions (i.e. plans), and executing and monitoring plans. The model is also built on structures featuring the importance of hierarchies and borders (e.g. internal vs external). The focus of the rational model is to produce a plan to be implemented.

The systemic approach is based on other principles. Some of those are prototyping, learning, cross-boundary dialogues, flexible, and ad-hoc processes. Developing an understanding of the strategic contexts, identifying and legitimising the strategic options, and mobilising strategic actions comprise an integrated learning process in which the organization (system) probes, tests, fails, and succeeds in understanding the situation at hand and how to deal with it. The Cynefin framework suggests a Probe-Sense-Respond approach. The process of strategizing, in the systemic model, is far from orderly. It is not built on clear roles and distinct steps. It is an open, inclusive, ongoing dialogue that in most instances is inseparable from other processes and activities in and around the organization. The roles and responsibilities are shifting and there are no permanent organizational structures to fall back on in the process. The focus of the systemic model is to facilitate an inclusive learning process and mobilise stakeholders.

To be perceived as legitimate, but also to earn and maintain legitimacy in the eyes of the public, is crucial when public managers are strategizing. To manage without describing the direction and what to do (vision and objectives) and without monitoring and communicating the performance is problematic. Managers in public services need visions and objectives as a platform both to leave from and return to when strategizing, due to the responsibility to execute the visions, but also to ensure political accountability and that politicians have an informed basis for making new political statements. They also need to assess the conditions for strategizing in the public service they manage. These conditions differ from service to service, and over time.

Below is a summary of different aspects of continuums elaborated in this chapter which are crucial for managers in public services to understand when strategizing. The

Simple	Complex
Rational strategic environment	Systemic strategic environment
Systematic and deductive	Exploratory and inductive
Foresight aiming to predict what **will** happen	Foresight aiming to explore what **can** happen
Rational school of thinking	Systemic school of thinking
Converging process	Diverging process
Strategy as plan/deliberate	Strategy as learning/emerging
Hierarchy as a method of strategy execution	Dialogue as a method of strategy execution
Orderly process based onSense – Analyze – Respond	A dynamic process based on Probe – Sense – Respond

Figure 3.1 Positioning of the strategic context and understanding the consequences for strategizing in public services

managerial implication to managers in public services is that they need to position their strategic context on the continuum from Simple (Relational strategic environment) to Complex (Systemic strategic environment) and honestly assess for themselves how well-adapted their approach to strategizing to the conditions is (Figure 3.1).

As mentioned at the beginning of the chapter, the strategic management of public services is shaped by some fundamental traits. The gap between ambitions and available resources, the shifts in political intention, the multifaceted objectives, the shifting public concerns and conditions, and sometimes the extremely long timeframes public services need to prepare for all create unique challenges for the public manager. There are no tested best practices for strategizing in public service. In addition, it can be argued that the strategic contexts of public services, to some extent, are migrating from the simple towards the complex. This underlines the need to find ways to strategically manage public services in more and more complex contexts while also addressing the unique institutional conditions (i.e. traits) of public services. The dilemmas and paradoxes of this, what we choose to call a *new* crossroads, are obvious and must be acknowledged and respected. On the other hand, applying a more inclusive, dialogue-based and exploratory approach to strategizing might lead to new ways of understanding how democratic, political, and managerial requirements can meet.

References

Acciarini, C., Brunetta, F. and Boccardelli, P. (2020) Cognitive biases and decision-making strategies in times of change: A systematic literature review. *Management Decision*, https://doi.org/10.1108/MD-07-2019-1006.

Andrews, K.R. (1971) *The concept of corporate strategy.* Homewood, Ill Dow Jones-Irwin.

Argyris, C. (2004) *Reasons and rationalizations: The limits of organizational knowledge.* Oxford University Press, Oxford.

Argyris, C. and Schön, D. (1978) *Organizational learning: A theory of action perspective.* Addison-Wesley, Reading, MA.

Bonn, I. (2001) Develop strategic thinking as a core competency. *Management Decision*, 39(1): 63–71.

Chevallier, A. (2016) *Strategic thinking in complex problem solving.* Oxford University Press, New York.

De Wit, B. and Meyer, R. (2010) *Strategy: Process, content, context.* 4th ed, Andover, Cengage Learning, Toebben Dr.

Dixit, A.K. and Nalebuff, B.J. (1991) *Thinking strategically: The competitive edge in business, politics and everyday life.* W.W. Norton and Company, New York.

Emmanuel, C., Otley, D. and Merchant, K.A. (1990) *Accounting for management control.* 2nd ed, Chapman and Hall, London.

Ezzamel, M., Robson, K. and Stapleton P. (2012) The logics of budgeting: Theorization and practice variation in the educational field. *Accounting, Organizations and Society,* 37(5): 281–303.

Gaddis, J.L. (2018) *On grand strategy.* Penguin Press, New York.

Heracleous, L. (1998) Strategic thinking or strategic planning? *Long Range Planning,* 31(3): 481–487.

Hofstede, G. (1981) Management control of public and not-for-profit activities. *Accounting, Organizations and Society,* 6(3): 193–211.

Kahneman, D. (2011) *Thinking fast and slow.* Allen Lane, London.

Kuhlmann, S. and Wollmann, H. (2019) *Introduction to comparative public administration: Administrative systems and reforms in Europe.* 2nd ed, Edward Elgar Publishing, Cheltenham.

Luke, J. (1998) *Catalytic leadership: Strategies for an interconnected world.* Jossey-Bass, San Francisco.

Mack, D.Z. and Szulanski, G. (2017) Opening up: How centralization affects participation and inclusion in strategy making. *Long Range Planning,* 50(3): 385–396.

McCarthy, I.P., Lawrence, T.B., Wixted, B. and Gordon, B.B (2010) A multidimensional conceptualization of environmental velocity. *Academy of Management Review,* 35(4): 604–626.

Mintzberg, H., Ahlstrand, B.W. and Lampel, J. (2009) *Strategy safari: The complete guide through the wilds of strategic management.* Pearson Education, Harlow.

Ohmae, K. (1982) *The mind of the strategist: The art of Japanese business.* McGraw-Hill, New York.

Pache, A.-C. and Santos, F. (2013) Inside the hybrid organization: Selective coupling as a response to competing institutional logics. *Academy of Management Journal,* 56(4): 972–1001.

Pierson, P. (2004) *Politics in time: History, institutions, and social analysis.* Princeton University Press. Princeton, New Jersey.

Pollitt, C. (2008) *Time, policy, management: Governing with the past.* Oxford University Press, Oxford.

Porter, M. (1985) *Competitive advantage.* The Free Press, New York.

Ramberg, U. (2017) Transformational change and the vacuum of performance measurement: How a story of success became a failure. *Financial Accountability & Management,* 33(3): 249–263.

Schoemaker, P., Krupp, S. and Howland, S. (2013) Strategic leadership: The essential skills. *Harvard Business Review,* 91(1–2): 131–134.

Simon, H.A. (1957) *Models of man.* Wiley, New York.

Simon, H.A. (1976) From substantive to procedural rationality, in T.J. Kastelein, S.K. Kuipers, W.A. Nijenhuis and G.R. Wagenaar (eds.), *25 years of economic theory.* Springer, Boston, MA: 65–86.

Simons, R. (1995) *Levers of control: How managers use innovative control systems to drive strategic renewal.* Harvard Business School Press, Boston, Massachusetts.

Sloan, J. (2006) *Learning to think strategically.* Butterworth-Heinemann, Oxford.

Snowden, D. (2002) Complex acts of knowing: Haradox and descriptive self-awareness. *Journal of Knowledge Management,* 6(2): 100–111.

Snowden, D.J. and Boone, M.E. (2007) A leader's framework for decision making. *Harvard Business Review,* 85(11): 68–76.

Speklé, R.S. and Verbeeten, F.H.M. (2014) The use of performance measurement systems in the public sector: Effects on performance. *Management Accounting Research,* 25(2): 131–146.

Tversky, A. and Kahneman, D. (1974) Availability: A heuristic for judging frequency and probability. *Cognitive Psychology,* 5(2): 207–232.

Vickers, G. (1965) *The art of judgement: A study of policy making.* Chapman & Hall, London.

Whittington, R., Molloy, E., Mayer, M. and Smith, A. (2006) Practices of strategising/organising: Broadening strategy work and skills. *Long Range Planning,* 39(6): 615–629.

Wildavsky, A. (1964) *The politics of the budgetary process.* Little, Brown and Co, Toronto.

4 Management of change

For better or worse?

Irvine Lapsley

Introduction

Change management may be enacted in different ways. A programme may be devised and implemented by an in-house team of experts. But this option becomes increasingly rare as public sector bodies are continually being expected to offer more services with fewer resources – a trend which intensified over a decade of austerity from 2009 to 2019. This resulted in reductions in staff in public sector bodies and the erosion or elimination of specific areas of expertise. This has also been accentuated at the central government level because of tensions between Ministers of Government and their civil service advisors (Aucoin, 2012). Given these kinds of constraints, many public sector bodies turn to management consultants to advise on or implement organizational changes. There has been a significant increase in expenditure on management consultants by public sector bodies (Craig, 2006; Committee of Public Accounts, 2007; Lapsley, 2009). Most recently, the UK government created a budget of £37 billion for the development of a test and trace system for citizens who have been in contact with or in the vicinity of people with Covid-19 infections. The programme for test and trace has been heavily reliant on management consultants to devise and carry out test and trace systems, although the amount of public expenditure is not yet in the public domain. The dominance of management consultants as a reference point in change management programmes in public services has been confirmed by Saint-Martin (1998), Lapsley and Oldfield (2000), KPMG (2010) and Lapsley et al. (2013). One distinct facet of the contemporary literature is the presumption of certainty: organizations can be changed by the power of managers in a way that results in everyone being better off (McCabe, 2020, p.2). In their discussion, Lapsley et al. (2013) identified three aspects of management consultancy in public sector bodies: (1) tensions over the motives of consultancy firms, (2) allegations of consultancy firms acting as colonising agents and (3) the use of consultants to support symbolic acts.

Regarding (1) tensions over motives, there is the likes of Armbruster (2006, p. 205), who asserts that management consultants have expertise which they offer to relevant organizations. On the other hand, Craig (2005, 2006), Pinault (2000) and Alvesson and Johansson (2002) all depict management consultants as manipulators, persuaders and exploiters of management weaknesses. There is a need for an awareness of these possibilities when approaching a management consultant. On (2), the colonising argument, this relates to the penetration of management consultancy across to entities such as hospitals, churches, theatres and kindergartens (Czarniawska and Mazza, 2013). The colonisation thesis relates to the critical mass of expertise within the organization and the inability of organizations to challenge outside experts. This is particularly true of

DOI: 10.4324/9781003154389-6

large IT projects (Brown, 2001; Pollock, 2013). On (3) the symbolic use of management consultants is captured by Brunsson (2006) in his book *Mechanisms of Hope*. This reveals the serial failure of a project in which both management and their consultants refuse to recognise the failure of the project. They keep driving on, despite all the evidence against the project ever working. Contrary to expectations, the consultants may offer a form of reassurance rather than an action programme, to bring the project to fruition (Arnaboldi, 2013). This outcome must be recognised for the failure it is – even if there are plaudits on what has and might be achieved.

An outline of the cases in this chapter are shown in Table 4.1. This includes discussion of an IT project and more general management changes with different approaches to the use of management consultants.

All three of the case studies have issues with mobilising sufficient expert staff, so they need external expertise. There are distinct approaches to these interactions with consultancy firms: Alpha university had a secret expert, Alpha Hospital formed a bond with their expert supplier which created an example of co-production and Alpha City Authority had contemporary management consultants who offered management in terms of visions, different practices and stories of success.

Alpha University: the secret consultant

In this discussion of change management at Alpha University, there is a narrative of (1) the motives for change; (2) the means of change; (3) the outcomes of the change programme and (4) the implications of these changes.

The motives for change

The Principal of Alpha University was the architect of a vision of Alpha as a more research-oriented university with a business-like approach to organization and management. The Principal was an eminent academic, but is no longer research active. He was recruited from a successful traditional university after a period as a senior academic manager. In his previous university, his experiences shaped his perceptions of

Table 4.1 Alternative means of change management

Entity	Nature of programme	Expert advice
Alpha University	Organisational design Devolved Budgets Performance Management	The Secret Management Consultant
Alpha Hospital	To resolve a longstanding challenge in many health care settings – the design of an information system which generates an Electronic Record Form (ERF) which captures data from many sources, including financial information systems.	An example of **coproduction** between the consultancy firm advising on and supplying the IT systems in a collaboration with medical staff.
Alpha City Authority	Redesign of a local authority with a structural deficit and challenges over its capacity to deliver services.	**Reinvention**: management consultants as storytellers and educators.

what a successful Alpha University should be like. In his view, successful universities should generate more income to undertake research and development projects.

When the new Principal took up his post, he was confronted by antiquated, bureaucratic structures. His previous university had been a progressive and forward-looking ancient university. His vision for Alpha was one of **transformation** into a research-led university with robust management systems to support it.

Alpha's control systems were typical of heavily bureaucratised universities, which had hierarchical management structures (Du and Lapsley, 2019). Alpha had highly centralised financial controls, with a Planning and Resources Committee which had overall responsibility for the planning and use of resources. At Alpha University, the Planning and Resources Committee (P&RC) was chaired by the Principal. This committee had all the Deans and the Director of Finance in its membership. This committee served as a central planning and financial control function for the entire university. There were limited budgets devolved to Deans for travel and incidental expenditures.

Financial control was exercised centrally by the Finance Director. This was achieved by typical credit management. For example, payment of creditors was delayed (or accelerated if the financial position allowed this), routine maintenance was reduced or delayed, and stocks of materials were run down or built up, with the objective of breaking even at the end of the financial year. Establishment control was exercised by the central P&RCs of the university. This blunt instrument was the major control device: new appointments had to be approved by this committee. Senior staff who resigned or retired were replaced by junior staff. Urgent re-appointments were delayed by months to generate cost savings. Where deemed relevant, vacant posts could be frozen until future planning periods. The above financial controls typify the centrally controlled bureaucratic administrative machine. Under this regime, central bureaucrats exerted control and there was little or no scope for delegation of powers to the operational parts of these entities. This meant middle and lower-level academic managers were continually looking to the centre for advice or instruction to address and resolve financial and academic management issues. These systems had persisted for decades.

The means of change

To devise a new approach, the head of a well-known management consultancy firm was hired. His remit was to advise the Principal on a new organizational design and on performance management systems. The Principal assumed personal responsibility for any changes. He was the point of contact for the management consultant and the main advocate for the reforms within the university. To university staff the management consultant was invisible. But the management consultant recommended a series of incremental changes to the university's organization and its performance management systems. At every element of change the consultant discussed the effectiveness of proposals with the Principal. This continued throughout the change management programme and included a six-month audit of the transformation programme to determine how it had worked in practice.

The outcome of change

The Principal of Alpha had addressed all staff before embarking on his change programme. He enlisted the help of the Director of Finance to elaborate on why a new business model was needed at Alpha. The Principal of Alpha University argued for

Alpha to become a "university of the future". To achieve this, he set out a clear agenda to transform his university from a traditional teaching institution into a more dynamic entity. This vision emanated from a desire to escape from the failings of the status quo. The Director of Finance informed staff that Alpha's funding situation was poor. In his view, the funding per student which Alpha received from the Government was insufficient for the university's needs. He explained its student income was constrained as undergraduate student numbers were capped and extra students from the UK or EU markets only attracted tuition-fee only students. This resulted in declining resources from Central Government. The Principal addressed this difficulty of limited resources for the university by introducing a new organizational structure with devolved budgets, and by identifying a growth strategy based on the recruitment of overseas students at both undergraduate and postgraduate levels. This placed finance at the centre of Alpha's strategy. In his talks, the Principal stressed the compulsory nature of these changes. He also introduced the idea of an engagement policy in which members of staff would seek to work with local organizations. This was envisaged as a means to build good community links, raise funds and encourage research. The Principal stressed to staff that this was a substantive project in organizational and cultural change. He acknowledged that members of staff might think he was moving too fast, but he revealed that he thought they were not moving fast enough. The challenge was great. The achievements of the Alpha Change Programme are set out in Table 4.2.

These results present a successful outcome for this change programme: a new vision, new structures, new procedures, new information flows, a fundamental rethink on the nature of this university, the adoption of a business model which has buy-in and support amongst the staff of this entity and changed behaviour patterns from staff.

Table 4.2 Outcomes of Alpha University Change Management Programme

Actions	Comment
1. A new business model was developed for Alpha	1. The senior management at Alpha are committed to this model
2. Strategic aims: (1) increased overseas students, especially postgraduate (2) increased research grants	2. Supported by all senior managers
3. Income generation by all staff members as an obligation	3. Accepted by staff
4. The recognition of the university *as a business*	4. Widely accepted by staff
5. Devolved budgets to enhance local accountability and control	5. Wide support
6. The information generated by the devolved budgets has been accurate, reliable and useful	6. Widely used
7. The prime objective of Alpha is its financial viability	7. Widely accepted by staff
8. Culture change to recognise the costs of all activities at Alpha	8. Accepted throughout Alpha
9. Performance Management – a focus on how activities impact on the bottom line: the use of staff/student ratios, space utilisation, targets on research output, research grants, commercialisation and on overseas student numbers	9. A new and widespread understanding of Alpha university as a business

Alpha university had ambitious plans for change. While the vision of the "university of the future" was presented to the staff as radical and different, in reality this vision had a lot in common with other universities which sought to improve their management and sense of direction. However, on the attraction of significant levels of research grant income, the ability to attract significant research grant income depends on staff having expertise, reputation and a track record of receiving research grants. Alpha had a strategy of focusing on niche areas for research which made it different. But this challenge is profound. Also, the model of attracting research funds would be affected by matters beyond Alpha's control. The UK decision to leave the EU (Brexit) meant UK universities no longer had access to EU research programmes. More importantly, the strategy of building the university by growing overseas student numbers was a pre-Covid-19 plan. Now universities face fundamental uncertainties over international travel, the incidence of the virus infection and its capacity to offer courses. In the face of the pandemic, universities have switched to online platforms for the delivery of courses. But many commentators see the twin threats of Brexit and particularly the pandemic as posing significant threats to UK universities which threaten their solvency (Baker, 2020; Bothwell, 2020). The new Alpha model may or may not survive.

Furthermore, there is the issue of resistance (McCabe, 2020, p. 94) to the change model. This narrative has presented the change model as having widespread acceptance. However, one Head of School said the university had simply replaced one bureaucracy with a new form of bureaucracy. He expressed concern that there was so much time-consuming form filling it could be displacement – eroding their time for core activities. This little resistance could become bigger – especially in an environment where Covid-19 threatens the continuation of the new Alpha model of "doing business".

Alpha Hospital: co-production

In this discussion of change management at Alpha Hospital, there is a narrative of (1) the motives for change, (2) the means of change and (3) the outcomes of the change programme and the implications of these changes.

The motivation for change

Hospitals are complex institutions. They have multiple services to provide, such as accident and emergency, with multiple care pathways for maternity patients, surgical patients and physician-led care. For example, Alpha Hospital has approximately 130,000 admissions per year, 620,000 outpatients per year and 115,000 accident and emergency patients a year. To care for these patients, they have a range of professional people in the hospital. This includes hospital doctors, nurses, medical support staff and a wide variety of other support staff, including administrators, financial specialists, transport managers and operatives and estates managers. Often these professions are described as operating as distinct hierarchies with tensions within and between different professions. These challenges of staffing hospitals overlay procedural complexity with significant interdependencies which cut across the different functions of the hospital.

One of the difficulties of hospital management is the traditional fragmentary IT systems with limited connectivity between different computing systems in different parts of hospitals (Ganesh, 2004; Kazley and Ozcan, 2007; Cucciniello, Lapsley, and Nasi, 2016). Hospitals tend to have significant legacy IT equipment, which is incredibly expensive and risky to change. Alpha had a specific case of fragmentary IT systems and the ambition of staff to make their systems operate in a much more integrated way. At Alpha, the principal advocate of an integrated information system was a clinician. He had an international reputation in his specialism. He was also an expert on IT.

To initiate this change, he addressed all staff. In his speech he asked the staff if they had ever received a handwritten note from a clinician which they found hard to understand. The staff all laughed aloud. Doctors have a certain notoriety for their bad handwriting. He then asked if staff would prefer such notes to be typewritten so anyone could read them. The staff overwhelmingly agreed.

The clinician then asked about reading handwritten notes which had been around some time and remained unreadable, but where the patient's condition had recurred after a lengthy period. The original team who had cared for this patient had moved on. The clinician asked if anyone had been in the situation of deciphering old handwritten notes where the original team had moved on. Many staff agreed that they had.

The clinician stressed the importance of typewritten medical records in a specific health care episode like his first example. But in the interests of providing continuity of care, typewritten medical notes would be enormously beneficial. The staff agreed unanimously.

The clinician observed that he wanted information that was accessible, timely and accurate. (ATA). He asked the staff if they would all join in a collective programme to create an Electronic Medical Record (EMR) system which would provide that quality of information. The production of effective EMR systems has proved elusive in many contexts (Boonstra et al., 2014), but the Alpha Hospital approach was most successful. The staff agreed unanimously, and this was the start of a three-year project to devise an integrated clinical information system at Alpha Hospital.

The introduction of EMRs is potentially one of the main innovations capable of securing the clinical process. It has the potential to yield major improvements in health care performance and service delivery. The main goal of the EMR system is continuity of care, especially if performed by different clinical teams, at different times and locations. Implementing an EMR system melds administrative processes and clinical information. It can result in more holistic delivery with different professions working more closely and more effectively.

Alpha Hospital was a receptive context with a competent IT project leader and a team with detailed professional knowledge of the organization's characteristics. The involvement of internal expertise in this project quickly flagged up the central idea of users' needs. Alpha established a significant user involvement in this project. This included the initial decisions on which system to acquire and the effectiveness of implementation, as discussed further below.

The means of change

From the outset the clinicians and the Alpha hospital IT specialists were keen to work with an external management consultant, but not to be told what to do and not to accept an off the shelf product. The group pushing for change wanted to work with their external consultant to devise a more customised information systems which all staff could contribute to in the development process as a "co-production" project. There were three strands to this: (1) the identification of a suitable IT system and a management consultant they could work with. (2) the definition of what an EMR might look like and (3) any structural or management changes to make this work. An initial Steering Group was established to address these three tasks. This comprised of Alpha's Director of eHealth and his programme manager, the architect of this proposal – the initial clinician. He was joined by another clinician, a senior nurse with high IT skills and an estates manager. The eHealth Director identified initial management consulting firms and this was whittled down to two by the Steering Group. The clinical staff made the initial draft of a target EMR. All of them worked on possible structures which were designed to be flexible and to have the widest participation possible.

The initial draft of the EMR was as follows: the first issue was the projected contents for an EMR. This started with the referral letter and the arrangements for attending hospital, e.g. whether the patient was an inpatient or outpatient. Then any preadmission checks, e.g. blood pressure, vital organs – heart, kidneys. All checks to go on the EMR. After admission, all details of interventions by physicians or surgeons. Any data collected on patients to monitor progress. Location of patient over the episode, e.g. ward, high dependency or intensive care. Any prescriptions from pharmacy. Any use of medical support services, e.g. physiotherapy. Outcome of treatment. Discharge details of patient, including patient follow up details and continuity of care.

The Steering Group offered the structure shown in Table 4.3 as the means to bring this to fruition. This involved key groups to drive forward the implementation of the project, to oversee the project and to gain feedback from user groups so the system could be adjusted for local needs. There were also key individual roles such as Clinical Advisors and Super Users to make this operational.

The two consulting firms met with the Steering Group. They were invited to present their approach at a workshop at which there was an open invitation for all staff. One of the speakers for the successful firm argued that the issue of integrating different streams of information in a single system was the most important IT, clinical and managerial agenda in health care. This consultant made it clear that he would be delighted to work with the health care professionals on this project. His wish was granted. He became a

Table 4.3 The mapping of key actors in Alpha Hospital Change Management

Key actors	Comment
Groups	
1. EMR Programme Board	This group oversaw the entire implementation of EMR
2. EMR Implementation Team	This group lead the implementation of the integrated information system
3. Key Users Group	Members of staff at the various implementation sites who had a keen interest in the development of the EMR and were willing to engage in discussions with the Implementation Team as the project progressed
Individuals	
1. Clinical Advisors	Members of the eHealth Department who had IT knowledge plus clinical experience
2. Super Users	Volunteers who had acquired experience of operating the EMR system. The Super Users are members of the various wards in the project. They are capable of training other members of staff in the use of the EMR system

member of the Implementation Group. The first task of this Implementation Group was a detailed operational plan which set out what they were implementing, when and how. The implementation of the system was structured. It started by implementing the most relevant functions across the entire hospital, and then continued by piloting additional functions in single wards to test them and get feedback from the staff working on the selected wards. This was useful for making any adjustments based on results and the progress made by using the system. Furthermore, by selecting wards for the pilot test of the new functions, it was possible to analyse how the system worked in different scenarios: inpatients, outpatients and emergency wards. Each ward had a Clinical Advisor and at least one Super User. The Clinical Advisor was part of the Implementation Team and fed back progress on the implementation. Key Users also gave feed back to the Implementation Team.

The outcome of change management

The outcomes of the change management programme are shown in Table 4.4.

It is evident that this project has been a huge success. It has delivered its prime objective of a meaningful EMR which is used by all the staff. The close working of different groups on this project has strengthened the staff's relationships with each other and with Alpha. There are wider benefits around training regimes and improvements on clinical audit. But there are also important impacts on planning which offer fundamental improvements on how this is handled. The design of this EMR has facilitated communications within wards and across the hospital to other units. The EMR offers ATA – accessible, timely, accurate information on all patients, at all times. The crucial factor in this success was the coproduction approach with all the relevant

Table 4.4 Outcomes of the Alpha Hospital Change Management Programme

Outcome	Comment
1. ATA – Accurate, timely and accessible information. Reduced waiting time for laboratory results and enabled diagnostic images to be viewed in real time	1. A successful implementation which achieved its major outcome
2. An enhanced level of communication – between nurses and clinicians on the same ward and between different wards and units	2. Another important objective is realised
3. Enhanced ability to plan admissions, more accurate diagnosis and treatment, fewer mistakes when prescribing tests and compiling reports	3. An improvement in all round efficiency
4. It is easy to trace who is using the EMR to access or exchange information about patients at any time	4. Enhanced security
5. Enhanced information for clinical auditing	5. A wider impact of EMR
6. Improved information for health care support services	6. A big improvement for discharged patients who continued to need medical support
7. The training programmes on the ward helped to integrate the different patient information flows	7. An intended benefit of the new system

Alpha staff heavily involved in both design and implementation and the embedding of the key management consultant within the Implementation Group, where his IT skills complemented those of the eHealth Director and the programme manager in exploring how the software could meet the needs of clinical staff. An outstanding success. But with one reservation. This project focused on patient information flows and clinical judgements. The next challenge is to integrate this information with the hospital's financial ledger. But this is a step of the utmost sensitivity.

Alpha City authority: reinvention

In this discussion of change management at Alpha City, there is a narrative of (1) the motives for change, (2) the means of change and (3) the outcomes of the change programme and the implications of these changes.

City Management has always been depicted as an area of complexity (Lowndes, 1997; Seal, 2000; Lapsley et al., 2002; Bracci et al., 2017; Thomasson, 2018a; Stafford et al., 2020). One aspect of this is the political nature of these organizations (Collin et al., 2017; Thomasson, 2018b). While there are full time officials to organise and deliver the complete range of local authority services, political control is exercised by the conveners of all services and the leader of the city – a full-time politician. There may be a management culture in cities, but the political dimension of city planning is ever present.

The political leader of Alpha City is an experienced politician in local government. He has a change agenda which is a shared vision with the Alpha Chief Executive Officer (CEO). They both work closely together on their agenda to make the city more effective in policy delivery. They are both consistent on the way to achieve this. The CEO says that the vision is from the political leaders, but he is too modest. Both these key actors have the highest regard for each other.

One pressing issue for Alpha is the integration of a smaller failing local authority which has been merged with Alpha, as directed by central government. The smaller authority has different aims, practices and a different culture. It has become a second dysfunctional tribe within Alpha City.

Both leaders recognised the enormity of their task. After a decade of austerity, Alpha City's budget had reduced year after year, with increasing expectations from the government on the range and quality of services it had to deliver. The central government directed local governments who experienced a loss of income in their government funding allocations to make up any loss from efficiency savings. This directive has become less viable after a decade of cutbacks. This meant the leaders of local authorities had severely constrained budgets with little opportunity for investments. For example, at Alpha the CEO and the political leader both recognised that their financial information system badly needed an upgrade, but they did not have the resources to chieve this. The Director of Finance acknowledged the difficulties of working with his antiquated IT system. His focus was on (1) budgets and (2) annual financial accounts. Alpha had to endeavour to break even financially, as a statutory duty, and it also had to provide annual financial accounts as a statutory requirement. However, despite the best efforts of the Director of Finance and his team, the target of breaking even on budget was a very difficult target to achieve in an era of austerity and sometimes they did not achieve this. Under these circumstances, the deficit was rolled forward into the next year's budget. The repetition of this carry-forward over time creates a structural deficit.

Therefore, the strained financial situation at Alpha casts a long shadow over the organization and its capacity to improve. This is both a constraint and a major motivation for change.

The motives for change

An evaluation of Alpha City by the Political Leader and the CEO identified a range of issues which needed to be addressed to make this City Authority effective. Their agenda for change included:

- A successful integration of small local authority into Alpha.
- A reduction in the number of front-line departments.
- An end to departments working as silos or fiefdoms which take little or no account of their relationships with other departments.
- The promotion of a "cross-cutting" approach which would stop departmental compartmentalisation and force them to work on policy and service delivery with other departments.
- A more effective restructuring of the organization, with a shift away from its heavy hierarchical structure to a slimmer structure with decision making pushed lower in the organization.
- A greater focus on working with stakeholders such as citizens and local businesses.
- A general approach of more openness and transparency.
- Changes to encourage more vibrant culture in management.
- A shift from being a provider of services to a facilitator of services.

The means of change

The CEO proposed the recruitment of a firm of management consultants to help Alpha to address some of these pressing issues. The Director of Finance outlined the financial difficulties of this option. The political leader belonged to a political party which had been critical of the extent of local government`s use of management consultants. This became a tense stand-off, but the CEO was given a remit to produce a proposal for top management which took their dire finances into account. After trawling the various well-established management consultants, he found they were too expensive for Alpha. However, he discovered a smaller consultancy firm which focused on change management. This was led by a former academic who did not live in Alpha, but who was born there. This management consultant had a distinctive approach to change management. He was a proponent of Strategy-as-Practice (SAP) (see Whittington, 2003, 2004, 2006, 2007), in which subjects are encouraged to use and reinvent current practices with a new performance improvement. The lead management consultant of the firm had a reputation of being an inspirational storyteller. His speeches were peppered with examples of change management – narratives or stories which members of organizations remembered, vividly. When he was briefed on the issues facing Alpha City, he said it had too many issues. He acknowledged the need to resolve finance availability, but this was outside his control. However, the design of the organization structure was crucial and he could help with that. Given the difficult financial circumstances of his hometown, this management consultant made an offer to Alpha City in which his own time was pro bono. He made two proposals:

1   He would make six lectures followed by Q and A sessions over an 18-month period.
2   All existing and intending managers would be provided with copies of his most recent book and other pamphlets which he had written on various aspects of change management in different functions, at cost.

His undertaking of the six lectures on a pro bono basis was with the understanding that for further consulting work at Alpha he would be the first consultant to be invited and this would be at his normal rates of payment. The CEO recommended this proposal to his top managers and it was accepted unanimously. The management consultant's six lecture topics were as depicted in Table 4.5.

The senior management team attended all these lectures and read the consultant's briefing material. They found them inspirational. In parallel with these events, they worked on proposed changes. Their output is evident in Figure 4.1, which shows a reorganised Alpha City Authority. The CEO was placed at the centre of the organization. This reflected his central role in offering strategic leadership, as being a key enabler and as having central resources which could be released to operational units to facilitate change. The number of departments at Alpha were reduced. The former hierarchical model was dispensed with and a new style of horizontal structure was introduced. Alpha called this new structure Radial Management.

This organization structure was presented as bold and new. This was presented to the staff and debated. There was a consensus that this was very different from previous practice and worth going for. This led to the creation of four divisions: the Back Office and three operational areas created critical mass which could collaborate without departmental boundaries impeding developments. The top management team also considered the organization was so big it needed extra dimensions. After careful consideration, they proposed two: firstly, Divisional Coordinators, who were not managers as such, but interpreters, translators and believers in the mantra of decentralisation. These coordinators were to address issues at the operational level and Alpha had three sectors for different activities with interdependencies. Secondly, they proposed localism within geographical areas. Alpha introduced lower-level coordinators who worked with and reinforced the messages of Divisional Coordinators. This retained the focus on a slim, tightly organised organization without departmental compartmentalisation. These changes were initiated, debated with staff, tested as pilot exercises and introduced as operational units over an 18-month period.

Table 4.5 The Management Consultant as Educator

Lecture number	Topic
1.	Interactions and Interdependencies
2.	Opening Up to Change
3.	Talking About Change
4.	When Things Get Difficult
5.	Keep Going
6.	Reflections on Things That Have Changed

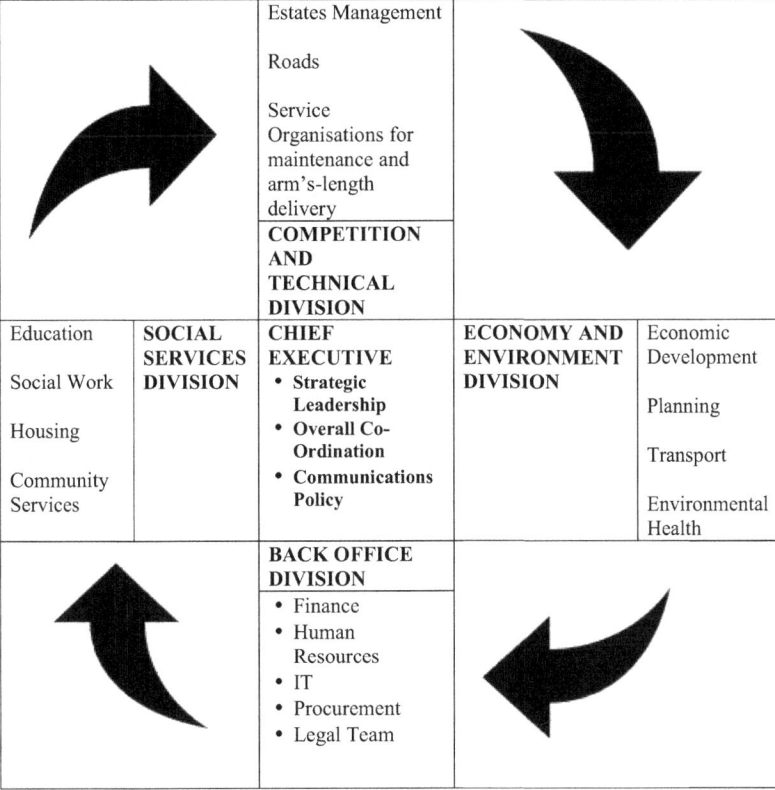

		Estates Management		
		Roads		
		Service Organisations for maintenance and arm's-length delivery		
		COMPETITION AND TECHNICAL DIVISION		
Education Social Work Housing Community Services	**SOCIAL SERVICES DIVISION**	**CHIEF EXECUTIVE** • **Strategic Leadership** • **Overall Co-Ordination** • **Communications Policy**	**ECONOMY AND ENVIRONMENT DIVISION**	Economic Development Planning Transport Environmental Health
		BACK OFFICE DIVISION • Finance • Human Resources • IT • Procurement • Legal Team		

Figure 4.1 Alpha City's Radial Management structure

The outcomes of change management

Alpha City had numerous outcomes – some good and some where its problems continued, as set out below:

1 The Alpha Authority now operated on a flatter organization structure.
2 Alpha shed almost 1,000 middle ranking officers over this period.
3 The Small Authority remained as a separate tribe in Alpha. They became a higher target for integration.
4 The restructuring of Alpha had reduced the proliferation of departments.
5 The departmental silos were weakened and there was more cooperation within and between departments.
6 Openness and transparency were deployed throughout the organization to good effect.
7 Modest improvements were made on 7.1 stakeholder engagement and 7.2 partnership working on service delivery.

However, there remained significant challenges to Alpha organization:

1 Its level of funding.
2 Its out-of-date financial information system.

Furthermore, in certain services, officers offered a very subtle form of resistance (see McCabe, 2020, pp. 94–112). When dealing with issues, officers would seek advice from the Director of their service, they would then disseminate this advice to others within their service as a direction from the Director. This was an attempt to recreate the former departmental structure. This "soft" challenge represents a significant challenge to the flat reorganization of Alpha. The Alpha Authority is further constrained by the range of these directorates which have statutory backing and in which citizens and other interested parties expect to have those responsible for education, social services and other major services as spokespersons for these services.

Therefore, this change management programme has worked, with the help of a respected management consultant – but significant challenges remain for Alpha City, such as the "soft" resistance of the reinvention of departments, the continuing severity of funding cuts and the need to get resources to update their financial information system to enable a policy-led approach to budgeting which would enable the political leader and the CEO to achieve their wider aims.

Managerial implications

The pressures for change in public services, in both the management and the delivery of services, are immense. These ideas for change may be a priority of citizens or business groups responding to an actual or perceived failure of an aspect of the organization's services. Or pressure may be exerted by the government or government agencies on standards and the means of providing services or the oversight of contracted out services to other providers.

However, while many of these voices express the urgency with which they see the need for change, there may be major issues over how the changes will be resourced. Management consultants have been a major reference point for change for many public service organizations for some time. However, many public services have had cutbacks in their core funding for many years and the option of buying in expertise from management consultants may be challenging. The continuous funding cuts also undermine the possibility of an internal consultancy project because of the need to slim down the workforce due to the cuts.

Nevertheless, in this chapter, there are discussions of examples of using management consultants to best effect in an environment constrained by a lack of funding. These are novel ways of drawing on consultancy expertise in modest but imaginative ways: the secret consultant at Alpha University, the embedded management consultant in the Alpha Hospital change programme and the use of the management consultant as an educator, rather than an agent of change in Alpha City. These examples merit careful consideration and they may lead to other innovative ways public services may utilise the expertise of management consultants. The key to the successes of Alpha University, Alpha Hospital and Alpha City: the management consultants may seek to secure a particular contract, doing what they are most comfortable with, but it's crucial that the public service organization thinks very carefully about what it is they actually need from external expertise and how best to achieve that.

References

Alvesson, M., and A. Johansson (2002) Professionalism and Politics in Management Consultancy Work, in T. Clark and R. Fincham, *Critical Consulting: New Perspectives on the Management Advice Industry.* Blackwell: 228–246.

Armbruster, T. (2006) *The Economics and Sociology of Management Consulting*. Cambridge University Press.

Arnaboldi, M. (2013) Consultant-researchers in Public Sector Transformation: An Evolving Role. *Financial Accountability & Management*, 29 (2), May.

Aucoin, P. (2012) New Political Governance in Westminster Systems: Impartial Public Administration and Management Performance at Risk. *Governance: An International Journal of Policy, Administration, and Institutions*, 25 (2): 177–199.

Baker, S. (2020) Covid Crisis Could Bankrupt UK Universities, *Times Higher Education Supplement*, July 6.

Boonstra, A., Versluis, A. and Vos, J.F.J. (2014) Implementing Electronic Health Records in Hospitals: A Systematic Literature Review. *BMC Health Serv Res*, 14 (370). https://doi.org/10.1186/1472-6963-14-370.

Bothwell, E. (2020) Coronavirus Could be 'Make or Break' for Universities' Finances, *Times Higher Education Supplement*, March 19.

Bracci, E., Maran, L. and Inglis, R. (2017) Examining the Process of Performance Measurement System Design and Implementation in Two Italian Public Service Organizations. *Financial Accountability & Management*, 33 (4): 406–421.

Brown, T. (2001) Modernization or Failure? IT Development Projects in the UK Public Sector. *Financial Accountability & Management*, 17 (4), November.

Brunsson, N. (2006) *Mechanisms of Hope: Maintaining the Dream of the Rational Organization*. Copenhagen Business School Press.

Collin, S.O., Haraldsson, M., Tagesson, T. and Blank, V. (2017) Explaining Municipal Audit Costs in Sweden: Reconsidering the Political Environment, the Municipal Organisation and the Audit Market. *Financial Accountability & Management*, 33 (4): 391–405.

Committee of Public Accounts (CPA) (2007) Central Government's Use of Consultants, 31st Report, House of Commons, Session 2006–2007, HC309, Stationery Office.

Craig, D. (2005) *Rip-Off! The Scandalous Inside Story of the Management Consulting Money Machine*. The Original Book Company.

Craig, D. (2006) *Plundering the Public Sector*. Constable.

Cucciniello, M., Lapsley, I. and Nasi, G. (2016) Managing Health Care in the Digital World: A Comparative Analysis. *Health Services Management Research*, 29 (4): 132–142.

Czarniawska, B. and Mazza, C. (2013) Consulting University: A Reflection from Inside. *Financial Accountability & Management*, 29 (2), May.

Du, J. and Lapsley, I. (2019) The Reform of UK Universities: A Management Dream, An Academic Nightmare? *ABACUS*, 55 (3): 452–482.

Fincham, R. and Clark, T. (2002) The Emergence of Critical Perspectives on Consulting, in R. Fincham and T. Clark (eds.) *Critical Consulting: New Perspectives on the Management Advice Industry*, Blackwell: 1–18.

Ganesh, J. (2004) E-health: Drivers, Applications, Challenges Ahead and Strategies: A Conceptual Framework. *Ind J Med Inform*, 1 (1): 39–47.

Kazley, A.S. and Ozcan, Y.A. (2007) Organizational and Environmental Determinants of Hospital EMR Adoption: A National Study. *Journal of Medical Systems*, 31: 375–384.

KPMG (2010) A Bitter Pill to Swallow: A Global View of What it Works in Health Care, KPMG International, Switzerland, April.

Lapsley, I. (2009) New Public Management: The Cruellest Invention of the Human Spirit? *ABACUS*, 45 (1): 1–21.

Lapsley, I. and Oldfield, R. (2000) Transforming the Public Sector: Management Consultants as Agents of Change. *European Accounting Review*, 10 (3).

Lapsley, I., Pallot, J. and Levy, V. (2002) *From Bureaucracy to Responsive Management: A Comparative Study of Local Government Change*. ICAS, Edinburgh.

Lapsley, I., Miller, P. and Pollock, N. (2013) Management Consultants: Demons or Benign Change Agents? *Financial Accountability & Management*, 29 (2): 117–123.

Lowndes, V. (1997) We are Learning to Accommodate Mess: Four Propositions About Management Change in Local Governance. *Public Policy and Administration*, 12 (2): 80–94.

McCabe, D. (2020) *Changing Change Management*. Routledge, New York and London.

Pinault, L. (2000) *Consulting Demons: Inside the Unscrupulous World of Global Corporate Consulting*. Harper Business.

Pollock, N. (2013) The IT Market Place, in N. Pollock and R. Williams (eds.), *Shaping Information Technology Markets and the Sociology of Business Knowledge*. Oxford University Press.

Saint-Martin, D. (1998) The New Managerialism and the Policy Influence of Consultants in Government: An Historical–Institutionalist Analysis of Britain, Canada and France. *Governance*, 11 (3).

Seal, W. (2000) *Beyond Incrementalism: Emergent Responses to Complexity in the Management of Local Government*. European Accounting Association, Annual Conference, Munich, March.

Stafford, A., Stapleton, P., Wei, H. and Williams, K. (2020) The Imaginary of the City Versus Messy Realities. *Financial Accountability & Management*, 36 (3): 380–391.

Thomasson, A. (2018a) Management Across Boundaries: A Municipal Dilemma. *Financial Accountability & Management*, 34 (3): 213–225.

Thomasson, A. (2018b) Politicisation of the Audit Process: The Case of Politically Affiliated Auditors in Swedish Local Government. *Financial Accountability & Management*, 34 (4): 380–391.

Whittington, R. (2003) The Work of Strategising and Organizing for a Practice Perspective. *Strategic Organization*, 1: 117–125.

Whittington, R. (2004) Strategy after Modernism: Recovering Practice. *European Management Review*, 1: 62–68.

Whittington, R. (2006) Completing the Practice Turn in Strategy Research. *Organization Studies*, 27: 613–634.

Whittington, R. (2007) Strategy Practice and Strategy Process: Family Differences and the Sociological Eye. *Organization Studies*, 28: 1575–1586.

Section three
Renewal of core practices

5 From cost accounting to strategic cost management

The experience of Italian higher education

Deborah Agostino and Michela Arnaboldi

From cost accounting to strategic cost management: the experience of Italian higher education cost management in public services has often been viewed with disenchantment. The perception of costs is associated with spending reviews and cuts in personnel, disregarding their strategic role. This chapter re-positions cost management at the strategic level. This repositioning is central to revaluate costs in their true essence: the calculation of how we use resources. This strategic view has two main benefits. The first is related to the results of cost allocation, that offer insights on how we consume our resources for service delivery. The second is related to the process for calculating these costs. There are several decisions in the process that might change the results; these decisions are not purely technical: they are a constitutive process in which managers, if involved, reflect on the services and products but also the organization and their responsibility centres.

This chapter poses the attention on these issues, presenting the experience of the Good Practice project. Good Practice is an Italian benchmarking initiative in which state universities voluntarily provide their costs, within the same protocol, in order to have a reference for their strategic management. The project started in 1999 under the initiative of the Italian Government, but from 2003 it has been brought forward and financed by universities directly. The project overall has involved more than 50 state universities during its 20-year life.

The chapter focuses in particular on three cases that are representative of how universities adopted a strategic approach to cost management. Three types of cost-strategizing configurations are identified: organizational reshaping, service balance and resource programming. The study offers a picture that is very distant from the often-employed cost-cutting approach. Cost data are instead part of a more strategic vision, although always coupled with other data.

The chapter is organised as follows. The next section illustrates the context and the method. Then, the distinctive features of the strategic approach to cost are presented. The empirical cases are illustrated in the third section, followed by a discussion of the managerial implications.

Context and method

This chapter is based on a longitudinal action research project carried out in Italian state universities. The research approach addressed the need to implement a reference framework for measuring and comparing costs associated with university support services, such as procurement, ICT services, libraries or research support.

DOI: 10.4324/9781003154389-8

The lack of consolidated frameworks on this topic pushed us to rely on the action research method. Interest in action research filtered down from social sciences, followed by renewed momentum in the 1980s, and its application in higher education studies (Cohen and Manion, 1980). Right from the beginning, there has been growing recognition for the way action research contributes to our understanding of practices in the various fields, where it can provide useful theoretical insights. The central issue of this approach lies in its interplay between science and practice, as both simultaneously influence the theoretical conceptualisation and the practical rules of the phenomena being studied (Argyris et al., 1985).

This chapter refers specifically to a 20-year project entitled "Good Practice". The project was initiated in 1999 on the initiative of the CNSVU, the Italian national committee for evaluating the country's university system. This independent body – established by central government – also provided its financial backing. The launch of the Good Practice project coincided with a lively period of reforms in Italy, especially for universities. Between 1993 and 1998, central government introduced a series of measures to move from a centralised model in higher education to a devolved system, giving universities greater autonomy to allocate their financial resources, define their curricula and decide on their research priorities. Against this backdrop, the CNVSU decided to tackle an area that had, at that time, been largely neglected in the reforms, that of support services. Administrative staff still worked according to the old public sector model, weighed down by cumbersome bureaucracy. Staff generally came from a background in law, had no management skills and there were no control systems in place.

After preliminary discussions with the directors of our selected universities, we embarked upon the first project. This first project cycle involved ten universities, our three-person research team and a CNVSU member acting as external observer. The aim of this project was to develop a performance measurement system (PMS) for support services, and to compare universities through this PMS. Cost data formed a central part of the PMS and was related to the cost of delivering support services. The results of the first Good Practice project and the positive backing of university managers prompted the CNVSU to finance two further projects and so achieve broader consensus and diffusion.

In 2002, the CNVSU ceased its financing of the project. The universities were, however, keen to press ahead with the project, and proposed to finance the research themselves, starting from 2003. The project is still running, starting its 13th edition in 2021. The number of universities involved has increased over time, and more than 40 universities are part of the group, which covers 60% of all state universities in Italy.

Strategizing cost: activity and benchmark

This research places a theoretical model for measuring costs at its centre. The choice of an activity-based management system was determined by our need to compare costs for support services from different organisations, our decision to construct a hierarchical model and findings from previous research (Arnaboldi and Azzone, 2002). The basic unit is a given activity (Anderson et al., 2002; Jones and Dugdale, 2002; Al-Sayed and Dugdale, 2016). In a basic activity-based framework, products and services are the consumers of activities and these activities, in turn, consume resources, and this ultimately drives up costs (Brown et al., 1999). An overview of this mechanism is given in Figure 5.1.

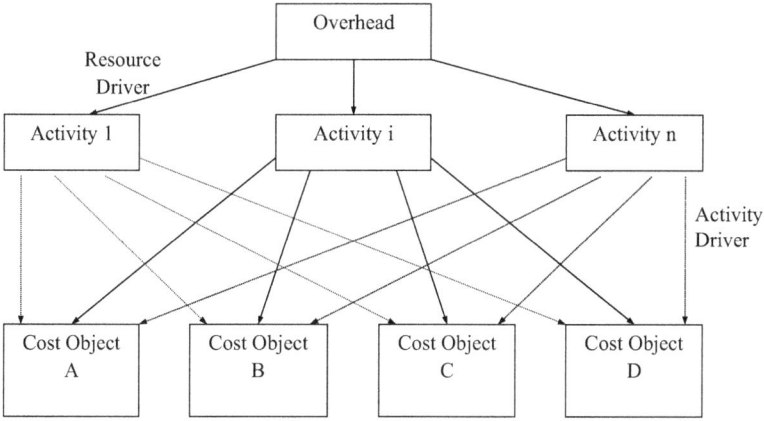

Figure 5.1 Activity-based scheme

This theoretical basis was used to build a tailored model for support services. The model was designed, revised and tested interactively, involving university managers and staff in the process, and the decision was taken to avoid standard package solutions. Because the model had to be flexible, this implied building a two-level framework divided into macro-activities and basic activities. By macro-activities, we mean services delivered for specific uses (e.g. procurement), and these can be further divided in sub-activities – or basic activities – which form our basic unit of analysis.

Figure 5.2 shows the key features of the system designed. First of all, from the very early stages, the model was always in the form of a hierarchical structure. This frame-work is intended to become a useful tool for managers wishing to find information at various levels of aggregation. The frame can also be used to design processes that give officers and operational staff selected access to the system. The second main feature of this control system is its modularity. Its graphic representation includes, as an example, three macro-activities (A, B and C), but the design of the architecture is such that other areas can subsequently be added along similar lines. This system modularity also operates at the lower levels of the architecture, with efficiency performance indicators (total costs and cost per driver) being designed and then fine-tuned on the basis of the managers' needs. The participants found it particularly interesting that an indicator could be used for all activities that worked with the same output/driver.

The two-level activity scheme brought additional flexibility through the option of including indicators of effectiveness, when needed, at the macro-activity or basic activity levels.

Efficiency is measured in terms of how wisely resources are used. For both basic and macro-activities, the choice of reference measurement was obvious: the cost of these activities. Resources consumed in universities were first divided into three macro-activities, and these potentially could be further split into their basic activities.

The first benefit of this measurement is that it can be used to compare universities with different organizational arrangements, ignoring their specific structure and extrapolating the costs from "virtual macro-activities" modelled from the set of their constituent basic activities. By focusing on the activity, it was also possible to relate the cost of an activity

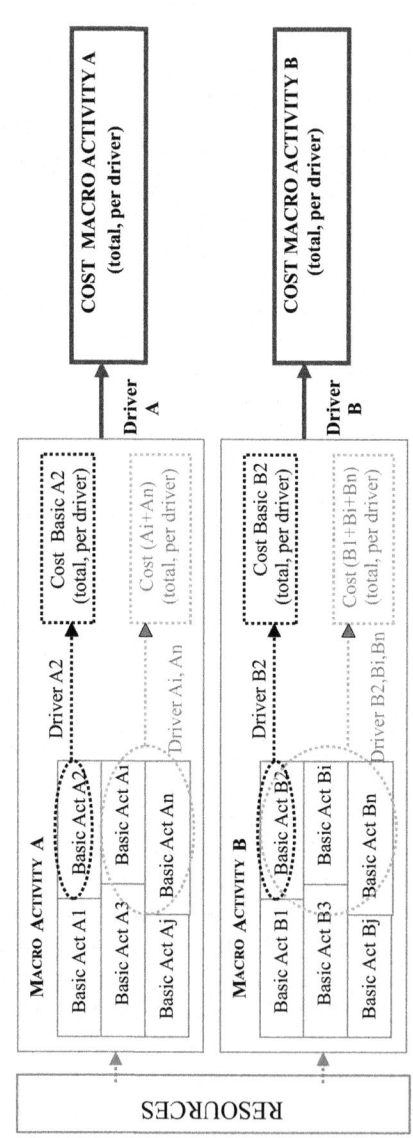

Figure 5.2 The reference model

to its product or to a measurement indicating how it is consumed – its driver (for example, personnel and the units of technical, administrative and teaching staff). Applying this Activity-Based Management (ABM) approach (Arnaboldi and Azzone, 2002), different organizations can be compared by dividing the total cost (cost of personnel) by the identified driver (no. of units of staff).

Clearly, allocating costs by macro-activity implies that the costs involved must be defined beforehand. We had to define the items in the chart of accounts that were taken into consideration and the methods used to evaluate them. The items used in this allocation exercise were defined on the basis of three criteria: (1) their bearing on administration costs; (2) whether the costs could be controlled by the offices in charge of administrative activities; and (3) the cost to extrapolate them. This led to us selecting the following cost items: internal personnel and outsourced staff.

Similar considerations were made when defining the method for evaluating the costs. Using the effective cost meant that we had the true figure for the resources consumed, but the burden to measure them was greater. Conversely, using standard costs was easier, but did not give the true expenditure for the universities. We turned again to our three criteria, deciding to measure the effective cost of each cost item.

Following the hierarchical model presented in the previous section, the design was developed and the single activities relating to each macro-activity identified. This is an essential step, as it is then that the elementary units are defined. These are then used to extrapolate costs and are the basis for the macro-activities and, therefore, for their performance. The system must, therefore, be given the necessary number of activities to provide sufficiently detailed information for management purposes, but not too many, as overly fragmented data would create difficulties both in terms of allocating the costs and in monitoring and using the measurements. During this phase, we worked very closely with internal university staff. Although we started from an initial proposal about the activities to include, the input of university operators was crucial and we modified the general activity-based model on the basis of their internal knowledge.

We used a similar approach for all the activities, identifying the drivers needed to calculate unit costs. At this point, we must note that we did not set up a driver for some of the activities (such as managing course equivalence in the Students Office or preparing financial statements in Accounting), as the information retrieved would have had little meaning.

Table 5.1 relates to the macro-activities involving the Students Office and gives the basic activities (in column 1), and the indicators or drivers that explain their level of consumption (in column 2).

Further steps were required to establish the cost of the activities considered. These involve defining the method for allocating the macro-activity costs to the basic activities and evaluating the drivers.

The overall costs of the macro-activities were divided among the basic activities on the basis of the quota of time spent by staff on each basic activity. Each of these quotas were then multiplied by the cost associated to each single person (loaded with all the items linked to placement, location and general services). The sum of the various contributions gives the cost of a given activity. Table 5.2 contains an example of the form we utilised.

Results

Good Practice-based research is heterogeneous in its use of costs, which are, in general, coupled with other performance indicators. We were able to highlight three

Table 5.1 Example of support services in teaching: activities and drivers

Activities	Drivers
1. Orientation and tutorship	No. students enrolled on degree courses
2. Matriculation	No. matriculated students
3. Enrolment	No. students enrolled on degree courses
4. Self-certification	No. students enrolled on degree courses
5. Record books/student cards	No. students enrolled on degree courses
6. Curricula	No. students enrolled on degree courses
7. Degree session management	No. graduates
8. State exam management	No. enrolled for state exams
9. Career management	No. students enrolled on degree courses
10. Attestation and certification	No. certificates issued
11. Transfers	No of transfers
12. Course equivalence and foreign students	None
13. Student activities	None
14. Research doctorate	No. students enrolled on PhD courses
15. Graduate schools and advanced courses	No. students enrolled to graduate schools and advanced courses
16. Agreements for work placements and internships	No. of agreements
17. Student grants, scholarships, fee exemptions and tax refunds	Total no. grants and scholarships (units)

Table 5.2 Example of costs allocated by activity

First and last name	Total cost for that person	Quotas			
		Orientation and tutorship	Enrolment	Grants, scholarships, fee exemptions	TOTAL
Name_1	€20,000	50%	10%	40%	100%
Name_2	€40,000	20%	30%	50%	100%
		Costs			
		Orientation and tutorship	Enrolment	Grants, scholarships, fee exemptions	TOTAL
Name_1		€10,000	€2,000	€8,000	€20,000
Name_2		€8,000	€2,000	€20,000	€40,000
	Total activity	**€18,000**	**€14,000**	**€28,000**	**€60,000**

configurations relating to cost usage, in the form of organisational reshaping, service balance and resource programming. The following figure shows how the universities are positioned for the three situations. Some universities adopted more than one type of logic.

Figure 5.3 The three strategic cost configurations

Below, we have described the three configurations, taking one university as reference for each case to explain our approach.

Organizational reshaping

The *organizational reshaping* configuration has, as its central element, the benchmarking of a university's cost data against those of other institutions, and this is taken as a reference point for assessing internal organizational efficiency. The case study in this configuration is Top-Small University. The General Director of Top-Small wanted to use costs, and in particular the unitary costs of support services, to assess how efficient their offices were. He intended to revise their organizational structure on that basis. Top-Small was keen to use detailed costs instead of following the typical linear spending review approach, and so apply a "precision intervention". In the words of the General Director:

> I didn't want to simply cut costs, and I probably won't cut costs, but my feeling is that some of our services are overstaffed and others are understaffed. There are historical reasons for this, but it is also down to gradual changes in the university's strategies.
>
> (General Director, Top-Small University)

This comment makes an important point: costs and their benchmarking with data of other universities is the first step and these are then integrated with elements that emerge from strategic considerations about the future direction of the university.

At the technical level, using costs for organizational configurations was carried out in three phases: (1) calculation of a benchmark value for the macro-activity and assessment of the efficiency for each support service; (2) analysis of the efficiency of the various offices and the activities they deliver and (3) definition of the university's strategy and re-allocation of personnel.

Phase 1 started by selecting a sub-sample of universities within the overall network of Good Practice universities, as this helped us to identify a target value of reference. The choice was directed and validated by the General Director who wanted both a technical fit (size, type of university) and a strategic fit:

> I know that some universities are very efficient, but this is because they decided to downsize some of their services. We can see this from the effectiveness data. For us, quality of support is central.
>
> (General Director, Top-Small University)

From our discussion with the General Director, we identified a cluster of nine universities to use for benchmarking the cost data. Within this sample, the unitary costs of each support service were compared against those of the universities in the cluster, allowing us to identify a target efficiency value for each service. The target value for efficiency was based upon two possible situations: the best target value in terms of efficiency and the median value, selected to avoid particular circumstances when costs were low due to a lack of resources.

By placing the unitary cost of each support service against a benchmark unitary cost, it was possible to identify situations where there was a deficit or surplus in resources. The results of phase 1 were elaborated in a graph to provide visual representation of each service, indicating whether each was over or under resourced (Figure 5.4). Each bar in the picture represents a support service and the numbers show the FTE (Full-Time Equivalent) in surplus or deficit for each service. As mentioned, this was achieved by comparing the median unitary value with the most efficient value for each service. This phase led to the identification of overstaffed and understaffed services.

The second phase was less straightforward. Top-Small wanted to have a reference cost for each office, not just for each support service (obtained in phase 1).[1] Starting from the Good Practice scheme, in terms of each support service, we calculated the efficiency for every office involved and identified a reference value for each (see Figure 5.5). Unlike the previous graph, each bar in this case represents an internal office, and its height gives the surplus or deficit in resources for any given office. As in the previous case, the delta analysis was carried out considering the most efficient value and the median reference value of efficiency.

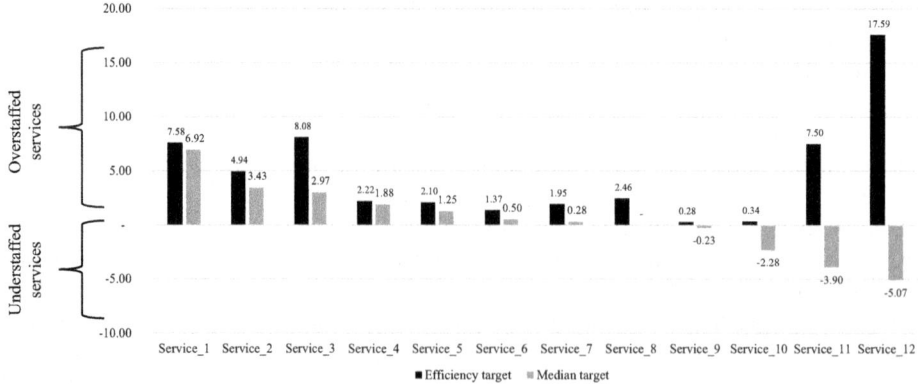

Figure 5.4 Services with relative surplus or deficit in resources

Figure 5.5 Offices with a relative surplus or deficit in resources

In this phase, the main challenge was to reconcile the cost data with the strategic objective of obtaining valuable references against other universities to support internal reorganization. In other words, the key question turned out to be: how should services be organised and prioritised? The Director wanted to identify the best university in terms of unitary costs, but he also wanted to find a reference that he could use strategically when making his own organizational choices. This was not possible since there was no "one best" university for all the services. A university could be efficient in one service, but not in another.

The "solution" was to highlight two major strategic choices that could be used to complement the unitary cost analysis. These were the centralisation-decentralisation of services, to be managed by central support services or departments, as appropriate, and the distribution of activities across central offices. Acting at this level allowed us to identify several organizational models of reference and their performance in terms of cost.

The third phase was more qualitative, but still based on cost data. At this point, the process consisted of redistributing personnel among the offices. Initially, the administrative staff responsible for the analysis thought that we could come up with some kind of sweeping "mathematical formula" based on cost data and use that for reallocating personnel. When presented with the benchmark of cost data, they realised that personnel could not be reallocated on the basis of costs alone. The main driver was to be the university's strategic direction, as highlighted during a meeting:

> Do we want to centralise our support service and save internal resources or is it better to place the service closer to students and academics? What are the Chancellor's strategic priorities? Our process to redistribute personnel should be coherent with the university's strategic choices.

This position changed the initial expectations of the working team, who refrained from immediately redistributing personnel, preferring instead to discuss the intermediate results with the Chancellor and define two other personnel redistribution plans based on the possible strategic choices.

Service Balance

The second strategic use of costs involved *service balance*. Here costs are used to assess if and how resources allocated to a specific support service generate value for users. Costs are reshaped around the provision of a service, and customer satisfaction is the main aggregation element of this activity.

At the technical level, this second example again makes use of unitary costs, but here activity aggregation relates to the users and the delivery of services. A good example of this configuration is Aspiring University. With the arrival of a new Chancellor and a General Director who came from the private sector in 2016, Aspiring wanted to change its model for delivering support services, putting users at the centre and seeing costs and efficiency as strategic levers to improve these services. Starting with an in-depth analysis, the first step was to construct efficiency and effectiveness maps for each service, relating to three different types of service users, i.e. students, academics and support staff. Universities are positioned on the matrix depending on their unitary cost (horizontal axes) and on the student satisfaction (vertical axes). The position of each university on the maps facilitates the relative comparison between the position of the university and that of the others in terms of efficiency and effectiveness. When looking at this matrix for student support services, results showed a position in the middle for Aspiring. The university's General Director commented this:

> This was acceptable in the past, today we want to compete with the best universities in Italy and be attractive to foreign students. If we do not improve our services, it will be hard to get there.
>
> (General Director, Aspiring University)

The first step brought up the need for an overall picture of all services. This was not easy to do given that the unitary cost metrics are different. At the end, we opted for a matrix solution, where the service costs were rescaled against benchmark costs. This choice had the two benefits of seeing all the services together and maintaining the benchmark with other universities. Figure 5.6 shows the matrix arrangement as follows:

Vertical Axis: this gives the position of a given service with respect to efficiency. Each unitary cost is normalised with respect to the average of all universities (set to 1). When the unitary cost for the university is above average, the value is greater than 1 and the service is placed in the bottom section of the graph.

Horizontal Axis: this gives the position of a given service with respect to the average customer satisfaction value for teaching staff, PhD students and fellows, technical/administrative staff and students. Here also, customer satisfaction points for each service are normalised with respect to the average of all universities (set to 1). When overall customer satisfaction in the service is below average, the value is less than 1 and the service is placed to the left of the graph.

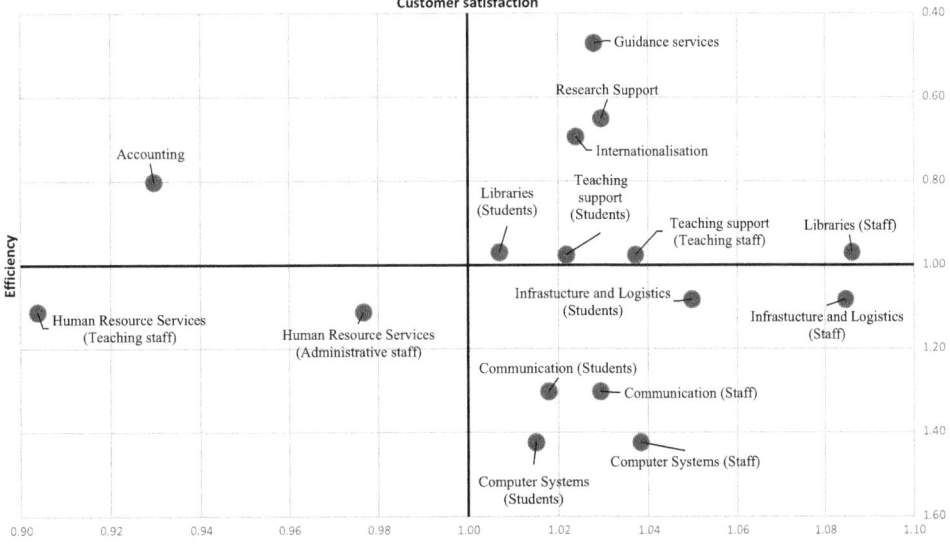

Figure 5.6 The integration between efficiency and effectiveness. Position of services

This gives us four quadrants:

- Top right: services where the unitary cost is below average and customer satisfaction is above average. These are what the University considers virtuous services.
- Top left: services where the unitary cost is below average and customer satisfaction is also less than average. These are services considered critical for customer satisfaction.
- Bottom right: services where the unitary cost is above average and customer satisfaction is also above average. These are services considered critical in terms of efficiency.
- Bottom left: services where the unitary cost is above average and customer satisfaction is below average. These are services considered critical for both efficiency and customer satisfaction.

Figure 5.6 gives a clear indication of the most critical areas, these being Computer Systems (IT) for the efficiency and Accounting for the perceived effectiveness. Human Resource Services are instead critical for both effectiveness and efficiency.

The third phase involved further in-depth interviews to focus on the main problems in each area and on possible solutions. Our organizational analysis meant that we could record several important facts about the role of the IT department in the university's vertical and cross-departmental processes. One point noted was the university's non-uniform approach to innovation projects. Firstly, we found that IT was still very fragmented, with an imbalance between the university's central – and more digital – structures, and the more peripheral areas. The reason was that there was no coordinated practice for innovative action.

The consequence of not having a single port of call in terms of computer management meant that each area was likely to go its own sweet way, generating inefficiencies and slowing work. This also meant that computer assets were also decentralised in their management, and this translated into duplication of data and information, with a waste of resources and an increase in mistakes. The problem was highlighted by several users:

> We have too many systems for managing student data. Sometimes, we have to trawl through different systems to get what we want because everything is so fragmented.
>
> (Education Department)

> We have to fill in four databases, but what if we could just input the data once and it got replicated automatically everywhere else? The process could be improved if it were computerised.
>
> (Technical Area)

For the university to achieve its objectives of rationalisation, efficiency and effectiveness, IT should be fully integrated into all university processes. What seemed to slow down this process mostly was a difficulty in communication and interaction between the IT department and the other organizational units.

This aspect was brought up by several departments and offices (see section 4.1). The people here felt marginalised, far from innovation initiatives and outside the process.

IT thinks only about IT and how to apply it. It doesn't look at organizational aspects, about knowing the processes or the users' needs.

(Director)

The IT manager also said that they were only marginally involved in designing and planning solutions. This situation was compounded when, as happened in some areas, there was an independent workgroup – not the IT Department – that managed IT.

We are not brought in at the design or planning stages.

(IT Department)

This seems to be confirmed by Back Office staff at the Education Office, who also found it difficult to be involved in processes or interact with end users of IT solutions, even at the design stage.

End users only ask me to come up with the product and don't want me to get involved in designing it.

(Back Office)

Overcoming these interaction and communication issues is an absolute must for setting in place ongoing and effective innovation.

Secondly, we found that IT had very little in place regarding user orientation, whether for external (students) or internal (other departments and offices) users. One example given made reference to the Strategic Annual Plan – which has the precise purpose of defining future projects – but they did not talk to other offices when preparing it. It could also be so much more effective if end users were involved.

[Software] is designed in a rigid manner, it can't handle special cases, but that is where it would be most useful.

(Unit Manager)

IT systems, in their very nature, must be allowed to evolve continuously and adapt to new technologies and to the new and amended laws that impose new models. However, the IT department had no unit dedicated to innovation projects and any R&D work in this area was often neglected as people were engaged in other routine work or busy coping with regular emergencies. On top of this, managing innovation requires organizational and management skills alongside IT and technical skills, but the former were given little consideration in the IT department.

Resource programming configuration

The *resource programming configuration* is the most controversial area, as cost data are used in negotiation, but are not inserted directly on the manager's individual dashboards – so they are not linked to their bonuses. The "measurements" partners used in strategizing are service standards and project outcome.

Our example here is Large, a big and ancient university. In 2014, its General Director decided to revise the university's budgeting process, linking it to a mid-year review process. This need emerged after a review of historical data highlighted that managers were engaged in building up pots of reserve resources, mainly for central support services, which had not been picked up earlier, as he noted:

> When I first analysed the data and budgeting cycle, I saw that every manager tended to overestimate the resources needed in their unit. Every year end, they find ways to spend the money in hurry even when this is not totally necessary.

The Director also gave his analysis about a possible solution:

> When I first tried to discuss this matter with the managers, they challenged my request to rationalise spending with their greater knowledge of the resources required. This convinced me that we needed to use benchmark costs and efficiency in our budgeting, together with output measurements.

The outcome of this was that the budgeting process became a budgeting-performance cycle, introducing monthly management reviews and a mid-year renegotiation. The revision was set within the wider framework of a revision to the performance cycle, which was presented and promoted inside and outside the university. The following figure shows one of the graphs used to present this approach.

The performance-budget process was divided into three phases. The first phase, which begins every October, consisted of the more traditional budgeting process. Managers were asked to set out their plans in terms of resources needed and results to be achieved. For the routine support services, the expected results (i.e. output) had to be expressed as customer satisfaction, or as the standard level to be maintained. The

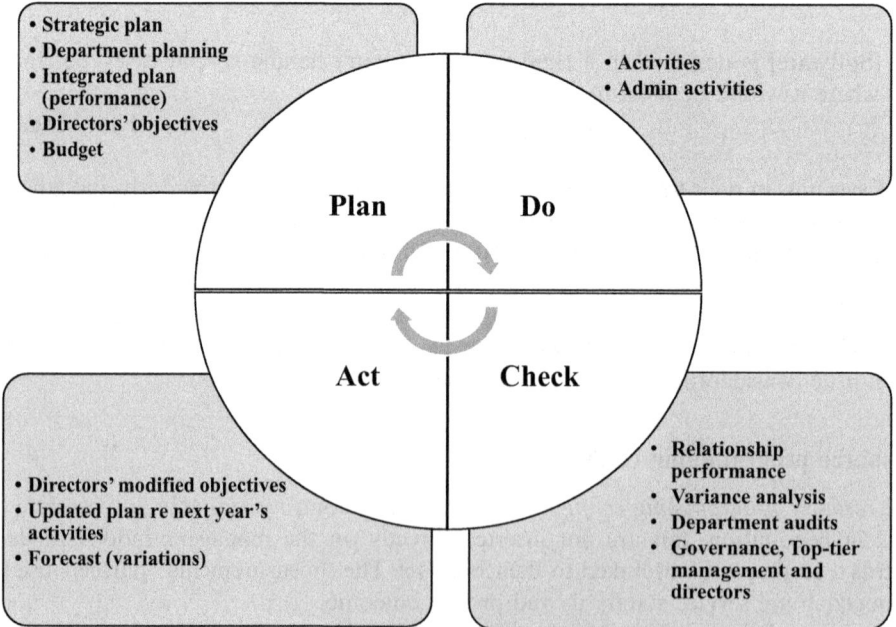

Figure 5.7 The Performance Management Cycle in Large (adapted – the original picture was in Italian)

resources (i.e. input) had, instead, to be expressed in terms of total costs and investments needed. Efficiency indicators (unitary costs for each service) were additionally used as a reference for negotiation purposes, as highlighted by this comment made by the head of Management Control:

> We do not use efficiency indicators explicitly when we budget resources. While they do not act as thresholds, they do play a role in our budgeting negotiations and can force managers to justify their budget requests.

Data from the Good Practice project were the main reference for customer satisfaction and efficiency. Benchmarked values are considered very important for central support services as there is no comparison data relating to other units, as the Director pointed out:

> Managers in central administration use the lack of comparative values as an excuse. So, I decided to use the benchmark value, but not too rigidly. When, for example, they asked for more resources to support academics in their EU research proposal, I challenged them by asking for clear results. Are they going to improve their funding? Are they going to improve customer satisfaction? They must tell me.

The second phase takes place in June the following year and is based on the analysis of the money spent and results achieved in the first part of the year.

The goals of this phase are to:

- Verify the progress of the planned activities (in continuity and discontinuity) and the deviations at that moment.
- Estimate the expected use of resources with reference to the end of the financial year.
- Estimate the resources that are not necessary for a manager's area of responsibility and evaluate the benefit of using these resources in future years for the same objectives or other requirements.

The impact on the university's budget is to identify the resources that can be used in the planning of the next financial year for the same objectives or for different requirements. These resources are used in the overall forecast for the financial year of reference (x+1) and are available as soon as they are included in the budget, as long as they are recorded in the statements for financial year x to ensure that the budget is covered.

During this phase, the General Director again held face-to-face meetings to revise the data. When considerably less money was spent than expected, the Director worked on agreeing an updated budget or a new proposal for using these funds during the next part of the year. As he pointed out:

> To be honest, so far, I've not cut anyone's resources, but these negotiations are very important to me. I have unearthed this practice of keeping surplus resources without any clear reason. Forcing managers to explain why the resources weren't spent and to think about their future use leads to much value added for both parties.

The cycle closes in the September of the same year, before the new cycle is due to start, with a review of the performance achieved and the remaining resources.

Commenting on the benefits of the new approach, the Director said that a big plus was promoting the use of variance analysis in a strategic way, where "the adjustments to annual planning form the basis of planning for the upcoming years".

To summarise, resource programming use of costs was shown to be useful in terms of:

- Verifying the use of resources allocated for the programmed activities and strategic plan actions.
- Formulating proposals to update the plans and confirm that there are available resources.
- Formulating proposals to review the plans, defining the various objectives, which must be consistent with the process of monitoring the status of the strategic plan.

Managerial implications

This study offers three cases of the strategic use of cost data, here referred to as organizational reshaping, service balance and resource programming. All three cases share a strategic approach to the use of cost data. Costs have no negative connotation, rather they support a broader strategic action, although there are differences between one case and another.

The *organizational reshaping configuration* uses costs strategically to support internal office reorganization. The principal cost element considered is the unitary cost for each support service, which is benchmarked with that of the other universities to give a realistic reference target. Given the end objective of reorganising internal offices, we are looking at the long-term for this type of cost usage and the unit of analysis is represented by each organizational unit. The main "partner" of cost data is the volume managed by each support service.

The *service balance configuration* uses costs strategically, but with the final aim of assessing whether resources are properly allocated in order to generate value for users. Therefore, the principal cost element is the unitary cost of the support service, with the main "partner" being customer satisfaction. Each support service is analysed by examining unitary costs and user perception (measured through customer satisfaction data) jointly. In this configuration, the organizational offices are of secondary importance, since the main unit of analysis is the support service itself. Unlike the previous case of organizational reshaping, this configuration was studied for the medium-term, and the reference value is set over a shorter period of time.

The *performance management configuration* uses costs strategically to allocate resources and support budgeting negotiations, although it is not linked directly to the managers' individual bonuses. In this specific setting, the attention focuses mainly on the total costs and on the resources assigned to each organizational unit, with the addition of benchmark values and output acting as the main "partner" to support budget negotiations with the directors in each university area. The period of time considered plays a major role in preparing the budget and in the ensuing negotiation process, relating mainly to the short term, and the cost data used relates to the budgeting cycle.

The three cost configurations presented above differ in several points concerning strategic elements, cost elements, time horizon, unit of analysis and performance "partner". Table 5.3 summarises these elements and their diversity across the three uses.

All the configurations, however, share two main building blocks that are common to a strategic approach to cost data. The first building block consists in connecting cost data to other "more qualitative" information. In all the cases covered, strategic decisions are based on cost data, but not only on costs. Cost data give an indication and this needs to be completed with other data and grounded in the existing organizational and strategic context.

The second building block is the process of benchmarking cost data. The unitary cost value is of limited added value and risks being linked to a negative perception of cost data. For cost data to be used strategically, the numbers should be connected to those of other organizations or recorded over time to show a trend. This real and substantial use of benchmarks is considered particularly valuable by the organizations involved, nevertheless, it is important to highlight some related issues. A first issue is the attention and time needed to carry out the benchmarking exercise, when data are used for actual organizational actions. It is known that benchmarking on costs needs a precise accounting from the technical staff, adapting internal costs to a common protocol (Arnaboldi and Azzone, 2004; Arena et al., 2009). What it is less pointed out is that the strategic use of costs needs the involvement of top manager not only in the decision-making phase but also in the "dirty" job of data collection. The cases highlighted that an effective approach was an open, reflective and interactive approach, where top managers and technical staff discuss cost results going back to the accounting rules (Agostino and Arnaboldi, 2015).

It is interesting to underline that this chapter presented the experience of Italian universities, but the same approach of activity-based management to cost analysis has been replicated in other two public settings: municipalities and state museums. The theoretical model has been the same, but activities have been tailored to the specific context (either local government or museums). The benchmarking logic has remained as well. The dynamics observed in the usage of costs data were found to be comparable

Table 5.3 Summary of strategic cost configurations

	Organisational reshaping	*Service Balance*	*Resource programming*
Strategic element	University positioning and development	Quality and efficiency of support services	Resource allocation and reduction in surplus
Costs element	Unit cost: reference for efficiency at the macro-level and micro-level	Unit costs at the service level	Total cost
Time-horizon	Long term	Medium term	Short term
Aggregation driver for activities	Organisational units	Services	Budget units
Performance "partner"	Volumes	Customer satisfaction benchmark data of other institutions	Benchmarking value related to outputs

with the three dynamics described here and, again, went beyond the cost-cutting approach. These additional experiences, although limited in time, underline and further confirm the opportunities for costs data to move beyond their traditional negative perception and serve a strategic function.

To conclude, strategic cost management is a precious tool for the reflective manager, who wants to put consolidated practices under discussion. Costs are a representation of the organization, derived from accounting rules; discussing costs openly with a future oriented vision creates the willingness in sharing ideas " in managers, who do not feel judged, but part of the creation of something new. After the creation of this collaborative, but technically grounded, environment, the challenge for top managers remains to make decisions, even though they will always disappoint someone. Here two strategies were evidenced as supportive: the use of benchmarking to highlight better or worse situations and the sharing of results inside universities with the final aim of showing administrative activities that are under performing and over performing.

Reflective managers have in cost data and benchmarking a strategic ally, but they need to be ready to enter the technicality of accounting and discuss controversies with higher and lower level staff.

Note

1 Note that there is no one-to-one relationship between support services and organizational offices. A given support service (e.g. procurement) may be managed by more than one office. This implies setting a target for both services and offices.

References

Al-Sayed, M. and Dugdale, D. (2016) Activity-based innovations in the UK manufacturing sector: extent, adoption process patterns and contingency factors. *The British Accounting Review*, 48 (1): 38–58.

Agostino, D. and Arnaboldi, M. (2015) How Performance Measurement Systems support managerial actions in networks: evidence from an Italian case study. *Public Organization Review*, 15 (1): 117–137.

Anderson, S.W., Hesford, J.W. and Young, S.M. (2002) Factors influencing the performance of activity-based costing teams: a field study of ABC model development time in the automobile industry. *Accounting Organization and Society*, April: 195–211.

Arena, M., Arnaboldi, M., Azzone, G. and Carlucci, P. (2009) Developing a Performance Measurement System for the Central Administrative Services of the universities. *Higher Education Quarterly*, 63 (3): 237–263.

Argyris, C., Putnam, R., and Smith, D. (1985) *Action Science*. San Francisco, CA, Jossey-Bass.

Arnaboldi, M. and Azzone, G. (2002) *Performance Measurement as Change Management Tool: the case of Italian New Public Administration*, PMA Performance Measurement Conference, Boston.

Arnaboldi, M. and Azzone, G. (2004) Benchmarking university activities: an Italian case study. *Financial Accountability and Management*, 20 (2): 205–220.

Brown, R.E., Myring, M.J. and Gard, C.G. (1999) Activity-based costing in government: possibilities and pitfalls, *Public Budgeting and Finance*, Summer: 3–21.

Cohen, L. and Manion, L. (1980) *Research Methods in Education*. London, Croom, Helm.

Jones, T.C., and Dugdale, D. (2002) The ABC bandwagon and the juggernaut of modernity. *Accounting, Organisations and Society*, 27: 121–163.

6 Rethinking performance management

Anders Anell

Introduction

Performance management is inherently complex (Arnaboldi et al. 2015). A central dimension of performance management is the need for effective performance measurement system, i.e. the regular collection and feedback of data concerning resources, activities and results of an individual, team or larger organization (Neely et al. 2005). Such collection and feedback of data can be used for different purposes and to support different forms of organizational control (Franco-Santos et al. 2012). In the standard management literature, it is often recommended that managers distribute rewards and sanctions based on deviations between actual performance and targets (e.g. Ferreira & Otley 2009). Targets are linked to key performance indicators (KPIs) which in turn are aligned with the vision and mission of the organization. A similar use of performance measurement, to support coercive control and compliance towards targets, has become common in public sector organizations (Siverbo et al. 2019). Rewards and sanctions include carrier opportunities and increased (or decreased) payment for services, possibly indirectly as transparency of performance influences the choice of provider by service users. These developments have been inspired by New Public Management (NPM) reforms (Diefenbach 2009; Arnaboldi et al. 2015), as well as increased transparency and accountability towards standards (Pollit & Bouckaert 2011; Bringselius 2017).

The outcomes of these performance measurement and control practices, and the impact on efficiency and quality in public sector organizations, are uncertain. In several professional services – e.g., healthcare, education and social services – professionals themselves seem to perceive increased demands for external accountability based on targets as an administrative burden with limited benefits. "External" here refers to payers, regulators and general managers not belonging to the profession(s) concerned. Criticism also comes from researchers who describe performance management in the public sector as the ultimate challenge for this section of the economy, both because of the need for such systems but also because of the complexity of designing effective systems (Arnaboldi et al. 2015) and because measurement is often limited to aspects that are easily quantifiable. More importantly, researchers describe the "measurement mania" as having far reaching negative consequences for people that work in public sector organizations, and for the services provided, due to staff demoralization, lower job-satisfaction, decreased motivation and increased employee turnover (Diefenbach 2009, p. 900). These empirical findings in the public sector are also supported by critical views developed by research in general. Experimental studies have found that coercive control using targets signals distrust and limits autonomy that in itself reduces

DOI: 10.4324/9781003154389-9

performance (Falk & Kosfeld 2006). Studies also suggest that coercive control combined with extrinsic financial incentives is not well adapted to complex tasks (Cerasoli et al. 2014). Financial rewards or sanctions linked directly to quality indicators may lead to distorted incentives, manipulation of the underlying data and irreversible and unintended effects on work related norms (Frey 1997; Gneezy & Rustichini 2000; Cerasoli et al. 2014). Ironically, such experiences may give NPM proponents justification (or a case which may not be merited) that even more coercive controls are needed (Diefenbach 2009).

During the past few years, policy interest in the wake of NPM criticism has turned towards new governance and management approaches, allowing for a higher degree of professional autonomy and participatory processes (see e.g. Bringselius 2017). It is far from clear, however, what this reversal of the NPM trend means in practice. One interpretation would be to stop measuring performance altogether, and to trust that professionals will do a good job without any form of external accountability. Although this may be a wet dream for some professionals, such proposals are unlikely to be accepted by payers or regulators, or indeed by society. Variations in the quality of services and problems, such as long waiting times for healthcare services or poor standards of schools, are regularly reported in media and much talked about. Politicians and general managers are expected to act.

So, is it possible to identify an alternative to even tighter controls focusing compliance towards general targets? In this chapter, it is argued that we need to rethink the purpose of performance management and focus more on learning and innovation rather than coercive forms of control. Performance management focusing on learning and innovation will be better adapted to a context characterized by increased uncertainty and rapid change. Negative side-effects undermining staff morale and motivation can be avoided. As will be discussed, rethinking performance management to support learning will have important implications for both performance measurement systems and relevant forms of accountability. Rather than focusing on a few key results or outcome measures, several measures describing both outcomes, results and processes are needed. Rather than using financial incentives, organizational change should be facilitated by strengthening autonomy, competence and relatedness and an appeal to the disciplinary mechanism of professionalism.

The arguments put forward in this chapter are relevant for professional services such as healthcare, education and social services. These services are similar in terms of recruiting professional workers with a university education that perform complex tasks requiring autonomy and self-governance, although conditions, the nature of services and the existence and strength of professional identities vary. The more general argument to rethink the purpose of performance management in support of learning and participatory processes – not least in uncertain and unstable times – also applies in other public services.

Performance management is not a new phenomena

Although described as a key component of modern management, performance measurement of human activities is as old as humankind, following the cognitive revolution. At a very basic level, performance measurement is the process of monitoring behavior and/or the output or outcome of behavior. If the purpose of performance management is to support control, actual behavior and/or outcomes are compared to norms and priorities. In case of a significant deviation, some form of accountability will follow. The technicalities of these processes as well as the mechanisms of accountability have varied greatly over time and across contexts. The search for cultural control in ancient nomadic tribes or communities specified by geographical or other borders, or more technocratic forms of control within large organizations employing thousands of people, is a common thread through history. Principles of performance management described as "new" when introduced as part of NPM reforms have often been used before, although in a different form.

One example is the use of pay-for-performance (P4P) implemented in many healthcare systems in the new millennium. A common background is dissatisfaction with previous payment mechanisms incentivizing a larger volume of care. With payment linked to quality indicators, e.g. improvement of care to patients with chronic conditions, it is believed that quality of care and health benefits will improve. Although often described as innovative, similar principles were in use during the Babylonian empire almost 4,000 years ago, even if consequences in cases of negative deviations were more severe and personal (see Box 6.1).

Box 6.1 The Code of Hammurabi

King Hammurabi (1810–1750 BC) carved laws for the Babylonian empire into stone columns. Included in the laws was a very early form of pay-for-performance of doctors.

> If a doctor has treated a gentleman for a severe wound with a bronze lancet and has cured him, or has opened an abscess of the eye for a gentleman with the bronze lancet and has cured the eye of the gentleman, he shall take ten shekels of silver.
> If a doctor has treated a gentleman for a severe wound with a lancet of bronze and has caused the gentleman to die, or has opened an abscess of the eye for a gentleman with the bronze lancet and has caused the loss of the gentleman's eye, one shall cut off his hands.

Source: Thatcher (2004, p. 457)

Although performance measurement for control purposes is not a new phenomenon, its use to support governance and management in public sectors has accelerated in recent decades. One explanation is that performance measurement and coercive control are seen as a proper response to increased demands for efficiency. Increased transparency regarding variation in the quality of public services indeed suggests that it is possible to achieve greater value for the same money. More and more, the performances of healthcare and social service providers, schools and other public service providers are measured and compared. Targets addressing individual quality and performance indicators are used to hold providers and managers to account.

Problems related to performance management in the public sector

Both in media and in the academic literature, it is not difficult to find examples where performance management did not achieve the intended outcome. Even worse, it is relatively easy to find examples where organizational behavior has developed for the worse as a result of implementing coercive controls using quantitative targets. Some examples are highlighted in Box 6.2. Similar examples of "reaching the target but missing the point" exist in the private sector and in human activities more generally. A more careful look at the logic behind the problems highlighted in Box 6.2 also reveal that the ones actually missing the point are those designing the targets, rather than the ones exposed to them. This has also been pointed out in a now classic article by Kerr (1975) with the informative title "On the folly of rewarding A, while hoping for B".

Box 6.2 "Reaching the target but missing the point" examples

Fixation on target achievement when monitoring activities, without due regard to policy and operational outcomes (Arnaboldi et al. 2015).

Waiting time targets introduced in the NHS in England from 1997 caused various forms of re-active gaming among health care providers (Bevan & Hood 2006, pp. 530–532). Providers sought to meet but not exceed targets (ratchet effect) and the distribution of reported data was influenced by targets (threshold effect). Other forms of opportunistic behavior were to require patients to wait in queues of ambulances outside A&E departments until hospitals were confident that waiting time targets of four hours could be met. Similar examples were that primary care would not book appointments more than 48 hours in advance following the introduction of a 48-hour maximum waiting time for patients to see their general practitioner (GP) target.

Road safety work by the Swedish police is described as so-called "pin hunting" in a previous audit report (Holgersson 2014). The follow-up system does not take into account when, where and why checks are performed. From a traffic safety perspective, controls are performed in the wrong places and at the wrong times. With the current follow-up system, the police authorities have good opportunities to make the appearance of their work efforts look efficient, because the quality of work is not visible.

Within universities, league tables, citation metrics and other forms of assessments for external accountability are reported to have adverse effects on the working environment for academics and marginalize independent thinking and collegiality (Du & Lapsley 2019). A "taste for science" is substituted for a "taste for publications" (Osterloh & Frey 2014).

Problems related to "reaching the target but missing the point" concern the measurement of performance but also the type of incentives introduced and its impact on people's behavior. Next, the problems of defining relevant and valid measures or indicators will be discussed. A discussion of problems related to behavior and motivation will then follow.

The difficulties of measuring performance

A general advice in the management literature is to develop a balanced score card combining both financial and non-financial measures (Franco-Santos et al. 2012). For public services, non-financial measures reflecting objectives and quality of services have special importance. If the purpose of performance management is to support coercive control, the ideal would be to focus on a few results or outcome measures, rather than measures reflecting the processes or activities needed to achieve the results or outcomes. A ranking of providers based on results or outcomes can then be used to determine rewards or sanctions and establish accountability. Alternatively, a provider's performance can be compared with a target that reflects what is expected.

In practice, results or outcomes are often very difficult to measure. Services provided in education, health care, social services and other public sectors can often be viewed as an investment that hopefully will have a beneficial impact on individuals and society in the future. Examples include teaching in schools, preventive health programs and good quality care for patients with a chronic disease, which reduce the risk of unfavorable events and complications. It will usually take a long time for such investments to pay off. This means that any performance measurement for control purposes "here and now" will have to focus on intermediary goals or process measures, e.g. regular tests and meetings with a specialist nurse or general practitioner (GP) when it comes to patients with a chronic illness.

Even if results and outcomes can be measured, it is far from certain that such indicators should be used for coercive control purposes. The link between the quality of services provided and actual performance in terms of outcome may be influenced by non-controllable contextual factors from the perspective of providers. Three key problems can be identified: 1) case-mix problems and the need for risk-adjustment, 2) attribution difficulties and 3) randomness.

Case-mix problems refer to a situation where characteristics of service users influence the outcome of services, as well as the quality of services provided. Results relating to a specific school are not only determined by the quality of education and the motivation and knowledge of teachers. An additional important factor is the selection of students that are attracted to a specific school. Similar examples can be found in other public services. A GP may have a good reputation in diabetes care, attracting patients with more difficult conditions. As a result, it will probably be more difficult for that GP to reach treatment objectives and good outcomes compared to GPs that attract patients with average conditions. To a certain degree, it will be possible to risk-adjust for case-mix differences, but any adjustment made is likely to be imperfect and difficult to interpret for non-professionals.

Results and outcomes may also be influenced by a chain or network of interrelated providers. This makes it difficult to attribute results or outcomes to a particular provider. Results from secondary schools depend on outcomes and the quality of primary schools. Good results and outcomes in cancer care can be attributed to excellence in surgery and oncology, but also to good standards when it comes to early detection in primary care and through screening activities. Even if perfect risk-adjustment and consideration of attribution is in place there will always be an element of random "noise" when measuring results or outcomes. For small organizations and providers in particular, reported results or outcomes for a particular time-period may be poor (or good) even if the quality of services are excellent, simply because of random variation. In the long-run, problems with randomness will even out or even disappear, as the volume of data increases and as the measured performance regress towards the mean. Performance management is frequently focusing on the short-term, however, which means that measurement of results or outcomes need to consider the degree of randomness involved.

To hold providers to account for non-controllable factors can be considered unethical and counterproductive (Terris & Aron 2009). Process measures that focus on activities and what providers are doing for service users offer an alternative that is less sensitive, at least when it comes to attribution difficulties and randomness. Such measures are, on the other hand, associated with other potential problems, as has been addressed previously as "reaching the target but missing the point" examples. A brief summary of pros and cons depending on the type of measure is provided in Table 6.1.

Table 6.1 Summary of pros and cons of results-/outcomes and process measures.

Pros of outcome (results-) measures	Cons of outcome (results-) measures
• Contribute to a focus on "true" objectives. • Are often more meaningful for payers and service users. Process indicators can often only be understood by the profession. • Promote innovations including new working methods. • Promote the development of long-term strategies that contribute to goal fulfillment. • Are often more difficult to manipulate.	• Are often difficult to measure, at least in the short term. In many contexts, intermediate results and outcome measures must be used. • Are affected by factors that cannot be controlled by individual providers. If several providers are involved (in a chain or network) it is difficult to determine to what extent each have contributed. • Good results and outcomes can occur despite poor quality of services (and vice versa). Random variation means that a large volume of data is needed to demonstrate a difference between providers.

Pros of process-measures	**Cons of process measures**
• Are often easy to measure and can be retrieved from existing registers of activities. • Are often easier to interpret through previous studies on the relationship between processes and results/outcomes. • Can often identify quality differences between providers more directly and based on a small sample of data. • Provide clear guidance on how quality can be improved. Efforts to improve processes can be implemented quickly, while shortcomings in results or outcomes only become apparent in the long run.	• In many contexts there is a lack of evidence, which may only apply to a specific process for a particular group of service users. • New evidence requires review and redesign of measures. • Can often be manipulated by providers. • Standardized services based on activities and processes (a protocol-driven service) may not be appropriate for individual service users. • Focus on process measures can prevent innovations.

Source: Adapted from Davies (2005).

An additional issue not covered in Table 6.1 is the administrative burden of performance measurement. Process measures, focusing the activities provided to service users, are often registered for legal and other reasons and in such cases are already available. Outcome measures often require the collection of new data that is not directly available for providers. Collection of results or outcomes may also run into ethical problems as it often concerns data at the individual level. The possibility to collect data using digital techniques has greatly simplified the process of measuring views, experiences and outcomes from the perspective of service users, e.g. using follow-up questionnaires or providing an open comments section on websites. This increased simplicity does not mean that the ethical problems disappear, however.

The "dark side" of extrinsic incentives

The previous section might give the impression that if we were able to define valid outcome and results measures that are reasonable easy to collect and administer, then it would be safe to use these measures for coercive control purposes. The problem is described as technical rather than related to the use of measures. Although developments of valid results and outcome measures would represent great value, such a position neglects the fact that extrinsic incentives used for coercive control purposes may have accidental and harmful effects on the motivation and behavior of people, even if measures themselves are "perfect". To some degree, this has already been exemplified in Box 6.2. Although cases from the British NHS and road and safety work in Sweden first of all illustrate the difficulties of developing valid measures and setting relevant targets, they also indicate that providers may be "willing" (or at least feel forced) to change their behavior in order to reach targets, even if this behavior is bad for service users and ignoring overall objectives.

The "dark side" of coercive control and extrinsic incentives has been extensively researched. Findings from both experimental work and empirical studies are presented using informative notions such as "hidden cost of control" (Falk & Kosfeld 2006), "hidden cost of reward" (Gneezy & Rustichini 2000) and "crowding out" (Frey 1997), with pay for performance described as being a Pandora's Box (Bevilacqua & Singh 2009). Several studies suggest that if the task is complex, difficult to measure and requires professional judgement and autonomy – as would be the case for several public sector services – the risk of accidental effects such as lower motivation, ignorance of non-incentivized tasks and other unintended changes in norms will increase (Cerasoli et al. 2014; Holmstrom & Milgrom 1991). Strong professional norms may to some degree counter-act extrinsic incentives linked to targets and imperfect performance measures, but only up to a point. In the long run, research suggests that inappropriate incentives in bureaucracies have harmful effects on the behavior and motivation of professionals (Ouchi 1979; Abernethy & Stoelwinder 1995; Du & Lapsley 2019).

Rethinking performance management

In summary, empirical studies and anecdotal cases suggest that problems related to performance management for coercive control purposes in the public sector are real and underestimated, especially when practiced in service areas focusing on complex tasks and involving the work of professionals. Societal developments towards increased uncertainty and more rapid changes, as well as increased socio-economic and geographical differences, also imply that it is increasingly difficult to determine universal targets that are valid and appropriate for all providers. The key question is then what can be done instead. One response would be to rethink the purpose of performance management and to support learning, innovation and quality improvement with a focus on local needs, rather than to demand coercive compliance towards general targets. Such a change will require new thinking when it comes to both the set of measures used and relevant forms of accountability. Rather than being coercive, performance management should have an enabling approach that supports local autonomy (Adler & Borys 1997). Rather than asking "what can we give providers that will motivate them", we should ask how intrinsic motivation can be facilitated through increased autonomy, competence and relatedness (Ryan & Deci 2000; Fowler 2014). Rather than trying to replace professionalism with extrinsic incentives, we should use, develop and appeal to existing professional identities as the primary disciplinary mechanism.

Similar to performance management for coercive control, performance management to support learning and innovation is not a new idea. In healthcare services, performance measurement was originally intended to support quality improvement work, rather than to support external accountability (Braspenning et al. 2013). A key question for any organization, in particular when facing rapid change and uncertainty, is how to combine the long-term interest of exploring and being innovative with the short-term interest of exploitation and being efficient (March 1991). Too much focus on learning may result in providers lagging behind since they lack the capacity or motivation to initiate and maintain quality improvement work. Too much focus on control can on the other hand be detrimental to both motivation and the possibility to explore new frontiers. Providers are motivated to *report* good performance or quality (to get the reward or to avoid the sanction), rather than having an interest in quality and quality improvement per se.

Implications for the set of measures to be monitored

Performance measurement for coercive control purposes seeks a summative evaluation of providers. Measures and the collected data need to be valid, reliable, robust and give "final answers" regarding a provider´s performance (Davies 2005). Ideally, only a few results or outcome measures that are able to cover all aspects of quality and performance should be used. When performance measurement focuses on learning, measures should support a formative evaluation of providers (Davies 2005). This means that both process and outcome measures are needed. Outcome or results measures alone cannot facilitate learning, as that will not provide clues to the processes and activities that explain results and outcomes. Without a combination of measures, no learning about possible relations can take place. Although non-professionals may be able to identify the end benefits of services, professional knowledge and experience is required to identify and understand relevant and valid process measures. This means that any performance measurement system used for learning purposes needs to be co-developed with the professionals concerned at a minimum. Co-development of the set of measures used may in itself contribute to increased understanding and motivation (Groen et al. 2012, 2017).

When using performance measurement according to a formative approach, the main ambition is to identify enough information that pinpoints areas that need attention and quality improvement work. This means that requirements regarding the reliability and validity of measures are less strict compared to a summative approach. Measures are used to "indicate" possible problems, deviations or emerging trends. These "indications" are not taken for granted. Additional information that includes experiences from staff and service users should support the analysis and contribute to decisions regarding the need for improvement work and changes. Staff and user experiences can be collected through surveys and focus groups, but also more informally and in face-to-face meetings. The views expressed through informal channels may not be representative or give a valid and reliable summative measure of performance, but this is less of a problem when performance measurement focus learning. A very good comment from a single service user may, from a learning perspective, provide more value than a summative statement based on surveys saying that 69.5% of service users were "satisfied" last year.

Implications for audit, feedback and accountability

For providers that are highly capable and motivated, the measurement of performance and transparent comparison with others may in itself trigger appropriate quality improvement work. For others, and not least for providers that really need to learn and change, the motivation and capability to implement quality improvement work needs support from carefully designed audit and feedback elements.

Evidence from 140 controlled studies in healthcare services shows that audit and feedback can contribute to improved quality, although the impact may vary depending on design and contextual factors (Ivers et al. 2012). The impact is usually greater among poor performers, when a service is over-used (like antibiotic prescriptions) rather than under-used and if the action required from providers is simple rather than complex. The impact is also moderated by the design of audit and feedback components; see Table 6.2. Findings suggest that audit and feedback should be provided regularly and use a multimodal approach, i.e. be provided in both text-based or graphic forms and through face-to-face meetings and seminars. Feedback should also be provided from a trustworthy source and linked to action plans with appropriate objectives for change. Even when audit and feedback includes all these components, the impact is far from certain. Parallel interventions and policies are needed, and not least support in the form of positive managerial attitudes towards change.

Most likely, the "best practice" of audit and feedback and the design of components will depend on the purpose of performance measurement. Previous research in the area of audit and feedback is not very explicit in this respect (Colquhoun et al. 2013). Frequently, the implicit idea is that audit and feedback should encourage providers to adapt to the existing knowledge base. This is indicated by the importance of targets, usually evidence based, as a key component of the design. The purpose is to facilitate implementation of existing innovations, i.e. diffusion of innovations, rather than to encourage providers to explore and come up with new ideas addressing local problems. These two approaches towards innovation have previously been referred to as the Science, Technology and Innovation (STI) mode and the Doing, Using and Interaction

Table 6.2 Evidence related to "best practice" of audit and feedback in health care services

Data components	• Data are valid and based on recent performance
	• Data are about individual/team's own behavior
	• New data presented over time
Feedback components	• Feedback is multimodal and repeated with new data
	• Feedback is delivered from a trusted source
	• Feedback includes comparison with others
Behavior change components	• Recipients are capable of and responsible for improvements
Goals, targets and action plan components	• Goals and targets are aligned with professional and organizational priorities
	• Targets are specific, measurable, achievable, relevant and time-bound (SMART)
	• An action plan is provided when discrepancies are evident

Source: Adapted from Ivers et al. (2014) and Brehaut et al. (2016).

(DUI) mode (Jensen et al. 2007). The linear STI mode of innovation has been the predominant perspective on innovation, not least in healthcare. Innovations are developed by someone else, frequently by university hospitals or by the pharmaceutical and medical device industries. If supported by enough evidence, innovations should be implemented more widely and the role of audit and feedback is to support this implementation. The two modes of innovation should not be seen as antagonistic (Jensen et al. 2007). The DUI approach, emphasizing practical experiences and oriented towards improvements in a local service delivery context, does not exclude that providers also can be recipients of innovations developed elsewhere. More often than not, innovations developed by someone else also need to be adapted to a local service delivery context.

In principle, audit and feedback components can be designed to support the development of innovations locally and adaptions of innovations developed by someone else. This would lean more towards an enabling approach to control and the DUI mode of innovation. Such a policy would be important in case evidence does not exist or if conditions at the local level vary. As has been addressed previously, support of learning and innovation locally should also be more important in uncertain and unstable times. A key difference between the approaches when it comes to audit and feedback is the role of targets and action plans. When used for diffusion of innovation and for coercive control, targets are being developed by someone else and providers are supposed to comply. When focusing on learning and innovation locally, audit and feedback should encourage providers to develop their own targets and action plans based on a local assessment of needs and conditions. The latter approach calls for a change in accountability. Standards and targets, if they at all exist, should be looked upon more as tools rather than something requiring strict compliance. The responsibility of local managers and professionals is to assess the data, including comparisons, interact and then develop their own targets and actions plans. The responsibility of general managers is to make this local managerial and professional responsibility clear and strong.

An obvious question is why local managers and professionals would be motivated to develop such targets and actions plans in the absence of financial and extrinsic incentives. This question then assumes that financial and extrinsic incentives work as planned, which is, unfortunately, frequently not the case in practice. On the contrary, studies indicate that audit and feedback have an impact on people's behavior, although studies are usually silent about the logic behind changes. Ironically, there is no explicit theory why audit and feedback without financial incentives should work, but they seem to work anyway. One possible explanation and logic is that professionals care about their reputation, even if this reputation is not associated with financial rewards (Kolstad 2013; Bevan et al. 2018). Professionals in public services are also motivated by empathy and commitment towards service users that are closely linked to this reputation.

The logic behind the importance of reputation can be explained through theories related to professionalism as a disciplinary mechanism and theories about the importance of human identity and intrinsic motivation in general (Frey 1997; Fournier 1999; Ryan & Deci 2000; Akerlof & Kranton 2000). More generally, providers may be motivated to change their behavior for a number of reasons besides financial rewards. One reason is that reward may come from the activity, behavior or change itself, i.e. motivation is intrinsic. There are strong reasons to assume that such rewards are more important in professional service firms involving complex tasks (Cerasoli et al. 2014). To facilitate intrinsic motivation, managers need to support competence and autonomy but also relatedness, i.e. that people feel connected to each other and the organization they work for. Over time, these processes will also support development of an identity, i.e. norms and social codes that reflect how people think of themselves and what they are. Such identities function as basic motivators at both individual and group levels (Akerlof & Kranton 2000, 2008). In organizations that function well, employees will identify with their work and organizations. Deviations between actual performance and what can be expected according to norms and social codes will create a dissonance and an ensuing motive to act. In organizations that function less well, employees are more likely to create a distance between themselves and the organization. In organizations without a trustful relationship with managers, employees are more likely to develop identities that resist managerial interventions. Such resistance may in turn lead to lower job satisfaction and decreased efficiency and quality. A trustful relationship is more likely to develop if employees understand actions by managers, which in turn requires some form of continuous interaction and dialogue (Frey 1997).

The identity of people is important for motivation and behavior in general and more so for people who identify with a profession. If audit and feedback from a trustful source suggests that recipients of data are "not professional", at least some form of behavioral change should be expected. This is in contrast to audit and feedback based on targets decided by "someone else" and delivered from a less trustful source. In this case, a response from professionals trying to preserve their own identity may very well be to simply be indifferent, to claim that data or measures are not reliable or to retaliate through passive or even active resistance.

Ideally, professionals should act on performance data and comparison with others as an integrated component of the professional identity. This clarifies why the ones providing the audit and feedback need to be trustful and legitimate as seen from the perspective of professionals and providers. Feedback can be provided through peer-review, i.e. by professional colleagues, or by an appointed team of independent professionals committed to the task. A team appointed by payers and regulators would have advantages as it facilitates double learning. Over time, the team will learn about conditions and any existing barriers for innovation and change when interacting with different providers. This knowledge can be used to support changes in the regulation of services that in turn will contribute to new service designs or more effective working methods.

Even if tasks are complex, inherently interesting and important for society, the motivation to perform and develop will vary across providers and individuals. Bevan & Hood (2006) suggest four categories or types that distinguish between the motivation of providers: saints, honest triers, reactive gamers and rational maniacs. Leaving the rare occasions of rational maniacs aside, these categories can be seen as a development of Le Grand's (2003) distinction between knights and knaves. Saints (as well as knights) have a strong public service ethos and voluntary driving force. For these providers, measurement and provision of data is usually enough to create a motivation to develop and change – they have a learning goal orientation. Honest triers are less capable and need more support but are not inclined to manipulate data or their practices in order to report good performance. Reactive gamers, on the other hand, will look for every opportunity to game the system. Examples include having ambulances wait outside hospitals in order to reach waiting time targets (see Box 6.1). This category would be more difficult to handle when the purpose of performance management is to support learning and innovation. Reactive gamers are on the other hand even more problematic if performance management focuses on coercive control, as providers can easily play the game of "reaching the target but missing (or not caring about) the point".

Similar to alternatives, the appeal to professionalism as a disciplinary mechanism is an imperfect form of government. Opportunistic providers and reactive gamers may misuse self-governance and the lack of external accountability towards targets and action plans. Possible ways to prevent such behavior include transparent comparison of data across providers and audit and feedback from trustful and legitimate sources. If nothing else works, the possibility to enforce targets and action plans – i.e. to use performance measurement for coercive control purposes – will still exist. For the majority of providers and professionals such a reciprocal policy would probably be welcomed, as any form of opportunism would threaten autonomy and self-governance in general.

Managerial implications and what might realistically be expected

The expected effects of performance management for learning purposes depend on possibilities to facilitate intrinsic motivation and the professional role orientation across public sector services. Although intrinsic motivation can be facilitated in any public sector providing services involving complex and inherently interesting tasks, the approach would be more important and valid in areas such as healthcare, education and social services. These services are homogeneous in that they involve a direct interaction with clients with different needs and preferences, which requires professional autonomy and decentralized decision-making. In any given geographical area, several local providers will exist, and payment and regulation of services is often determined by a single principal in the form of a local or national agency. It will be possible for payers, regulators and general managers to co-develop performance measures with professionals. In many cases, development of performance measures can be left to professionals, as is already practiced within healthcare services. It will also be possible to develop similar policies for audit and feedback, including dedicated professional teams that conduct face-to-face meetings and seminars to support learning, innovation and initiation of quality improvement work locally.

To support a shift towards learning and innovation locally, processes need to be backed up with reflective managers. Such managers should have characteristics that are likely to support enabling rather than coercive control, i.e. have a positive attitude towards decentralized decision-making, place a greater emphasis on internal and external communication and be supportive of development and change. The crucial thing is how performance measures and targets are developed and used. A reflective manager will not take measures and indicators literally. Rather than "final answers", measures and indicators will be the starting point of a development process that includes qualitative and experience-based data. The outcome of this process will support incremental and local workplace changes, rather than radical innovations across providers. Many small continuous steps will represent significant leaps in quality and performance over time, however. Performance management systems that focus on learning and innovation also facilitate professionals that actually enjoy their work and become more motivated to develop their performance. This is the essence of successful reflective management.

References

Abernethy, M.A. and Stoelwinder, J.U. (1995) The role of professional control in the management of complex organizations. *Accounting, Organizations and Society*, 20: 1–17.

Adler, P.S. and Borys, B. (1997) Two types of bureaucracy: Enabling and coercive. *Administrative Science Quarterly*, 41 (1): 61–89.

Akerlof, G.A. and Kranton, R.E. (2000) Economics and identity. *The Quarterly Journal of Economics*, 65 (3): 715–753.

Akerlof, G.A. and Kranton, R.E. (2008) Identity, supervision, and work groups. *American Economic Review*, 98 (2): 212–217.

Arnaboldi, M., Lapsley, I. and Steccolini, I. (2015) Performance management in the public sector: The ultimate challenge. *Financial Accountability & Management*, 31 (1): 1–22.

Bevan, G. and Hood, C. (2006) What's measured is what matters: Targets and gaming in the English public health care system. *Public Administration*, 84 (3): 517–538.

Bevan, G., Evans, A. and Nuti, S. (2018) Reputations count: Why benchmarking performance is improving health care across the world. *Health Economics, Policy and Law*. doi:10.1017/S1744133117000561.

Bevilacqua, C.M. and Singh, P. (2009) Pay for performance: Panacea or Pandora's box? *Compensation & Benefits Review*, Sept/Oct: 20–26.

Braspenning, J., Hermens, R. and Calsbeek, H. (2013) Quality and safety of care: The role of indicators. In Grol, R., Wensing, M., Eccles, M., Davis, D. (eds.), *Improving Patient Care: The Implementation of Change in Health Care*. 2nd edition. John Wiley & Sons.

Brehaut, J.C., Colquhoun, H.L., Eva, K.W., *et al.* (2016) Practice feedback interventions: 15 suggestions for optimizing effectiveness. *Annals of Internal Medicine*. doi:10.7326/M-2248.

Bringselius, L. (2017) Tillitsbaserad styrning och ledning – Ett ramverk. Tillitsdelegationen.

Cerasoli, C.P., Nicklin, J.M. and Ford, M.T. (2014) Intrinsic motivation and extrinsic incentives jointly predict performance: A 40-year meta-analysis. *Psychological Bulletin*, February 3.

Colquhoun, H.L., Brehaut, J.C., Sales, A., *et al.* (2013) A systematic review of the use of theory in randomized controlled trials of audit and feedback. *Implementation Science*, 8: 66.

Davies, H. (2005) Measuring and reporting the quality of health care: issues and evidence from the international research literature. Discussion paper. NHS Quality Improvement Scotland.

Diefenbach, T. (2009) New public management in public sector organizations: The dark side of managerial "enlightenment". *Public Administration*, 87 (4): 892–909.

Du, J. and Lapsley, I. (2019) Reforming UK universities: A management dream, an academic nightmare? *Abacus*. doi:10.1111/abac.12167.

Falk, A. and Kosfeld, M. (2006) The hidden cost of control. *The American Economic Review*, 96 (5): 1611–1630.

Ferreira, A. and Otley, D. (2009) The design and use of performance management systems: An extended framework for analysis. *Management Accounting Research*, 20: 263–282.

Fournier, V. (1999) The appeal of "professionalism" as a disciplinary mechanism. *The Sociological Review*: 280–307.

Fowler, S. (2014) What Maslow's hierarchy won't tell you about motivation. *Harvard Business Review*, Nov 26. Digital article.

Franco-Santos, M., Lucianetti, L., Bourne, M., *et al.* (2012) Contemporary performance measurement systems: A review of their consequences and a framework for research. *Management Accounting Research*, 23: 79–119.

Frey, B. (1997) On the relationship between intrinsic and extrinsic work motivation. *International Journal of Industrial Organization*, 15: 427–439.

Gneezy, U. and Rustichini, A. (2000) Pay enough or don't pay at all. *The Quarterly Journal of Economics*, August: 791–810.

Groen, B.A.C., Wouters, M.J.F. and Wilderom, C.P.M. (2012) Why do employees take more initiatives to improve their performance after co-developing performance measures? A field study. *Management Accounting Research*, 23: 120–141.

Groen, B.A.C., Woutersa, M.J.F. and Wilderom, C.P.M. (2017) Employee participation, performance metrics, and job performance: A survey study based on self-determination theory. *Management Accounting Research*, 36 (1): 51–66.

Holgersson, S. (2014) Polisens trafiksäkerhetsarbete. Rikspolisstyrelsens utvärderingsfunktion Rapport 2014:1.

Holmstrom, B. and Milgrom, P. (1991) Multitask principal-agent analyses: Incentive contracts, asset ownership and job design. *Journal of Law, Economics & Organization*, 7, Special Issue: 24–52.

Ivers, N., Jamvedt, G., Flottorp, S., *et al.* (2012) Audit and feedback: effects on professional practice and healthcare outcomes. *Cochrane Database of Syst Rev*, Issue 6.

Ivers, N.M., Sales, A., Colquhoun, H., *et al.* (2014) No more "business as usual" with audit and feedback interventions: Towards an agenda for a reinvigorated intervention. *Implementation Science*, 9 (14).

Jensen, M.B., Johnson, B., Lorenz, E. and Lundvall, B.E. (2007) Forms of knowledge and modes of innovation. *Research Policy*, 36 (5): 680–693.

Kerr, S. (1975) On the folly of rewarding A, while hoping for B. *The Academy of Management Journal*, 18 (4): 769–783.

Kolstad, J.T. (2013) Information and quality when motivation is intrinsic: Evidence from surgeon report cards. *American Economic Review*, 103 (7): 2875–2910.

Le Grand, J. (2003) *Motivation, Agency, and Public Policy*. Oxford University Press.

March, J.G. (1991) Exploration and exploitation in organizational learning. *Organization Science*, 2 (1): 71–86.

Neely , A., Gregory, M., and Platts, K. (2005) Performance measurement system design. *International Journal of Operations & Production Management*, 25: 1228–1263.

Osterloh, M. and Frey, B. (2014) Ranking games. *Evaluation Review*, 39 (1): 102–129.

Ouchi, W.G. (1979) A conceptual framework for the design of organizational control mechanisms. *Management Science*, 25 (9): 833–848.

Pollit, C. and Bouckaert, G. (2011) *Public Management Reform: A Comparative Analysis – New Public Management, Governance, and the Neo-Weberian State*. Oxford University Press.

Ryan, R.M. and Deci, E.L. (2000) Intrinsic and extrinsic motivation: Classic definitions and new directions. *Contemporary Educational Psychology*, 25: 54–67.

Siverbo, S., Cäker, M. and Åkesson, J. (2019) Conceptualizing dysfunctional consequences of performance measurement in the public sector. *Public Management Review*. doi:10.1080/14719037.2019.1577906.

Terris, D.D. and Aron, D.C. (2009) Attribution and causality in health-care performance measurement, in P. Smith*et al.* (eds), *Performance Measurement for Health System Improvement*. Cambridge University Press.

Thatcher, O.J. (2004) *The Library of Original Sources: The Ancient World*. The Minerva Group.

7 Public procurement a vehicle for change?

Anna Thomasson and Jörgen Hettne

Introduction

There is a belief that public procurement can be an instrument for change. The public sector is a large procurer and the idea is that if public procurers demand better products or new types of solutions, the market has no choice but to provide more environmentally and socially sustainable products. However, many public procurers in the EU consider public procurement a complex procedure and a source of frustration. The idea behind the legislation was to prevent corruption in public sector procurement, improve competition and the growth of the EU's internal market. The legislation thus encompasses three different interests: that of the public sector, that of the legislator and finally that of the market.

This balancing of interests is based on good intentions, but, in spite of this, public procurers and private suppliers alike (especially smaller companies) find it difficult to understand and interpret the legislation, and perceive the procurement process as cumbersome and resource demanding (Uyarra and Flanagan 2010; Erridge and Greer 2002; Morgan 2008). Consequently, the legislation, instead of improving competition has the opposite effect as smaller companies are unable, due to a lack of resources, to participate in call for tenders. At the same time, public procurers, fearing costly appeal processes, shun the possibility of increasing demand on the market and include other criteria besides the price in the evaluation of tenders (Uyarra and Flanagan 2010; Morgan 2008; Schapper et al. 2006). In many cases the problems perceived by the public procurer however stem from misconceptions that hinder not only the ability to use public procurement as a strategic tool, but also exclude potential bidders from responding to a call either because of a lack of resources or because they feel that they cannot compete on price alone. This hinders the development of the procurement process in a way that supports development in a market, as well as in public service provision.

One possible explanation for the effects the legislation has had could be the combination of interests that not only contribute to making the legislation complicated, but also require that actors on the market understand political intentions and that public procurers understand the market logic (Sinclair 2000). Part of the frustration felt by companies as well as public procurers could thus be understood as difficulties in understanding interests that are not their own.

Public procurement thus imposes challenges on public sector organizations. Still, research shows potential for public procurement to be a useful tool for public sector organization to stimulate innovation, including the development of new and improved products and services as well as to move political policies related to environmental

DOI: 10.4324/9781003154389-10

goals and ethical considerations into action (Uyarra and Flanagan 2010; Aschhoff and Sofka 2009). To illustrate the magnitude of public procurement, statistics from the European Commission from 2008 show that, on average, a public authority within the European Union spends 16 percent of the GDP on procurement (Lundberg et al. 2015). With these figures and given the wide range of products procured by the public sector, it is not surprising that public procurement has the potential to become an important strategic tool for public sector organizations (Hall et al. 2016; Risku-Norja and Loes 2017: Lundberg et al. 2015; Cheng et al. 2013).

In order for public procurers to be able to turn procurement into a useful tool that can help them develop quality in public services provision and delivery, there is a need to increase understanding of the legislation as well as the conditions on the market targeted by a specific call for tender. Further, there is a need to reconsider how public procurement is organized and governed in relation to the possibilities that the legal framework actually provides (Dalpé 1994; Schapper et al. 2006: Caldwell et al. 2005; Green 2010).

In light of this, this chapter focuses on how public managers can, with an increased understanding of legislation, turn public procurement into a strategic tool. In order to accomplish this, we use the public procurement law (as it has developed within the EU) as a backdrop. The rest of the chapter deals with these issues in the following way:

- Firstly, we will provide the reader with an overview of the legal framework surrounding public procurement and how it has developed over time.
- Secondly, we will discuss how on a governance level public organizations can work with public procurement.
- Thirdly, we will discuss the managerial and organizational aspects of developing the procurement process.
- The final and concluding part of the chapter consists of a discussion surrounding how politicians at the governance level can work with managers at the organizational level in order to improve the public procurement process in order to convert the procurement process into a strategic tool.

The legal framework

The goals of public procurement can, according to Schebesta (2018, p. 318), be summarized by the following bullet points:

1 To work against public corruption and increase transparency
2 To ensure value for money in procurement
3 To provide authorities with a policy instrument in order to support social and environmental considerations in the procurement process.
4 To manage competition
5 To create an internal market for EU

As already pointed out, regulation of the public procurement process is highly complex and cannot be described in detail in this context. For our purpose it is sufficient to point out that there are two distinct processes regulated: the selection of tenderers and the award of the contract. The selection of tenderers is a process based on a list of technical and financial requirements expressly stipulated in the relevant Directives. The selection process is followed by an award procedure, in which the contracting authority decides which of the qualified selected tenderers has submitted the best tender.

When is the legislation applicable?

The public procurement process is regulated in detail in several EU Directives which are implemented in all the EU Member States as well as the EEA states, Norway, Iceland and Liechtenstein. The most relevant for our purpose is Directive 2014/24/EU on public procurement. The EU Directives contain certain monetary thresholds, which implies that the detailed provisions of the Directives only have to be applied if the value of the public contract in question exceeds those thresholds. For social services, for example elderly care, the threshold is €700. However, it should be pointed out that, in Sweden for example, the EU rules are applied also below these thresholds, even if the Swedish Riksdag has recently decided to simplify the procurement rules below the thresholds (Prop. 2017/18: 158). At the same time, general principles of EU law are always applicable in relation to public procurement procedures. Indeed, the Court of Justice of the European Union (CJEU) has clarified in several cases that the requirement of equal treatment and transparency must be met also in procurement or similar procedures not covered by the Directives (see, for example, Case C-324/98, Telaustria and Telephone Address, para 60). The only limit to the application of these EU principles is that the contract lacks a cross-border interest (see, for example, Cases C-147/2006 and C-148/2006, Secap, para 31). This example alone shows how complicated it is, especially for a smaller municipality in a European country, to keep up to date with what occurs at the institutional level.

Criteria for awarding contracts

From an economic perspective, EU public procurement regulation has for a long time been influenced by neo-liberal theories. According to Bovis (2015), such influences embrace the merit of efficiency in the relevant market and the presence of competition, mainly price competition, which would create optimal conditions for welfare gains. The connection between public procurement regulation and this approach to economic integration is reflected upon the criterion for awarding public contracts based on *the lowest offer* (Bovis 2015, p. 2).

However, as Schebesta (2016) points out, public procurement regulation in the EU has been much more pre-occupied with the creation of a common market (now internal market) than with optimal outcomes of procurement procedures (Schebesta 2016, loc. 830–831). The main objective has been to follow the assumptions made through the internal market process that procurement represents a significant non-tariff barrier and its regulation could therefore result in substantial savings for the public sector (Bovis 2015, p. 6).

This neo-liberal approach is not the only foundation for the public procurement framework. As outlined above, over time, the perspective has shifted towards aims other than price competition and the lowest offer.

In support of the above stated goals of public procurement, the EU introduced new and common criteria concerning Green Public Procurement (GPP) in 2008 (Schebesta 2018). These criteria are not binding but can be seen as another way of increasing the strategic part of public procurement and also as a way for public procurers to use their bargaining power to influence market supply. GPP is also an important component in the broader term strategic procurement, or strategic use of procurement, indicating that the procurement is about more than just saving money. Thus, the Member States may use their purchasing power to procure goods and services that foster innovation, respect the environment and combat climate change, while also improving employment, public health and social conditions (Hettne 2013, p.1).

In the current rules, this is marked by a greater focus on "the most economically advantageous offer". By allowing discretion to the Member States, an element of public policy is inserted into the equation, which often has decentralized features. The public sector can award contracts with reference to "qualitative" criteria, in conjunction with price, and thus can legitimately deviate from the strict price competition environment set by the lowest offer criterion (Bovis 2015, p. 8). This has created the scope for the development of green procurement and strategic procurement.

The most economically advantageous offer as an award criterion has also provided the CJEU with the opportunity to balance the economic considerations of public procurement with policy choices. We consider that a good example of this development is the case EVN and Wienstrom (see Box 7.1), which illustrates how environmental considerations can largely influence what is considered to be the most economically advantageous offer.

In the most recent EU public procurement rules, this balancing of interests is clearly outlined. For instance, in recital 123 of the Directive 2014/24/EU on public procurement it is stated that in order to fully exploit the potential of public procurement to achieve the objectives of the Europe 2020 strategy for smart, sustainable and inclusive growth, environmental, social and innovation procurement will also have to play its part. To balance all the different goals inherent in the present European public procurement regime, summarised in the challenges outlined above, is however a complex legal task which requires legal expertise not available in all public sector organizations.

Box 7.1 Case EVN and Wienstrom (C-448/01)

In this case, questions arose as to whether a contracting authority could apply, in its assessment of the most economically advantageous tender for a contract for the supply of electricity, a criterion requiring that the electricity supplied be produced from renewable energy sources, and, if so, under what conditions that criterion could be used. In principle, that question referred to the possibility of a contracting authority laying down criteria that seek advantages that cannot be objectively assigned a direct economic value, such as advantages related to the protection of the environment. The Court held that not all of the award criteria used by the contracting authorities to identify the most economically advantageous tender need to be of a purely economic nature. The Court therefore accepted that, where the contracting authority decides to award a contract to the tenderer who submits the most economically advantageous tender, it might consider ecological criteria. This, provided that these criteria are linked to the subject matter of the contract, is expressly mentioned in the contract documents or the tender notice, and comply with all the fundamental principles of Union law, in particular the principle of non-discrimination.

In the case at hand, the Court concluded that Union legislation on public procurement does not preclude a contracting authority from applying, in the context of the assessment of the most economically advantageous tender for a contract for the supply of electricity, an award criterion with a weighting of 45% which requires that the electricity supplied be produced from renewable energy sources. On the other hand, public procurement law does preclude such a criterion where it is not accompanied by requirements, which permit the accuracy of the information contained in the invitation to tender document to be effectively verified and where the factors for its assessment are not directly linked to the subject matter of the procurement in question.

To summarize: the criteria for awarding contracts thus can be said to encompass two different interests: that of the market and that of the public sector. The first interest is reflected in the original idea to give support to the lowest bidder. The second interest on the other hand is reflected in the more recent development towards opening up for other criteria besides price, that open up the ability to also consider politically set goals.

Enforcement rules

Another feature of the EU public procurement regime, which adds to this development, is *the strong enforcement rules*. The enforcement of EU law in public procurement is made up of two components, *public* and *private enforcement*. Public enforcement is carried out by the European Commission and national authorities responsible for the supervision of the public procurement rules, while private enforcement is pursued by individuals at Member State level, for example through damages claims or other remedies. Public procurement is – next to Competition law – one of the few domains in which enforcement rules are laid down in detail at the EU level (Schebesta 2016, loc. 872–875). This regime is spelled out in secondary legislation in the so-called Remedies Directive (Directive 2007/66/EC, which amends Directive 89/665/EEC). In accordance with the Remedies Directive, the Member States shall establish appropriate procedures so that decisions in breach of the procurement rules can be set aside and compensation paid to those injured by the infringements. However, the member states are not compelled to apply the EU enforcement rules for contracts under the thresholds. Therefore, in Germany, Ireland and the UK the system is applicable only to contracts over the thresholds. However, in Sweden and some other Member States, the same system applies to all public contracts (Matei 2016, p. 365).

One fundamental purpose behind the Remedies Directive is to strengthen private enforcement by mobilizing the interested contractors in order to supervise the application of the public procurement Directives (Bovis 2015, p. 49). Hence, parallel to competition law,[1] the EU legislator has sought, through the Remedies Directive, to stimulate private enforcement in public procurement, i.e. that individuals who are dependent on the correct application of the substantive rules are given the opportunity to take legal action if they consider that these rules are not respected. However, a distinction that is not to be ignored is that, contrary to competition law, contracting authorities are not private companies, disposing of their own capital, but public authorities spending public money. Thus, on one hand, private enforcement would induce compliance with procurement rules, and therefore theoretically contribute to safeguarding the public interest in prudent spending of public money (Schebesta 2016, loc. 899). On the other hand, unfounded challenges to bid procedures and the resulting time delays are costs which are ultimately born by the public (Ibid, loc. 899–903). The damages, like other remedies available to individuals, must therefore be weighed against efficiency interests, in other ways than in competition law. The prime interest must be that the public procurement framework functions as planned and that the intended aims are achieved. The objective is certainly not to have speculative litigation with the adverse side effects of delaying procurement processes, making contracting authorities more reluctant in engaging with the private sector and, finally, increasing the cost of procurement as a result of the potential of contractual ineffectiveness and damages to aggrieved parties (Bovis 2015, p. 536).

Against this background, the CJEU has emphasized that legal processes that are contrary to or inadequate for the fulfilment of the public interest pursued by the EU procurement Directives should not be allowed. Therefore, Member States shall not make those review procedures available to any person wishing to obtain a public contract, but may require that the person concerned has been or risks being harmed by the infringement he alleges (Case C-249/01, Hackermüller, para 18). Indeed, the CJEU has shown an increasing understanding for the need of the Member States to limit, to some extent, procedural rights for private parties in the public interest. In *Universale-Bau* (Case C-470/99, para 75), the Court stated that the setting of reasonable limitation periods for bringing proceedings must be regarded as generally satisfying the requirement of effectiveness, since it is an application of the fundamental principle of legal certainty. Thus, the CJEU has stuck a balance between the interest in a fast and efficient procedure (public interest) and the ability of individual suppliers to complain when they are dissatisfied (private interest).

To summarize; when looking at the enforcement policies we can thus also see here that different interests are present. In this case there is, on the one hand, the public interest to carry out procurements in an cost-efficient way and ensure the supply of necessary products and services and, on the other hand, the private interest to ensure that all individual tenderers are treated fairly and have access to appeal procedures. From the description of enforcement policies given here it is clear that the private interest is non-compatible with the public interest to reduce public spending and thus to avoid costly and time-consuming legal processes. Therefore, the legal interest here falls somewhere in between the public and the private interest. Given the different interests that strive in different directions, it is not surprising that the legislation for public procurers and private companies alike is perceived as difficult to grasp.

The public procurer

The public procurer has to consider not only the interests of the politicians, but also the private interests and the interests of the legislation when applying the legal framework of public procurement. A public procurer can, as mentioned in the introduction to this chapter, perceive this as difficult, since it requires knowledge about the market as well as the legislation. When analyzing the public procurer there is therefore a need to consider not only the procuring organization, but also what occurs on the governance level where the goals and policies are set. This section is thus divided into two parts: the governance level and the managerial/organizational level.

The governance level

The previous section showed how changes at the EU level of public procurement policy and Directives facilitate the inclusion of goals focusing on sustainability and environmental considerations in the procurement process. There is thus for the procuring organization possibilities to use the procurement process as a tool for implementing public policy. The implementation of the new criteria is however a different thing (Schebesta 2018; Lundberg et al. 2015). To change the content of public procurement by the inclusion of new strategic goals starts at the governance level with a political decision. When a decision has been made at the governance level to consider social and environmental aspects, or make other considerations in the procurement, strategic goals for the procurement process are set. To have political support for using the procurement process as a tool for implementing an organizational strategy has in recent studies been proven to be important (Cheng et al. 2018; Palm and Backman 2017; Knutsson and Thomasson 2013). Political support is perhaps especially important given the risk averse nature of public organizations with a limited access to competent legal expertise (Erridge and Greer 2002; Morgan 2008). This is also supported by more recent research (Palm and Backman 2017; Cheng et al. 2018).

The governance level is thus of great importance for how individual organizations in the public sector work with public procurement. The governance level is however not only of importance when it comes to setting the goals and support purchasing units, but also when it comes to allocating resources that enable the development of processes necessary to conduct procurements in a way that corresponds with the needs of the public organisation (Cheng et al. 2018; Palm and Backman 2017; Knutsson and Thomasson 2013).

These results are supported by other studies showing that political support from within the procuring organization is the key factor for successful procurement (Hall et al. 2016; Knutsson and Thomasson 2013). Thus, political goals and political support for new procurement methods are important in order to manage the risk adverse tendency in the public sector. Verbal support from the political level is however insufficient, since goals need to be backed up with the resources necessary to accomplish them. This is true for financial resources as well as human resources, including know-how and the right type of competence.

The procuring organization

As previous section points out, support from the governance level, including access to resources, is thus of importance when it comes to converting public procurement into a strategic tool (Cheng et al. 2018). A special challenge for public organizations when it comes to changing the procurement process and including strategic goals related to sustainability issues is the procurers' lack of sufficient knowledge and financial resources (Cheng et al. 2018). The latter is likely to require a new type of organization to be formed that supports strategic procurement. The need to adapt the organization to the challenges a new procurement strategy imposes on the organization is supported by previous research within the field of public sector tendering (Bance 2003; van Syke 2003; Hefetz and Warner 2004; Padovani and Young 2008; Chen 2009; Gottfridsson and Cámen 2012). These studies show the need for public organizations to adapt organizational processes in order to adjust the organization to the need to monitor compliance with existing contracts and evaluate tenders. This is important not only to avoid contracts being breached, but also for the organization to improve the procurement process and the content of the contract before the next call for tender. This is a part of the process of public sector organizations "learning how to be a procurer" (Knutsson and Thomasson 2013).

Another challenge for public procuring units/organizations is the difficulty with adopting other criteria besides price in the tender. Price is easy to measure, while quality criteria is more difficult not only to measure but also to develop (Rönnbäck 2012). Criteria that are difficult to measure, however, expose the procuring organizations to situations where the procurement is questioned and the award of the contract risks being appealed. It also takes more time as they require a new way of working (Palm and Backman 2017). Political support is one way forward, established standards another (Rönnbäck 2012). As described in the section above outlining the institutional framework, the EU procurement framework now supports the inclusion of other criteria beside price. The challenge is, for public procuring units and organizations, to learn how to use it in practice. The problem is thus once again the level of knowledge in the organizations (Schebesta 2018). Knowledge here refers to not only the legal expertise in the organization, as has already been mentioned, but also the knowledge regarding the products or services being purchased (Hall et al. 2016).

This leads us to the next challenge, which is the size of the individual procuring organization (Cheng et al. 2018; Hall et al. 2016), for even if public procurement amounts to a large share of public spending, a large part of these purchases are conducted by individual public organizations, that is, small local authorities or municipalities. Since these procuring organizations are not collaborating, the advantage of the size of public procurement in terms of the share of GDP or another measure is not present. Adding to this is that it is difficult for these smaller organizational units to attract or develop within the organization the knowledge and resources necessary to enable a strategic focus on purchasing (Cheng et al. 2018; Palm and Backman 2017; Erridge and Greer 2002; Morgan 2008). It is once again not only about securing the legal expertise, but also knowledge about the needs of the organization that is to use the purchasing products or services (Hall et al. 2016).

One way to manage this problem is through collaboration between purchasing units in different local authorities. As shown by literature on procurement as well as public sector collaboration, that kind of collaboration also occurs (Palm and Backman 2017). One such example is the creation of Central Purchasing Bodies (CPBs). They provide goods, services and works to a large number of contracting authorities in their Member States and their accumulated procurement volumes are extensive. However, if the procurement unit becomes too centralized and distant from the organizations or units on behalf of which they are conducting the procurement, they risk not having the knowledge required to make the right type of purchase (Hall et al. 2016). Another way to manage this problem could be through collaboration between public and private sector organizations prior to the procurement and the tendering process. This kind of collaboration could result in an increased understanding on behalf of the procurer of the market situation, as well as allow for suppliers to learn more about the needs of the public procurer. One way to do so is through innovation procurement. The Swedish National Agency for Public Procurement supports these kind of attempts for public–private sector collaboration regarding innovation, as well as efforts made to initiate a dialogue between supplier and procurer early in the process. This is since such a collaboration might lead to enhanced quality in the development of public service delivery. This strategy has support in current legislation as well as at the European level.

Managerial implications

When managing the procurement process, one needs to bear in mind the fact that it is not only a tool for accomplishing a strategy or fulfilling the goals and needs of a specific organization. It is a legal framework put in place to secure legal interest, spur competition and improve how public money is spent. Thus, the legal framework has been developed with three different interests in mind. For public procurers to use the framework as a strategic tool, there is therefore a need to understand what each of these interests consists of and how they can be combined. However, for a public procurer with perhaps little or no knowledge about market conditions and limited access to legal expertise, this is, as also identified in the previous section, a challenge.

In order for public procurement to be a valid strategic instrument, several issues need to be taken under consideration and dealt with by organizations in the public sector. One of these issues is related to the legal framework and the fact that it is considered by many public procurers to be too complicated to fully comprehend, resulting in precautionary measures being taken (Erridge and Greer 2002; Morgan 2008). The EU Directives contain no rules on what should be procured. The public procurement Directives do not prescribe in any way what contracting authorities should buy, and consequently are neutral as far as the subject matter of a contract is concerned. The problem is that the legislation is considered complicated and difficult to grasp, and a smaller public procurer might find that difficult to manage. This complexity, in combination with general risk aversion, directs the contracting authorities towards the safer alternative, i.e. to award the contract on the basis of the lowest offer (lowest price). To avoid this from happening and to be able to develop public procurement into a strategic tool, there are several challenges that the procuring organization needs to manage.

This leads us into other issues, among them issues related to how procurement is governed and organized, which was discussed in the previous section and summarized here. Table 7.1 thus provides the reader with an overview of the conclusions that can be drawn from this chapter.

We have in this chapter discussed the need for the procuring organization to secure access to knowledge not only when it comes to legal expertise in the organization, but also regarding the products or services being purchased. For example, to what extent public procurers are supported by policy makers has been considered as important (Risku-Norja and Loes 2017; Cheng et al. 2018), as well as how the procurement function is organized and the knowledge and expertise available in the organization (Risku-Norja and Loes 2017; Knutsson and Thomasson 2013). These issues require that organizations in the public sector actively consider how they manage procurement processes (Dalpé 1994; Schapper et al. 2006: Caldwell et al. 2005; Green 2010), especially in those cases where the ambition is to use procurement as a strategic tool to gain access to products that are in line with the goals set by policy makers at the governance level.

One way to access resources and increase leverage on the market is to create a network consisting of public procurers from different public organizations. It is also possible to work with innovation procurement and to establish a dialogue between the procurer and potential suppliers. Yet another possible solution is for public organizations to collaborate, form support centres and hire expertise necessary or even to have joint calls for tenders (Cheng et al. 2018). Collaboration should however not be seen as a panacea since it might require extensive coordination as well as compromises. The latter could mean that one organization would have to compromise its own needs or policy in order to comply with the interest of the larger group (Palm and Backman 2017).

Table 7.1 Summary of challenges at the governance and organizational level for the procuring organization

Challenges	Governance level	Organizational level
Understand different interests	Acknowledge different interests when deciding on policies	Need to acquire knowledge about legislation and market conditions.
Provide resources for public procurers	Allocate sufficient resources	Managers need to support the development of the procurement process and the procuring organization
Convert political policies into assessable and transparent criteria	Challenges need to be acknowledged by the ones deciding on policies.	Public procurers need to understand underlying policies – managerial support to develop knowledge
Support the development of the procuring process	Allocate resources and acknowledge procuring as an important strategic tool. Allow for some risks to be taken	Managers needs to adapt organization and work processes
Access to knowledge and resources – use size to leverage	Find ways to collaborate with other public procurers as well as suppliers – policy decisions made by politicians	Managers enable and support networking and knowledge sharing across organizational boundaries and sectors

To conclude, in this chapter we have, with the point of departure being the legal framework for public procurement, identified and discussed the challenges related to public procurement from a public procurer's point of view. These challenges have been summarized in Table 7.1 and suggestions have been made on how the procuring organization can on the governance as well as the managerial level address these challenges.

Note

1 See in particular Directive 2014/104/EU of the European Parliament and of the Council of 26 November 2014 on certain rules governing actions for damages under national law for infringements of the competition law provisions of the Member States and of the European Union (OJ 2014 L 349, p. 1).

References

Aschhoff, B. and Sofka, W. 2009. Innovation on demand: Can public procurement drive market success of innovations? *Research Policy*, 38: 1235–1247.

Bance, P. 2003. Opening up public services to competition by putting them out to tender. *Annals of Public and Cooperative Economics*, 74 (1): 33–61.

Bovis, C. 2015. *The Law of EU Public Procurement*, 2nd ed, Oxford University Press.

Caldwell, N., Walker, H., Harland, C., Knight, L., Zheng, J. and Wakeley, T. 2005. Promoting competitive markets: The role of public procurement. *Journal of Purchasing and Supply Management*, 11: 242–251.

Chen, C.-A. 2009. Antecedents of contracting-back-in: A view beyond the economic paradigm. *Administration and Society*, 41: 101–126.

Cheng, W., Appollini, A., D'amati, A. and Zhu, Q. 2018. Green Public Procurement, missing concepts and future trends: A critical review. *Journal of Green Production*, 176: 770–784.

Dalpé, R. 1994. Effects of government procurement on industrial innovation. *Technology in Society*, 16 (1): 65–83.

Erridge, A. and Greer, J. 2002. Partnerships and public procurement: Building social capital through supply relations. *Public Administration*, 80 (3): 503–522.

Gottfridsson, P. and Camén, C. 2012. Service development in outsourced public service networks: A study in the public transport sector. *International Business Research*, 5 (5): 26–34.

Green, P. 2010. Efficiency Review by Sir Philip Green. Key Findings and Recommendations. Independent report, Cabinet Office, UK Government.

Hall, P., Löfgren, K. and Peters, G. 2016. Greening the street-level procurer: Challenges in the strongly decentralized Swedish system. *J Consum Policy*, 39: 467–483.

Hefetz, A. and Warner, M. 2004. Privatization and its reverse: Explaining the dynamics of the government contracting process. *Journal of Public Administration Research and Theory*, 14 (2): 171–190.

Hettne, J. 2013. *Strategic Use of Public Procurement: Limits and Opportunities*, Swedish Institute for European Policy Studies, SIEPS:7epa.

Knutsson, H. and Thomasson, A. 2013. Innovation in the public procurement process: A study of the creation of innovation-friendly public procurement. *Public Management Review*, Innovation special issue: 2–14.

Lundberg, S., Marklund, P.-O., Strömbäck, E. and Sundström, D. 2015. Using public procurement to implement environmental policy: An empirical analysis. *Environ Econ Policy Studies*, 17: 487–520.

Matei, E. 2016. The remedies directive in public procurement, in Bovis, C. (ed.), *Research Handbook on EU Public Procurement Law*. Elgar.

Morgan, K. 2008. Greening the realm: Sustainable food chains and the public plate. *Regional Studies*, 42 (9): 1237–1250.

Padovani, E. and Young, D. W. 2008. Toward a framework for managing high-risk government outsourcing: Field research in three Italian municipalities. *Journal of Public Procurement*, 8 (2): 215–247.

Palm, J. and Backman, F. 2017. Public Procurement of electric vehicles as a way to support a market, examples from Sweden. *International Journal of Electric and Hybrid Vehicles*, 9 (3): 253–268.

Risku-Norja, H. and Loes, A.-K. 2017. Organic food in food policy and in public catering: Lessons learned from Finland. *Org Arg*, 7: 111–124.

Rönnbäck, Å. 2012. Quality in the public procurement process. *The TQM Journal*, 24 (5): 447–446.

Schapper, P. R., Veiga Malta, J. N. and Gilbert, D. L. 2006. An analytical framework for the management and reform of public procurement. *Journal of Public Procurement*, 6 (1&3): 1–26.

Schebesta, H. 2016. *Damages in EU Public Procurement Law, Studies in European Economic Law and Regulation*, Springer.

Schebesta, H. 2018. Revision of the EU Green Public Procurement Criteria for Food Procurement and Catering Services: Certificate schemes as the main determinant for public sustainable food purchases? *European Journal of Risk Regulation*, 9: 316–328.

Sinclair, T. 2000. Governmental purchasing in the public policy process: Orienting theory and practice. *Journal of Public Budgeting, Acounting & Financial Management*, 12 (2): 291–306.

SOU. 2015. *12 Överprövning av upphandlingsmål mm*. Stockholm, Statens offentliga utredningar (Swedish Government Official Investigation).

Syke, van D.M. 2003. The mythology of privatization in contracting for social services. *Public Administration Review*, 63 (3): 296–315.

Uyarra, E. and Flanagan, K. 2010. Understanding the innovation impacts of public procurement. *European Planning Studies*, 18 (2): 123–143.

8 Governing in a digitalized era

Anna Thomasson and Jonas Ledendal

Introduction

In the era of "big data", "Internet of Things" and "social media" digitalization and information and communications technology (ICT) solutions, organizations in the private and public sector alike strive to explore and exploit the possibilities provided by this new technology. Cross-border digital public services is also a key area in the European Union's Digital Single Market strategy (COM, 2015, 192). Furthermore, according to the UN E-Government Survey (2018), the introduction of these new technologies plays an important role in accomplishing the Agenda 2030 goals. The survey further states that the introduction of new technologies signifies a paradigm shift in the public sector which have implications for citizen relations, accessibility and the ability to accomplish a more sustainable and resilient society.

At the same time, there is a need for governments to be ready for this transformation (UN E-Government Survey, 2018). As early as in 2005, Dunleavy et al. (2005) discussed digitalization as the new trend in public management and other researchers have followed suit, which is noticeable, not least in the number of sessions dedicated to digitalization of government in international conferences and research as well as trade journals.

Generally, digitalization and implementation of ICT has been regarded as something positive and an asset to the organization and the citizens alike. In the public sector, digitalization and ICT solutions are regarded as a way to alleviate the burden of a sector that is under pressure in times of austerity (Klievink et al., 2016). In such times, the incentive to innovate and be creative increases (Klievink et al., 2016). Digitalization reforms are thus and perhaps not surprisingly often discussed and analyzed with support in research on public sector innovation processes (Scupola and Zanfei, 2016).

The suggested solutions are many, from improving collaboration and communication with citizens through social media and digital platforms (Klievink et al., 2016) to computers making decisions and robots substituting teachers. Regardless of the type of reform and solution implemented, ICT solutions are a new type of infrastructure that open up new ways of providing public services, organizing work processes and developing new ways of interacting with citizens (Legner et al., 2017). That is also how digitalization reforms have been defined as:

> sociotechnical phenomena and processes of adopting and using these technologies in broader individual, organizational and societal contexts.
>
> Legner et al. (2017, p. 301)

DOI: 10.4324/9781003154389-11

Thus, through digitalization, resources can be freed up and public service provision delivered more efficiently (Andersen et al., 2012; Linders, 2012). This transformation is, however, far from unproblematic. As the definition by Legner et al. (2017) reveals, digitalization is complex and involves different parts of an organization. Consequently, implementing digital solutions is complicated and therefore not always the panacea it is portrayed as being.

It is, however, only during the last couple of years that researchers have started to pay attention to the consequences of digitalization on public service. For example, digitalization not only facilitates interaction, it might also exclude certain groups of citizens from accessing services and information (Berger et al., 2016). Additionally, the implementation of new solutions has consequences for organizations and employees (Hofmann and Ogonek, 2018), as well as the conditions under which public services are delivered and how transparent information is (Cuccinello et al., 2015; Ranerup et al., 2016). It is thus clear that digitalization and the introduction of ICT is not only about the technology, but also requires that the human dimension and organizational processes, as well as issues related to information security, are taken into consideration before new digital solutions are implemented (Cuccinello et al., 2015; Hofmann and Ogonek, 2018).

With the above as a backdrop, this chapter aims to discuss challenges related to the governance and management of public services in a digitalized era. The rest of the chapter is organized in the following way:

- Firstly, we provide the reader with a background to the development of digitalization in governments.
- Secondly, we give the reader an overview of the legal aspects of digitalization together with a presentation of how digitalization affects the governance and management of public sector organizations.
- Finally, a summary of the discussion of the implications of digitalization for governance and management is provided, along with a discussion of how managers in public sector organizations can approach challenges related to digital reforms.

Digitalization of governments

There is a growing body of research on the topic of digitalization and the introduction of ICT solutions in the public sector. Digitalization and the introduction of ICT reforms can be regarded as government reforms aiming at improving service provision either by increasing efficiency or by improving quality, or both, through the change of structures and processes in government (Pollitt and Bouckaert, 2004; Linders, 2012; Andersen et al., 2012; Hofmann and Ogonek, 2018). However, and in line with other types of reforms implemented in the public sector, the outcome is not always the expected one (Pollitt and Bouckaert, 2004). One explanation for why digitalization reforms fail to live up to our expectations is that when implementing these reforms the complex relationship between organizational processes, technologies and contextual factors, including legal aspects, are often ignored (Legner et al., 2017; Gil-Garcia et al., 2018), in particular in relation to the specific aspects of the public sector context as research on ICT solutions so far mainly has been focusing on the private sector organizations (Cordella and Bonina, 2012; Hofmann and Ogonek, 2018). To successfully implement ICT solutions thus requires knowledge and insight into these different areas, as well as understanding the relationship between them (Berger et al., 2016).

This is also illustrated in the growing body of literature on digitalization and ICT reforms in the public sector (Cordella and Bonina, 2012). The question is what we put into these reforms and how they can be better understood. As mentioned in the introduction, the digitalization of governments has different meanings and encompasses different types of reforms, from the use of ICT technologies to more wide-ranging reforms of organizational processes and how public services are delivered. The use of ICT in a way that leads to substantial changes in governments can be defined as Digital Government, DG (Gil-Garcia et al., 2018). DG reforms are multifaceted and as such they involve different areas of government. According to Gil-Garcia et al. (2018, p. 635) DG reforms raise managerial issues in terms of their implications on organizational efficiency and effectiveness as well as on human resource management. At the same time, DG reforms also have implications for the political side of government as they influence the relationship between elected officials and citizens (Linders, 2012; Cordella and Bonina, 2012; Bertot et al., 2012). Finally, since DG reforms have implications for information security and privacy, DG reforms also have a legal side.

Based on the above background we can conclude that DG reforms are a multifaceted phenomenon concerning not only the implementation of new technological solutions, but also have implications for how they are implemented:

- Organizations manage flows of information and data, including how to secure compliance with existing legislation and adaptation to new legislation specifically targeting digital solutions.
- The relationship between elected officials and citizens, especially the need to manage inclusion as well as exclusion of citizens due to different degrees of knowledge of and access to digital solutions.
- Organizational processes, including human resource management, change management and competence in organizations.

In the following, we will focus on the above challenges relating to DG solutions and will do so against the backdrop of previous studies and experiences from DG reforms. When doing so we will draw upon the definition of DG reforms presented above.

Challenges related to DG reforms

Legal implications of DG reforms

Governance of the public sector is a matter of constitutional and administrative law. For example, the principle of legality, which requires that all public power is exercised under the law. It is enshrined in the European Convention on Human Rights and in the constitution of many countries. Hence, decision-making in the public sector is subject to and constrained by both procedural and substantive provisions in constitutional and administrative law. Since digital transformation of the public sector to a large extent is driven by the need to reduce public spending, public sector bodies are increasingly exploring how automated decision-making (ADM) can be used to shift routine work from humans to machines, the goal often being to use ever-scarcer human resources for tasks which cannot be automated. ADM has, for example, been employed by the social services in some Swedish municipalities to automate decisions regarding social welfare payments (Spielkamp, 2019).

However, the use of ADM in the public sector, as noted above, must comply with constitutional and administrative regulations. Procedural rules that require signatures or even stamps or seals to be legally valid are still an obstacle to digitalization in many countries. This is, for instance, common in the public administrative law of many continental European countries. Efforts have been made in some countries to remove such obstacles. For example, in Sweden and Estonia, which are at the forefront of digitalization of the public sector. Estonia is the first country in the world that offers e-Residency, a digital identity that gives anyone, regardless of nationality, access to certain public services in Estonia. For example, the ability to start an EU company and declare taxes electronically. In Sweden, administrative law up until recently prohibited ADM, except for cases where it was specifically provided for in statutory law. However, this changed with the new Public Administrations Act of 2017, which entered into force in 2018. The new act explicitly allows decisions to be made by automatic means (Article 28 of the Public Administrations Act). However, the act does not cover public sector bodies at all levels of government, for example, municipal authorities are not covered, and algorithms (or rather governments) still need to respect fundamental rights and ensure legal certainty and good governance. EU data protection law, for example, prohibits automated individual decision-making, which is based solely on automated processing and produces legal effects concerning or similarly significantly affects individuals (Article 22 of EU Regulation 2016/679). Hence, on the one hand algorithms must be adapted to comply with legal requirements and on the other hand regulations must be adapted to the need for digital transformation of the public sector.

Digitalization can also greatly increase the availability of public sector information (PSI), which improves transparency and enables re-use of government data. Cloud computing and the internet has made storage and supply of information very cost-effective, allowing government data to be made available at near zero marginal cost (EUT C 240 2014). However, the digitalization of public sector information is not just a technical issue, it also has significant legal and financial implications. Access to public documents is determined by law and depends on whether rules of access are technology neutral. Digitalization can make governments less transparent, especially if the law treats all information alike, regardless of it is on paper or stored digitally. Hence, as the Swedish public administration was going through the early stages of digitalization in the 1970s, significant efforts were made by the legislator to preserve the principle of openness (SOU 1972:47). The Freedom of Press Act, which ensures broad access to public documents, was changed to cover government databases and electronic documents (Prop. 1973:33). However, the rules on access have not been adopted to more recent technological changes, for example, the internet (Ledendal et al., 2018).

The digitalization of public sector information also enables increased re-use of government data, not merely for transparency purposes, but also for commercial re-use. For example, the Swedish government produces high-quality geographical data for the original purpose of societal planning, but this data, which have already largely been funded by taxpayers, also has a significant value for digital service providers and other commercial actors (Ds 2009:44). The EU legislator has recognized this and adopted a series of directives on the re-use of public sector information (Directive 2003/98/EC as amended by Directive 2013/37/EU and soon to be recast by a new directive). The PSI directive forces public sector bodies to make government data available at the marginal costs incurred for their reproduction, provision and dissemination (Article 6 of Directive 2003/98/EC), which is often near zero in the digital environment. It also prohibits exclusive arrangements, making re-use open to all potential actors (Article 11 of Directive 2003/98/EC). Since governments had previously relied on charges and exclusive arrangements, the PSI rules significantly limit how the public sector can fund or recover costs of producing information.

Digitalization of the public sector also produces potential risks for the fundamental rights and freedoms of individuals, in particular the right to privacy and protection of personal data, which are enshrined in the Charter of Fundamental Rights of the European Union. The right to privacy has been protected in the union since the late 1990s through the adoption of the Data Protection Directive (Directive 95/46/EC). To modernize the rules and adopt them to the internet, the EU legislator enacted the new General Data Protection Regulation (Regulation 2016/679) (GDPR) in 2016, which became directly applicable in all member states on May 25, 2018. The GDPR builds on the basic data protection principles and rights of the directive, but also strengthens the protection and introduces high administrative fines. Public sector bodies must comply with the GDPR, but member states have some flexibility to adopt derogations in national law as long as those rules are compatible with union law. The purpose of the GDPR is to protect the fundamental rights of individuals with regard to processing of personal data, but also to ensure the free movement of personal data in the union (Article 1 of the GDPR). Hence, rather than obstructing the digitalization of the public sector, the regulation recognizes that differences in the regulation of personal data in the member states can "impede authorities in the discharge of their responsibilities under Union law" (recital 9 of the GDPR). However, under the GDPR the responsibility to ensure that data protection does not impede digitalization of the public sector ultimately falls on the national legislator, which must adopt supplemental national legislation to close the gap between union and member state law.

Table 8.1 summarizes the outcomes of DG and ICT solutions from a legal perspective, including the potential positive and negative effects of the outcome from a legal as well as organizational perspective. The legal challenges presented in Table 8.1 need to be managed at the governance as well as the management level of governments implementing ICT and DG solutions. Preferably, they need to be considered when the decision to implement or not implement ICT or a DG reform is taken. The legal side of DG and ICT reforms thus constitute a set of prerequisites that governing politicians as well as managers need to relate and navigate around. That, however, requires access to legal expertise within the organizations where the reforms are implemented. For smaller municipalities this could be a challenge, especially since they already struggle with this in daily activities.

Table 8.1 Legal challenges related to DG and ICT reforms

Outcome of DG and ICT solutions	Positive effect	Negative effect
Availability of public sector information (PSI)	Transparency, accountability and democratic values.	Legal restriction and new legislation necessary. Issues of privacy. Exclusion of non-digital citizens.
Automated decision making (ADM)	Increases efficiency and free-up resources.	Legal restriction, human aspects. Re-use of data.

Implications of DG reforms for political governance

We have already established that the implementation of DG reforms and ICT solutions in government alters the relationship between public authorities and citizens (Dunleavy et al., 2005). The question is how? ICT solutions and new infrastructure are considered to provide the public sector with new means to increase transparency as well as citizen participation (Jho, 2005; Bertot et al., 2012; Andersen et al., 2012; Linders, 2012), especially as they reduce the costs for politicians to communicate with citizens (Jho, 2005) as they, for example, can use social media to do so. To share information and increase transparency can result in an increase in public trust in the political government and also enhance democracy as it enables more people to participate in influencing decision making (Cordella and Bonina, 2012).

Social media has become a popular tool for politicians to inform citizens about political decisions and current events. Studies on ICT solutions and DG reforms from the U.S. for example shows how the use of social media was implemented as a deliberate strategy by the Obama administration (Bertot et al., 2012). The idea was to increase transparency and include citizens in the political process. The problem is that the use of digital solutions for communication excludes those that do not have access to internet or feel comfortable using social media. It can also cause problems with how data and information is treated (Jho, 2005).

The challenges can be summarized in the following four points:

1 Accuracy. What happens if the information in the system is not accurate or information is missing?
2 Integrity. How is information shared, managed and stored?
3 Security. Who has access to the information?
4 Adequacy. How adequate is the information that is shared and gathered?

Jho (2005) is not the only one raising issues regarding how to secure information when introducing ICT solutions. Already Dunleavy et al. (2005) raised concern about information security in their seminal article on governance in the digital era. In particular, in studies focusing on health care there is a great concern about how to involve patients and stakeholders in health care and at the same time ensure that privacy and security issues are taken care of (Tresb et al., 2016).

Consequently, at the same time as ICT solutions can be used to improve the dialogue between elected politicians and citizens, they also impose challenges on organizations and in particular those responsible for organizational activities. In order to handle the challenges imposed by the new technology, there is a need to create awareness at the political level of not only the positive effects of ICT and DG reforms, but also the potential pitfalls. That in turn requires access to know-how and legal expertise. The latter in particular might be challenging for smaller municipalities that are in general struggling with keeping up with new legislation, directives and access to expertise needed to enable informed decisions (Allers and de Greef, 2018; Blaeshke and Haug, 2018; Kalu, 2012; Warner, 2011; Margerum, 2007). The introduction of ICT solutions in government is thus far from clear-cut and therefore needs to be carefully planned and considered.

Not only is it a challenge to manage the flow of information, another area that is discussed in the literature is that of exclusion. Citizens that do not have access to high-speed internet, computers or have not acquired the knowledge necessary to use ICT solutions are not given the same opportunity to access public services or the information presented by politicians (Berger et al., 2016; Scupola and Zanfei, 2016; Siren and Knudsen, 2016). Examples of how e-governance can be used to increase democracy and include citizens in the decision-making process are thus perhaps not considered as good solutions by everyone. There are even occasions when ICT solutions and DG reforms can lead to exclusion from the democratic process. This assumption is supported by two recent studies on internet use, one conducted in Sweden (Internet Stiftelsen, 2018) and one conducted by the UN (UN E-Government survey, 2018). According to the UN E-Government survey (2018), there is a correlation between social exclusion and the inability to access E-Government services (inability due to no access to high-speed internet service, no access to computer or lack of the required knowledge). One consequence of the increasing use of ICT solutions might therefore be that citizens no longer feel like full members of society (Siren and Knudsen, 2016). What is needed is thus an awareness on behalf of governing politicians as well as managers of public services of the level of access to internet and knowledge about ICT solutions among their clients (Siren and Knudsen, 2016). The study conducted by Siren and Knudsen (2016) in Denmark demonstrates how the elderly in particular run the risk of being excluded from public service provision due to lack of internet access and/or knowledge about ICT systems. Another interesting result from the study by Siren and Knudsen (2016) is that exclusion not only emerges because of lack of access to high speed internet or knowledge about how to use the new technology, but also due to a lack of trust in new technology. The latter is also supported by a study conducted in the U.S. that in particular looked at the reforms implemented by the Obama administration (Bertot et al., 2012).

It is necessary to secure information, solve questions regarding who gets access to data and to ensure that data gathered on platforms and online systems is protected and that risks are analyzed (Bertot et al., 2012; Klievink et al., 2016), especially to establish and maintain trust in ICT solution and digital reforms. Governments need to keep control over the data gathered on platforms and in systems (Klievink et al., 2016). This is not least challenging when considering that a large part of the data stored is controlled by social media providers, for example Facebook, Twitter and YouTube, as well as suppliers of cloud computing and other types of ICT solutions. Sometimes this requires in-depth knowledge about the infrastructure and the new technology, knowledge that needs to be acquired by the government (Klievink et al., 2016).

In Table 8.2 the challenges DG reforms and the use of ICT solutions impose on the political governance level is summarized. The challenges presented in Table 8.2 have

Table 8.2 Challenges for political governance when implementing ICT and DG solutions

Outcome of DG and ICT solutions	*Positive effect*	*Negative effect*
Use of social media and E-governance	Transparency, accountability and democratic values.	Issues of privacy and problems related to the use of social media. Exclusion of non-digital citizens.
Implementing ICT solutions	Increases efficiency and free-up resources. Increases transparency of and influence on democratic processes.	Exclusion and distrust in governance. Security and control over data and processes.

implications for governing politicians in their communication with citizens and in the set-up of new solutions for democratic processes, including ways for citizens to influence the decision process. It is particularly important to consider how to avoid a democratic deficit among the group of citizens that for one reason or another are unable to use the new technology.

Managerial implications of DG reforms

Several studies stress the effects that the implementation of ICT solutions have on organizations and on organizational processes. As captured in the definition by Legner et al. (2017), ICT solutions do not only mean a change of technology, but also affect organizational processes and the social dimension of an organization. ICT solutions are complex systems and as such the implementation involves different parts of an organization at the same time. According to Hofmann and Ogonek (2018), the implementation of ICT solutions is not only a matter of being able to handle IT, rather, what is needed is more soft skills. The author for example mentions competences related to being able to understand the impact of digitalization in general, being aware of the social aspects of digitalization in regard to how it influences interaction and relations within organizations, as well having an understanding of the legal consequences.

Additionally, it takes time for the organization to adapt to the above-mentioned implications and learn how to manage information security, relationships with system suppliers and the secure supply of and access to the new solutions (Berger et al., 2016). Digitalization also requires new forms of collaboration between different parts of the organization (Klievink et al., 2016; Scupola and Zanfei, 2016). Managers need to be aware of this and enable the organization to adapt. Further, there needs to be an understanding within the organization that when employees acquire new competences and skills on their own and take the lead, others risk falling behind (Klievink et al., 2016; Berger et al., 2016). It is thus not strange that literature on digitalization show mixed results in regard to how employees perceive these types of reforms. Staff are, for example, negative towards ICT solutions if they feel such systems will increase the workload.

It is, however, not only the relationships within organizations that change and need to adapt to the implementation of different ICT solutions, but also how the organization interacts with external stakeholders. ICT solutions require a holistic view on organizations and service provision. According to Dunleavy et al. (2005), ICT solutions require a more profound transformation of service provision that goes beyond the use of a new technology, and also transforms how services are provided. A recent study conducted among university students in Australia is a good example of the issue addressed by Dunleavy et al. (2005). According to the students, the main benefit from the implementation of ICT solutions was not related to the learning situation, but how students structured and planed study activities (Henderson et al., 2015). The reason for this, according to the authors of the article, was that the learning process and the teaching activities remained the same when the learning platform was implemented. Consequently, the full potential benefits of the ICT solutions were not accomplished as they were not integrated with organizational processes (Henderson et al., 2015). Instead, ICT solutions were used only for communicating with students and for developing online platforms for courses and schedules.

The use of ICT solutions has also been discussed as a way to turn citizens into co-producers of public services (Linders, 2012). By including citizens in the production of public services they can contribute with their knowledge and competence (Linders, 2012). One way to do this is through the use of social media or different kinds of software applications. One example of the latter is a smartphone application developed by the municipality of Cascai, located south of Lisbon, Portugal. The application is aimed at including citizens in the improvement of the social as well as physical development of the municipality. By reporting problems, taking on responsibility or helping out in the community, citizens can gather points that later can be used for accessing different types of activities and services in the city. One example provided is that if you donate a book to a library or adopt a stray dog you can gather points that can be converted to a concert ticket. Through the application, the municipality can use their knowledge of the citizens and their resources to improve the municipality at the same time as having citizens included in the process. A Danish study of the use of social media in healthcare is another example of how ICT solutions can lead to co-production and improve service provision (Andersen et al., 2012). In the Danish study, the case was the use of social media for interacting with and increasing the knowledge among cancer patients in order to make them feel more included and in control during the treatment process.

The two abovementioned examples thus show how ICT solutions can be used as a means to transform and improve processes and relationships between providers of public services and the citizens in need of these services. What is required though is a transformation of processes in order to implement and make full use of the ICT solutions. It is not sufficient to merely purchase the technology and make it available to the organization and stakeholders, as the example of higher education in Australia shows.

Even though ICT solutions are successfully implemented, as in the example from the Danish health sector and the municipality of Cascai, ICT solutions can still lead to exclusion among citizens that for one reason or another are not able to use the new technology. Further, issues of security arise regarding how information is handled and stored by the providers of the ICT solutions. Another issue that emerges is how to secure the provision of digital solutions in situations of a power shortage or crisis. A power shortage caused by a natural disaster or terrorism not only results in a loss of power, but also a loss of access to the internet and, consequently, ICT solutions. This interdependency between systems needs to be recognized as well and the need for a plan for how to manage a situation within the government during which ICT solutions like hospital online journal systems or surveillance systems are not available. These situations can quickly turn into a larger crisis if not managed correctly (Henstra, 2010). As research within crisis management shows, organizations that have developed plans for how to manage a crisis are better equipped to handle the situation and therefore recover sooner and with less damage to the society at large (Basu et al., 2013; Sellberg et al., 2015). Preparations include knowing who to contact and who to collaborate with in a case of crisis (MacManus and Caruson, 2011). When it comes to ICT solutions this means the suppliers of systems, platforms and high-speed internet. For governments to keep track of all suppliers and know who to contact, as well as making provisions in contracts on how responsibilities are shared in case of a crisis, is a complex and cumbersome task, a task that requires collaboration between departments within the government as well as access to expert knowledge. The latter is something that smaller municipalities have problems accessing.

Table 8.3 summarizes the managerial challenges identified here in relation to the implementation of ICT and DG solutions. The impact on organizations and the need to fully transform organizations in order to adapt processes and knowledge to the new technology is especially apparent and is also addressed in the literature as the main managerial challenge.

The reality lies somewhere in between the fact that ICT solutions can be used to control and gather information at the same time as it can improve interaction and communication. Politicians that support decisions to implement ICT solutions need to be aware of this and consider this when making the decisions. Additionally, politicians in collaboration with managers need to discuss how to manage this duality and to balance the critique against the new technology with the advantages that it brings.

To summarize there are for managers as well as politicians on the governance level several aspects that need to be taken into consideration when planning for and implementing ICT solutions in order to digitalize public service provision. The issues are related to the "what" is being digitalized, the "how" it is going to be implemented and also the "why" it is relevant and for whom. More specifically, and perhaps also most importantly, the organization needs to be ready for the change and have access to the right type of resources. Also, the citizens need to be prepared for the change and equipped to manage it. To have pilot projects like the one that the small Swedish municipality carried out might thus be a way to approach these issues and find answers to the questions of "how", "why" and "what".

Firstly, the need to adapt the organization and the type of resources, mainly competence, the organization has access to. Secondly, how to prepare employees as well as citizens for the change that digitalization means. Thirdly, and perhaps most importantly, there is a need to plan for how digitalization is to be carried out in the organization, i.e. a digitalization strategy and plan is needed.

Managerial implications of the implementation of ICT solutions

In the previous sections of this chapter the challenges related to the implementation of ICT solutions were discussed from a legal perspective, a political governance perspective and finally a managerial perspective. In Tables 8.1 to 8.3 the challenges related to each perspective were summarized. From the previous discussion, we can derive a set of effects of the implementation of ICT solutions that each raise issues that need to be addressed by managers and politicians. These issues or implications are summarized in Table 8.4. Implications for the organization represent issues that the managers need to

Table 8.3 Managerial challenges of implementing ICT and DG solutions

Outcome of DG and ICT solutions	Positive effect	Negative effect
ICT solution implemented in organizations	Increases efficiency. Innovation and service development.	Implications for employees. Knowledge level in organization – exclusion. More vulnerable in a crisis.
Implementing ICT solutions for service provision	Improves service level. Co-production of services.	Exclusion. Risk of no real impact. More vulnerable in a crisis.

Table 8.4 Implications for public organizations and democracy form implementing ICT solutions

Implications for the organization	Implications for democracy
Know-how and competence adapted to the new technology	Exclusion vs inclusion of citizens
Transformation of processes necessary to reach full effect	Increased transparency vs privacy issues and information security
Co-production and increase quality vs exclusion of certain groups of users	Increased dialogue vs loss of credibility and exclusion
Risk management and supplier relations	Adaptation to new legislation

address, while implications for democracy are considered as issues that the political governance level needs to consider.

As Table 8.4 shows, implications related to the implementation of ICT solutions to a large extent consists of the ability to manage trade-offs at the governance as well as the managerial level. Even though digitalization has several merits, it is thus far from uncomplicated and implementation of new solutions requires careful consideration and also extensive work and transformation of organizational processes. Digitalization is thus not a quick fix that will solve public sector challenges related to austerity, increased demand on service provision and improve democratic processes overnight. Rather, digitalization requires extensive work from managers and also an awareness of the known effects of digitalization as well as the fact that there still are unknown effects. To conclude, digitalization has several advantages and the potential to reform public service provision in a way that serves the citizens as well as public organizations. There are, however, also several challenges that come with the digitalization reforms. Some of these challenges are known, some are still for us to find out. The challenge for politicians as well as managers is that they have to prepare for the known as well as the unknown when implementing the new technology, especially since it is likely to transform the public sector as we know it today.

References

Allers, M.A. and de Greef, J.A. 2018. Intermunicipal cooperation, public spending and service levels, *Local Government Studies*, 44 (1): 127–150.

Andersen Normann, K., Medaglia, R. and Henriksen Zinner, H. 2012. Social media in public health care: Impact domain propositions. *Government Information Quarterly*, 29: 462–469.

Basu, M., Srivastava, N., Mulyasari, F. and Shaw, R. 2013. Making cities and local governments ready for disasters: A critical overview of recent approaches. *Policy Studies Organizations*, 4 (4): 250–273.

Berger, J.B., Hertzum, M. and Schreiber, T. 2016. Does local government staff perceive digital communication with citizens as improved services? *Government Information Quarterly*, 33: 258–269.

Bertot, C.J., Jaeger, P.T. and Hansen, D. 2012. The impact of policies on government social media usage: Issues, challenges, and recommendations. *Government Information Quarterly*, 29: 30–40.

Blaeshke, F. and Haug, P. 2018. Does inter-municipal cooperation increase efficiency? A conditional metafrontier approach for the Hessian wastewater sector. *Local Government Studies*, 44 (1): 151–171.

COM2015. Meddelande från kommissionen till Europaparlmantet, rådet, Europeiska ekonomiska och sociala kommittén samt regionkommittén. En strategi för en inre digital marknad i Europa SWD(2015) 100 final, Bryssel 6.5.2015 COM(2015) 192 final.

Cordella, A. and Bonina, C.M. 2012. A public value perspective for ICT enabled public sector reforms: A theoretical reflection. *Government Information Quarterly*, 29: 512–520.

Cuccinello, M., Lapsley, I., Nasi, G. and Paglian, C. 2015. Understanding key factors affecting electronic medical record implementation: A sociotechnical approach. *Health Service Research*, 15 (268): 1–19.

Dunleavy, P., Margetts, H., Bastow, S. and Tinkler, J. 2005. New public management is dead-long live digital-era governance. *JPART*, 16: 467–494.

EUT C 240 (2014) Kommissionens tillkännagivande – Riktlinjer om rekommenderade standardlicenser, datauppsättningar för vidareutnyttjande av handlingar. EUR-Lex.

Freeman, J. and Hancock, L. 2017. Energy and communication infrastructure for disaster resilience in rural and regional Australia. *Regional Studies*, 51 (6): 933–944.

Gil-Garcia, R.J., Wawes, S.S. and Pardo, T.A. 2018. Digital government and public management research: Finding the crossroads, *Public Management Review*, 20 (5): 633–646.

Henderson, M., Sely, N. and Aston, R. 2015. What works and why? Student perception of 'useful' digital technology in university teaching and learning. *Studies in Higher Education*, 42 (8): 1567–1579.

Henstra, D. 2010. Evaluating local government emergency management programs: What framework should public managers adopt? *Public Administration Review*, March/April: 236–246.

Hofmann, S. and Ogonek, N. 2018. Different but still the same? How public and private sector organizations deal with new digital competences. *The Electronic Journal of E-Government*, 16 (2): 127–135.

Internet Stiftelsen 2018. Svenska och internet 2018. www.svenskarnaochinternet.se.

Jarman, A., Sproats, K. and Kouzmin, A. 2000. Crisis management: Toward a new informational "localism" in local government reform. *International Review of Public Administration*, 5 (2): 81–97.

Jho, W. 2005. Challenges for e-governance: Protests from civil society on the protection of privacy in e-government in Korea. *International Review of Administrative Science*, 7 (1): 151–166.

Kalu, N.K. 2012. All that glitters: Competing narratives and transaction costs in complex collaborative environments. *Administration & Society*, 45 (4): 420–442.

Klievink, B., Bharosa, N. and Tan, Y.-H. 2016. The collaborative realization of public values and business goals: Governance and infrastructure of public–private information platforms. *Government Information Quarterly*, 30: 67–79.

Ledendal, J., Larsson, S. and Wernberg, J. 2018. *Offentlighet i det digitala samhället: Vidareutnyttjande, sekretess och dataskydd*. Stockholm, Norstedts Juridik.

Legner, C., Eymann, T., Hess, T., Matt, C., Böhmann, T., Drews, P., Mädche, A., Urbach, N. and Ahlemann, F. 2017. Digitalization: Opportunity and challenge for the business and information systems engineering community. *Sus Inf Sys Eng*, 59 (4): 301–308.

Linders, D. 2012. From e-government to we-government: Defining a typology for citizens coprdocution in the age of social media. *Governance Infromation Quarterly*, 29: 446–454.

MacManus, S. and Caruson, K. 2011. Emergency management: Gauging the extensiveness and quality of public and private sector collaboration at the local level. *Urban Affairs Review*, 47 (2): 280–299.

Margerum, R.D. 2007. Overcoming locally based collaboration constraints, *Society and National Resources*, 20 (2): 135–152.

Pollitt, C. and Bouckaert, G. 2004. *Public Management Reform: A Comparative Analysis*, Oxford, Oxford University Press.

Ranerup, A., Zinner Henriksen, H. and Hedman, J. 2016. An analysis of business models in public service platforms. *Government Information Quarterly*, 33: 6–14.

Scupola, A. and Zanfei, A. 2016. Governance and innovation in public sector services: The case of the digital library. *Government Information Quarterly*, 33: 237–249.

Sellberg, M.M., Wilkinson, C. and Peterson, G.D. 2015. Resilience assessment: A useful approach to navigate urban sustainability challenges. *Ecology and Society*, 20 (1).

Siren, A. and Grönborg Knudsen, S. 2016. Older adults and emerging digital service delivery: A mixed methods study on information and communications technology use, skills and attitudes. *Journal of Aging and Social Policy*, 29 (1): 35–50.

Spielkamp, M. 2019. Automating society: Taking stock of automated decision making in the EU. Bertelsemannstiftung Studies.

Tassabehji, R., Hackney, R. and Popovic, A. 2016. Emergent digital era governance: Enacting the role of the "institutional entrepreneur" in transformational change. *Government Information Quarterly*, 33: 223–236.

Tresb, V., Overhage, J.M., Bundschus, M., Rsbizadeh, S., Fasching, P.A. and Shipeng, Y. 2016. Going digital: A survey on digitalization and large-scale data analytics in healthcare, *Proceedings of the IEEE*, 104 (11): 2180–2206.

United Nations 2018. United Nations E-Government survey: Gearing E-Government to support transformation towards sustainable and resilient societies. Retrieved from: https://publicadminis tration.un.org/egovkb/Portals/egovkb/Documents/un/2018-Survey/E-Government%20Survey% 202018%20Preliminary%20pages.pdf.

Warner, M. 2011. Competition or cooperation in urban service delivery? *Annals of Public and Cooperative Economics*, 82 (4): 421–435.

Section four

Innovations in management practices

9 Brand orientation

Tensions and conflicts in public management

Jon Bertilsson, Jens Rennstam and Katie Sullivan

Introduction

Public institutions such as cities, the police or schools are increasingly adopting a brand orientation, understood as an approach to organization aiming to create coherence around image and identity, such that consistent, precise and coherent messages can be presented about the organization to internal and external stakeholders. This may be seen as an expression of what is sometimes called "brand society," meaning that branding affects ever more aspects of human life, including public sector organizations (Kornberger, 2010). Similar to other management techniques – like Lean Management or TQM – branding has its roots in private organizations. Although private and public organizations may gain from exchanging management practices, it also creates tensions between corporate and civic rationales and practices. For instance, whereas the corporate branding ideal is to seek to reduce complexity via a coherent or unified identity and presentation to *customers*, public organizations are complex and must communicate with and serve a diverse *public* (Wæraas, 2008). In the wake of this development toward brand orientation, it is important to understand intended and unintended consequences for organizations, public employees, citizens and other stakeholders.

Branding is both timely and relevant for public employees to consider. Given the ubiquity of branding in the public sector it is possible that a brand orientation begins to organize how managers make decisions. For instance, a director of public health may be asked to engage in branding healthcare, a school principal might need to respond to threats to the "brand" when managing diminishing resources or a city manager might begin to think of citizens and businesses as either a "good or bad" fit for the brand. The point here is that branding is no longer only the purview or responsibility of communication professionals in marketing departments, but rather something that public managers, in general, are being asked to consider.

Drawing on illustrative examples of branding in the public sector, this chapter highlights tensions that emerge between a brand orientation and the following public sector ideals: organizational transparency, inclusion and reflexivity. By tensions, we mean that a brand orientation and public sector ideals may not mix, but rather create conflict and discord. The examples shed light on how a brand orientation may discourage whistleblowing in a school, how a brand orientation may encourage cities to compete to house so-called "good" organizations like Amazon and discourage them from housing so-called "dirty" organizations like prisons and how police officers may be sacrificed to protect the brand. The chapter concludes by encouraging reflective managers to engage in more critical and conscious practice when considering brand related issues. As

DOI: 10.4324/9781003154389-13

heuristic support, we suggest a value-based framework that articulates a more critical understanding and encourages analysis of branding based on multiple values.

Brand orientation and the public sector

Brand orientation refers to a managerial approach, or philosophy to organization "in which the processes of the organization revolve around the creation, development, and protection of brand identity in an ongoing interaction with target customers" (Urde, 1999, p. 117). Put differently, a brand orientation aims to create coherence around image and identity (Hatch & Schultz, 2003), such that a consistent, precise and homogeneous message can be presented about the organization to internal and external stakeholders (Wæraas, 2008). As a managerial technique, branding is therefore associated with the management of the meaning and values associated with an organization, its products and its activities, both to external stakeholders and to members of the organization (e.g. Kärreman & Rylander, 2008; Kornberger, 2010).

Brand orientation has traditionally been an integral part of the private sector. However, partly stemming from a New Public Management approach to public administration, brand orientation has found its way into the public sector and public sector organizations (Marland, 2016; Moor, 2007). Researchers from several disciplines such as political science and organization studies (Wæraas & Maor, 2015) address the rise of brand orientation in cities, municipalities, police, universities and public hospitals (Bjørnå & Salomonsen, 2016). Literature on brands and branding in the public sector largely proclaim the benefits and positive sides of brand orientation (Gromark & Melin, 2013). For instance, brand orientation is credited with helping public sector organizations communicate their organizational identity to other societal actors (Rochette, 2015); conducting their operations more efficiently, more profitably, as "strong brands" attract people, commerce and investment potential (see for example Asbury et al., 2008; Evans et al., 2008) and securing legitimacy in the eyes of other societal stakeholders (e.g. Karens et al., 2016). Brand orientation is also justified as a rational and effective response to increases in competition for resources (Braun, Kavaratzis & Zenker, 2013).

Although a relatively positive and promotional ideology surrounds questions of whether public institutions should adopt a brand orientation, skepticism has been voiced. Wæraas (2008), for instance, is wary of branding because it is based on communicating a single, aestheticized identity. This might not fit the needs of public organizations, which are inconsistent and contain multiple identities. Because they typically have a wider societal mission, serving a range of public stakeholders, public organizations must often balance public and individual interests, and both control and serve their clients. In addition, potential conflicts may arise between a public sector mission and a brand orientation because the former should be permeated by similarity and equality, while the latter forwards uniqueness and differentiation (Sataøen & Wæraas, 2015).

A key concern is that introducing the private-sector practice of branding to the public sector will divert energy and resources away from broader issues around civic governance and care for all people, including marginalized populations. Mumby, for instance, points at the risk that "brands come first and everyday organizing and work processes follow" (2016, p. 886). A concern is thus that the brand is granted too much constitutive power: public agencies decide what their brand will be and then engage in developments to support it, running the risk that the core tasks of the organization become dominated by the brand. Scholars within this strand of research not only question the advice that public organizations copy ideas of branding from the private sector, but also more generally problematize the value of a brand orientation in public organizations.

In this chapter we align with scholars who take a cautious and reflective approach to branding in the public sector. In particular, we encourage reflection on what could happen to public debate, diversity and inclusion, transparency and critical reflection when a brand orientation exists. We engage these as "tensions" and propose that scholars and practitioners ask what type of values are at stake when a brand orientation is adopted by public management. In what follows, we highlight and concretize tensions that we believe practitioners should consider before, or when, following a brand orientation in order to provide insight into some conflicts that may arise for public employees and values that might be compromised as a consequence of brand orientation in public organizations.

Tensions for practitioners to consider

Tension 1: Brand orientation and transparency

The public sector and its many stakeholders value transparency as a democratic foundation, serving as an important principle for good governance (Ball, 2009). Brand orientation, on the other hand, involves understanding transparency and openness as potential threats to a well-crafted image and identity. As we noted above, brand orientation (among other things) involves *protection* of the brand identity (Urde, 1999). Or, as Fournier and Avery (2011, p. 203) note:

> In a world governed by social empowerment, hyper-criticism, and instant transparency, management's traditional focus on brand building becomes supplanted by an ever-present need to protect brands from attack and demise.

Thus, tensions between transparency and protection may emerge when a brand orientation is pursued in the public sphere. Although there are certainly positives – branding may assist in balancing excessively negative images of the organization produced in traditional as well as social media – public sector principles such as openness, transparency, the right to open communication and whistleblowing might go against the best interests of the brand. In other words, branding has the potential to legitimize the impulse to back away from transparency when it challenges the brand.

In both the literature on branding in the public sector and our own empirical work, we have found that the challenges to transparency can be subtle or overt, but a common factor is that practitioners must decide how to manage the tension between transparency and brand protection. In a world of both hype and hyper-criticism, brand managers are encouraged to protect their brands from attack. Therefore, in situations where external pressures – such as public debate – call for transparency, this may constitute a threat to the brand identity.

A Swedish school experienced this tension particularly relating to (brand) image-thinking, communication freedom and whistleblowing. In 2008, the school's municipality launched the brand campaign "Knowledge-City". Like many other places, the municipality was concerned with competition stemming in part from the rise in the number of private schools, and as part of protecting their brand and securing a competitive advantage they urged public employees to keep their concerns and criticism private. However, in 2011, tensions rose to the surface. In a series of articles published in the local newspaper, public sector employees' legally protected right to whistleblowing was debated alongside the need to care for schools' brand images. In one of the articles, 'Critique is sealed off at work' (Pehrsson & Gravlund, 2011), anonymous teachers testified to the increased fear of retributions for publicly voicing criticism against their organization.

Keeping concerns to oneself went beyond refraining from talking to media; it also applied to everyday practices such as talking with colleagues and friends, or when answering questions at parent-teacher meetings in ways that went against a positive brand image. Administrators asked teachers to demonstrate "loyalty" to the brand by performing silence and deference in the face of critique. One teacher conveyed that although they were encouraged to bring up criticism internally, people appeared afraid to do so when top management was present. Instead, colleagues shared discord in a whispering manner, and they continued to fear reprimands, such as not getting pay increases and, in the worst case, facing termination of employment.

The teacher's fears appear to be justified, as the head administrator of education department's messages about transparency are rife with ambiguity. In a follow-up article (Gravlund, 2011), the administrator conveyed that he supports and defends employees' rights to whistleblowing and bringing issues to the media. However, he also expressed that employees should convey discord internally, and suggested that employees be "careful" about how they talk about the organization. After stating, "We encourage an atmosphere of openness, but foremost internally", the administrator invokes a branding rationale to argue against employees talking to the media, by noting:

> It could weaken our abilities to compete and that has negative consequences for our employees because we will be receiving less resource (income) if students transfer to the private independent schools. I don't mean that you can't go to the media but one should be concerned with our own conditions. From a brand perspective, attacking your own employer is not positive.
>
> (Gravlund, 2011)

The journalist pointed out that the head of the education department displayed two inconsistent opinions, and therefore asked him what stance the teachers ought to assume. The head of school replied:

> I think it's ok with the right to whistleblowing, but I don't think it's good to publish criticism that could damage the brand ... I can't prioritize, both are equally important. I think most teachers understand what I'm saying.
>
> (Gravlund, 2011)

Although the administrator says that transparency and whistleblowing are valued as much as the brand, he leaves readers (and teachers) with the impression that the brand must be protected, as it is what protects jobs and resources. What is left unsaid is what and who is sacrificed when the brand is centralized as the important feature to protect, above the needs of students, teachers, parents or communities. For public managers, this example highlights an instance where principles of the market and/or branding may end up on a collision course with democratic principles of transparency and openness. Public sector managers may therefore find themselves in positions where they not only have to negotiate, but also prioritize between these conflicting principles.

Tension 2: Brand orientation and inclusion

A central tension between a corporate brand orientation and the public sector is that branding seeks to highlight pristine elements while the public sector often deals with multiple elements of society, some which are considered "dirty or undesirable", such as poverty, homelessness or unattractiveness. These differences highlight a tension between what a community seeks to include and exclude. We illustrate this tension by presenting two contrasting examples involving the establishment of new organizations in municipalities, differing in their perceived attractiveness. The first organization is Amazon, the other is a prison.

In late 2017, the U.S. corporation Amazon put forth a call, dubbed H2Q, for North American cities to submit proposals to be considered for the location of Amazon's second headquarters. In an unprecedented move, Amazon's call was public and highly publicized. Yet, although the organization sought to bring attention to the "competition", they also required that cities and city employees sign confidentiality agreements, dictating that the proposals, including any incentives promised to Amazon, remain secret. On offer from Amazon was the promise of as many as 50,0000 high-paying jobs – i.e., those paying approximately US$100,000 per year, as well as tens of thousands of jobs created by building and infrastructure for the operations, and tens of billions of dollars in additional investments in the community. In designing their proposal, Amazon encouraged city employees to "think big and be creative" in their pitch. (Amazon Request for Proposals, 2017). In November, 2018 Amazon announced that their new headquarters would be split between two locations on the East Coast of the United States: New York City and Arlington Virginia, although in early 2019 the company pulled out of the New York City deal due to ongoing citizen protests and critique.

The case of Amazon highlights tensions regarding branding and inclusion/exclusion in the public sector in three ways. First, Amazon provided clear indications of what constitutes an "ideal" metro area, and, in doing so, implicitly defined what ideal cities are and, importantly, what they are not. Second, the sheer volume of cities seeking to be Amazon's second home speaks to how eager cities are to brand themselves to attract big business. Third, backlash from citizens concerned about who is left behind in the race to land Amazon highlights tensions between corporate growth and public service.

In seeking a new headquarters, Amazon had the opportunity to brand what it means to be an ideal city by putting specific parameters around their preferred site (Amazon Request for Proposals, 2017):

- Metropolitan area with more than one million people
- A stable and business-friendly environment
- Urban or suburban locations with the potential to attract and retain strong technical talent
- Communities that think big and creatively when considering locations and real-estate options (for Amazon).

By detailing what they desired, and labelling these attributes as "ideal", Amazon influenced city branding, including what aspects of a city managers must highlight or downplay.

Amazon received a staggering 238 proposals in October of 2017 (Del Rey, 2017). Only seven of 50 U.S. states declined to submit bids, meaning over 85% of states wanted to win the contract. In January of 2018, Amazon selected 20 cities as finalists. Although Amazon mandated that proposals remain confidential, some cities did publicly share proposals, and many others created public branding campaigns around the proposal, such as websites or videos, which a city consultant in Denver, Colorado referred to as a "Love Letter" to Amazon (Colorado Loves, 2019). Other city officials engaged in stunts designed to draw attention. For instance, city officials from Tucson, Arizona sent CEO Jeff Bezos a 21-foot-tall cactus, and officials from Stonecrest, Georgia promised to rename their city Amazon, should they be chosen. The bid to get Amazon encouraged cities to brand specifically for the corporation (Garfield, 2018a).

However, not everyone is in "love" with the idea of Amazon coming to their communities. Several city employees, watchdog agencies and citizens questioned the cost of such tremendous growth – including a glut of housing, the impact on transportation and infrastructure and the further fragmentations around class and inequalities should home prices rise as a result. The dissent over the H2Q process sheds light on branding, inclusion/exclusion and the public sector by providing an alternative to the overwhelming message that "good" cities should vie for unfettered business growth, seek to land "the big fish" and to offer incentives to companies who wish to do business there. Of the 20 finalist cities, nine offered major economic incentives; the largest package from Montgomery Maryland was valued at US$8.5 billion (Garfield, 2018b). While the Amazon case highlights, overall, the energy and excitement that can exist around bringing a new enterprise to a city, the next case about a prison demonstrates the inverse – that energy can also exist around keeping an enterprise out of a city.

Svedala is a municipality in southern Sweden that decided to build a prison. The decision caused various reactions. Broadly speaking, some thought it was good because the prison would provide employment, while others worried about increased criminality, and a reduction of home values (Sydsvenskan, 2017). In response to citizens' requests for further analysis, the municipality hired a communication consultancy to do a brand analysis of the prison plans, in order to "see how the establishment [of the prison] will affect the Svedala brand, as a place to live, work and visit" (Identx, 2018, p. 3). The consultancy report educated readers on what a brand is ("that which others associate with you") and outlined questions that affect the brand (for instance: What does the media write about? What is written in social media? How is it to live and work in the area? What are we known for? Why do people come here and live here? What impression do visitors get?). It also defined the purpose of considering a place as a brand, and the challenges place brands face:

> The purpose of a place brand is to create positive associations in order to create pride, attract new inhabitants, attract new businesses and visitors. The challenge for place brands is that nobody fully owns the brand. On the contrary, many actors must come together beneath the same brand. Businesses, politicians, public organizations and citizens all have to identify with the values of the place to communicate the right image to the environment.
>
> (Identx, 2018, p. 6)

The report analyzed the prison plan from six different perspectives, including:

- Housing perspective – how will housing prices be affected by the prison?
- Citizen perspective – how will the well-being of the citizens be affected by the prison?
- Business perspective – how will business entrepreneurs experience the establishment of the prison?
- Tourist perspective – how will tourism be affected by the prison?
- Employer perspective – may the prison affect the employer brands of Svedala employers seeking new employees?
- Media perspective – will the prison lead to more negative publicity in the media?

To address these questions and predict the effects on the city brand, the consultancy analyzed other municipalities with prisons, and drew the general conclusion that none of the above perspectives would be affected negatively by the prison except possibly the publicity in social media, but only in the short run.

The report was strongly criticized by a citizen initiative called "prison-free Svedala". One of their representatives – a place branding professional – published an article in the local newspaper, criticizing the report for lacking validity because it used municipalities with prisons that were *not* associated with their prison. It would be more relevant to compare with places that *are* associated with their prisons. She also argued that this was not an adequate brand analysis because the report relied on "hard" data, and branding is essentially an emotional association. The representative suggested instead that:

> It's scientifically proven that people make choices on emotional grounds. Choices that are retrospectively supported by rational arguments. That's the cornerstone in all branding. So, which emotions emerge by Sweden's second largest prison connected to a city? Does it create positive associations? Does it lead to proud citizens and ambassadors? Does it contribute to attracting new inhabitants and visitors? Does it make the landscape more beautiful? Does it create the conditions that families and others who are searching for peace and calm in the countryside want? This is what must be found out in a brand analysis.
>
> (Östberg, 2018)

The Amazon vs. Prison case demonstrates that enterprises necessary to the functioning of a city, such as businesses and prisons, are evaluated through a branding lens, meaning that their value is assessed as it relates to (or fails to relate to) an ideal city image. Importantly, this case provides insight into how city managers might be "pulled" in various directions around what is valued when cities use a brand orientation to make decisions about who and what can enter. Sataøen and Wæraas (2015) highlight this value tension when they state, "When public organizations … engage in corporate branding work, a tension emerges between corporate branding's specific demand for uniqueness and differentiation on the one hand, and public institutions' general need for equal services and legitimacy on the other" (444). In other words, the purpose of a city (i.e., law enforcement) might be at odds with the brand (which may prefer to be known for being linked to Amazon), leaving public managers to decide upon and defend their actions from within a branding framework. At heart, then, are issues of the inclusion and exclusion of certain stakeholders, businesses or services as a means of constructing the right brand.

Tension 3: Brand orientation and reflexivity

A third tension regards organizational reflexivity, that is, an organization's ability to take into account and reflect on its own way of understanding and acting in the world (Cunliffe, 2003, p. 51). While we probably want public organizations to ponder over their processes before making decisions, and encourage their stakeholders to do so too, a brand orientation tends to encourage reflex reactions designed to develop or protect the brand rather than reflective thinking. This tension is particularly expressed when an organization's reputation is at stake in the wake of a scandal, as in the following case from the police (for a more detailed outline of this case, see Rennstam, 2013).

In December 2008 there were riots in the city of Malmö, Sweden. The situation was severe. Cars were set on fire and people threw cobblestones and homemade bombs at the police. Media called the area a war zone. Inside a police van operating the area, police officers made utterances with racist connotations, directed toward the riot makers (e.g. calling one of them a "fucking ape"). This would not have been heard by anybody outside of the van if it were not for the fact that the officers filmed the situation, and the film was later used in a trial against one of the riot makers. At the trial, the film was played, the utterances were heard, and the focus of the trial shifted instantly from focusing on the riot maker to focusing on the utterances of the officers. Journalists were present in the courtroom and the utterances quickly made it into the news.

The police management reacted swiftly. The same day as the trial, they reported the officers to the National Police Related Crimes Unit, they stressed when interviewed by journalists how upset they were about the utterances and how disturbing it was that "there exists such an attitude to human beings among our employees" (Sydsvenskan Web-TV, 2009). The management also reassured journalists that they would take the officers off the streets (which they did), isolating them from any contact with the public until the investigation was finalized. It was 15 months until the officers were allowed to go back to their regular service.

Arguably, the police management reacted by reflex rather than reflexivity. This becomes clearer if we consider how they talked about this incident internally. Within the organization (and to the researcher doing the study), they communicated that they knew that the officers were aware that they had done wrong, and that they were good officers. The police management had fairly good grounds for this. The officers had worked on the streets for 8 and 19 years respectively, had no previous remarks with racist connotations and were known among their colleagues as "correct" (for instance, one of the researcher's respondents, a former manager of one of the officers, called one of them "one of the most ethically correct officers I have ever worked with"). Obviously, the utterances were not "correct" and most of the colleagues seemed to think they were highly inappropriate, but also to be seen as stupid mistakes by otherwise competent officers. The fact that the utterances were made inside the van and in a very stressful situation – many of the officers in service reported that they had never experienced anything like it – also made colleagues believe that the officers did not mean what they said. Altogether, the punishment of the officers was deemed disproportionate.

Our point here is not to discuss the guilt or innocence of the officers, but to show how the police managers followed a brand orientation by focusing on what they *thought* the outside wanted instead of acting based on what they thought was reasonable. The case indicates that the police management's understanding of the situation was far more complex than suggested by their communication to the outside world. As a result, the brand orientation stimulated the "sacrifice" of the police officers, expecting this to establish peace with the outside (the public and media). What was also "sacrificed" in the process, however, was the potential for reflexivity – deepened analysis – about the role of racism/raced talk in the police organization: Were the officers' utterances an exception or a significant cultural expression? And if there are problems, are those perhaps due to management rather than backstage utterances by single officers?

In sum, the brand orientation seemed to lead the managers to act by reflex rather than engage in reflective thinking. A key lesson from this case is that following a brand orientation may imply a "sacrificial mode" of organizing (Rennstam, 2013) that leads to emphasis on simple solutions to complex problems. This is a potential problem because public managers may often find themselves in complex situations, or even scandals. Following a brand orientation, the impulse will likely be to protect the brand. Sometimes this protection involves sacrificing people, policies or programs that can be redeemed. Although this may be good in the short run – because it can save managers' backs, and/or avoid time-consuming reflection on current managerial or street-level practices – it may also limit the possibilities of long-term organizational learning and improvement.

A value-based tool for understanding the pros and cons of brand orientation

So far, we have explored, through examples, three tensions that public employees who are also branding practitioners might face when they seek to follow a brand orientation. In the following section, we will suggest a value-based framework that can be used as a "heuristic" tool to analyze the pros and cons of concrete branding initiatives. By "heuristic" we mean a tool that does not prescribe action but seeks to help analysts to discover and understand new aspects of a phenomenon, such as brand-oriented behavior. In the wake of the development towards brand orientation in the public sector, it is important to discover and understand intended and unintended consequences for organizations, public employees, citizens and other stakeholders. The "tool" is intended to assist in this work.

Our framework is based on the work of French sociologists Luc Boltanski & Laurent Thévenot (2006) and has previously been applied to branding in Bertilsson & Rennstam (2018). Here, we will describe it with particular attention to public sector organizations. In short, the framework is based on the idea that the activities in such organizations can be analyzed based on different "worlds", or perspectives, which all have their own basic principle for measuring value. In other terms, whether an activity is valuable cannot be decided objectively and once and for all, but depends on the "world"/perspective from which the activity is analyzed.

Boltanski and Thévenot have outlined eight "worlds" and here we outline the four that have the most relevance to our case: market, civic, fame and industrial. Each has its own way of measuring value, as we briefly outline below:

- Market world: value is measured by price/increased revenues (increased sales, tourism, consumption).
- Civic world: value is measured by the extent to which an activity contributes to "the common good".

- World of fame: value is measured by the degree to which a person or organization is recognized by others.
- Industrial world: value is measured by efficiency (efficiency as in minimizing the input/output-ratio. For instance, does branding contribute to the efficiency of public practices like schooling and public transport?).

In Table 9.1 we have outlined how our three cases may be analyzed based on the framework, suggesting how value might increase or decrease in the different "worlds". A few comments are appropriate to clarify how we intend that the framework is used by public managers.

First, the framework does not *predict* if value will increase or decrease but only directs the analyst's (e.g. a practitioner) attention to different ways of thinking about a particular activity (such as silencing whistle blowers, attracting/repelling large organizations or punishing misbehaving employees). Each case requires its own situated analysis. Exactly what will happen in terms of value cannot be known beforehand.

Second, and relatedly, the framework does not add up to a result in terms of an aggregated value increase or decrease. In other words, it does not provide a measure for *how much* the value might increase in X world and decrease in Y world. It might be tempting for decision makers to engage in such a mathematical exercise, but the values in all but the market world do not lend themselves very well to quantification.

Third, the worlds may interact. One world can use another to its own advantage. For instance, in the school case, the market world can "coopt" the world of fame in the sense that a more well-known school will attract more pupils, which enables increase of the school tuition (if the political system allows it). Or, in the Amazon case, if the city attracting Amazon becomes "famous" as the ideal city for business, the increased value in the world of fame spills over to the market world if other businesses follow Amazon's lead.

Fourth, the market world has a special stance because that is where branding originates. Although the price mechanism does not always directly correlate to the public sector, it is important to note that a brand orientation creates both pressure and urgency to demonstrate growth and production in the public sector. This means that public managers may primarily be held to the standards of the market world, rather than the civic world in which they are meant to manage and develop.

Managerial implications

Public managers play a crucial role in their communities. Often, the job requires public managers to be flexible, engaged, and responsive to contemporary trends and fashions, such as branding. As we have discussed in this chapter, branding has become ubiquitous in the public sector, making it both timely and relevant for public sector employees to consider as a policy option. As our cases articulate, a brand orientation often factors into how public managers think, make decisions and communicate with stakeholders. Importantly, brand orientation may generate conflicts between the principles of the market and the foundational principles of the public sector. In what follows, we offer suggestions that encourage managers to think about the potential conflicts that may exist between the market and civic worlds, and to prioritize the ideals and principles of the public sector ahead of brand considerations.

Table 9.1 Value-based framework for analyzing pros and cons of a brand orientation

	Transparency/school	*Inclusion/Amazon-Prison*	*Reflexivity/police*
Market – how does our brand orientation affect the revenue of our organization or our products?	Value may increase in the market world as a result of an attractive school brand through the suppression of whistle blowing or critique that could threaten the attractiveness of the brand.	Value may increase as a result of attracting Amazon due to increased tax revenue. Value may increase as a result of attracting a prison due to increased tax revenue.	Value, including employer brand value, may decrease as a result of poor recruitment or retention abilities due to the sacrificial mode of branding.
Civic –how does our brand orientation affect the way in which we contribute to the common good?	Value in the civic world may decrease as problems and mal-practices in schools/ education never reach the public/public authorities (because of brand-induced suppression of critique and whistle-blowing), and therefore cannot be rectified. It is for the common good to have a school and education system that performs its role well, including enhancing the role and expectations of future advisors.	Value may decrease if attracting Amazon drives out affordable housing, increases traffic, stresses infrastructure or diverts tax support away from stakeholders in need (i.e., marginalized populations). Value may increase when a public organization fulfills its obligation to manage criminal justice in a responsible and humane manner, irrespective of the "dirty" association of the service.	Value may decrease as a result of the brand orientation. It is for the common good to have a police organization that reflects on their own actions. In contrast, the behavior of the police management strived for a "quick fix" (blame everything on the police officers, punish them and hope that will be the end of the discussion); a reflex reaction when the news "came out". It is also for the "common good" to stimulate public reflection on how the police functions, while the "sacrificial mode" may silence important discussions about police culture and how the police organization is managed.
Fame – how does our brand orientation affect the extent to which we are recognized by others?	Value in the world of fame may increase if the suppression of (both internal and external) critique against a school brand is successful in maintaining or elevating the recognition of that brand.	Value may increase if a city can attract or "win" in the contest to attract Amazon, in which case the city might be recognized as an "ideal" business-friendly city. Value may decrease if a city opens a prison, in which case the city may be recognized as "dirty" or assumed to be less attractive.	Value may increase. If the "sacrificial mode" of branding "works", in the sense that it makes people think that the police are able to minimize racist expressions in the organization (by sorting out "bad apples"), then the police will gain recognition. In particular, the improved recognition value will have a positive effect on the managers who sorted out and punished the "bad apples".

(Continued)

Table 9.1 Cont.

	Transparency/school	Inclusion/Amazon-Prison	Reflexivity/police
Industrial – how does our brand orientation affect how efficiently our core processes are carried out?	Value in the industrial world may increase if the silencing/suppression of the whistle blowers is successful, because it enables management to run the organization more efficiently – not having to deal (spend time and resources) with internal dissent and external critique.	Value may increase as securing Amazon demonstrates an efficient process of integrating business into the city. Value may increase if effective prison management could demonstrate an efficient process of integrating business/organizations into the city.	Value may increase if the sacrificial mode of branding is successful, because it requires resources to engage in a public discussion about racism in the police.

Drawing from the heuristic tool offered above, we offer four takeaways for public managers to consider. Again, while we cannot say with certainty how a manager should *act* in all situations, we can put forth advice on how managers can *think* through a variety of situations where a brand orientation creates tensions with public sector ideas. In essence, what we are advocating is that managers embrace and disseminate a culture of critical thinking as a means of managing branding in the public sector.

1   Managers can acknowledge the distinctions between managing public and private organizations, and the different values or principles guiding each realm. We suggest that public managers should return to the foundational principles of the "world" in which the public organization finds itself and use those values as a base for their decisions and priorities. Put simply, managers should understand when the context requires them to prioritize public values over brand values. The cases above all demonstrate situations where a brand orientation supersedes or challenges public sector values. In these cases, managers face a tension or dilemma between the brand and principles such as openness and transparency, equality and inclusion and reflexivity versus responding by reflex. Public managers ought to prioritize the value of the civic world above the value of the market world – should they collide.
2   Managers can encourage dissent and doubt. Managers can encourage a culture of critical thinking by embracing stakeholders who are willing to communicate doubt or dissent around decisions, policies or practices. In particular, managers can encourage doubts around a brand orientation as a managerial philosophy. From our perspective, doubters, such as internal critics or whistle blowers, should be acknowledged and offered consideration rather than ignored or silenced. Doubters can shed important light on the ways in which a brand orientation may run against the very values and principles the public organization is expected to live up to. For example, the perceived need to protect the brand image by circumventing whistle blowing and preventing critique, such as in the school example above, ought to be resisted, perhaps by making continuous reference to principles of openness and transparency.
3   Managers can engage in reflexive management. Managers can be mindful of the ways in which a brand orientation encourages certain actions and discourages others. By thinking of protecting the brand as merely one way of operating,

amongst many others, managers begin to realize that branding intentions may backfire. For instance, in the case above regarding the police, the intention of punishing the officers was to "save the brand". However, this brand-oriented decision-making does not mean that the strategy will always be successful, and it ignores other management principles, such as taking a hard look at occupational and organizational culture and the importance of managing and guiding employees to do and be better. In other words, sacrificing a few so-called bad apples likely does not protect a brand in the long run, and it certainly has implications over the long term regarding organizational culture.

4   Managers can look beyond the market and civic worlds to consider the social and global impacts of a brand orientation. Doing so enables managers to consider "grand problems", or the big issues facing society (Shockley-Zalabak et al., 2017). This links to the value of what Boltanski and Thévenot (2006) call the "green world", in which value is measured by the extent to which actions are in line with the principles of environmentalism (such as reducing pollution and CO_2 emissions, protecting the wilderness and animal health). However, being mindful of grand problems also allows managers to be aware of how a brand orientation might impact broader social issues, such as environmentalism, conservation or the downsides of unfettered growth.

As noted at the beginning of this chapter, public institutions such as cities, the police or schools are increasingly adopting a brand orientation. This trend has both micro and macro implications for public managers and the stakeholders they serve. On a micro or daily level, public managers may notice that a brand orientation is embedded in a variety of tasks and decisions, and as such, it may impact public-sector ideals. On a macro or societal level, a brand orientation in the public sector may challenge a manager's abilities to tackle grand problems that speak to broader environmental and social issues. Via the three cases above, we demonstrate how a brand orientation can impact transparency, inclusion and reflexivity, or critical thinking. We end this essay by encouraging managers to prioritize public and civic values, to support dissent and critical thinking and to consider broader implications at stake when branding and public sector governance co-exist.

References

Amazon Corporation (2017) Amazon HQ2 RFP: 1–7.

Asbury, L.D., Wong, F.L., Price, S.M. and Nolin, M.J. (2008) The VERB Campaign: Applying a branding strategy in public health. *American Journal of Preventive Medicine*, 34: 183–187.

Ball, C. (2009) What is transparency? *Public Integrity*, 11 (4): 293–308.

Bertilsson, J. and Rennstam, J. (2018) The destructive side of branding: A heuristic model for analyzing the value of branding practice. *Organization*, 25 (2): 260–281.

Bjørnå, H. and Salomonsen, H.H. (2016) Reputation and brand management in Scandinavian municipalities. *Scandinavian Journal of Public Administration*, 20 (2): 3–5.

Boltanski, L. and Thévenot, L. (2006) *On justification: Economies of worth*. Princeton University Press.

Braun, E., Kavaratzis, M. and Zenker, S. (2013) My city – my brand: The role of residents in place branding, *Journal of Place Management and Development*, 6 (1): 18–28.

Colorado Loves (2019) Colorado Loves Amazon – Get Involved. Available at: https://colora dolovesamazon.com/. Accessed 23 April 2019.

Cunliffe, A. L. (2003) Reflexive inquiry in organizational research: Questions and possibilities. *Human Relations*, 56 (8): 983–1003.

Del Rey, J. (2017) Amazon received more than 200 proposals from places that want to host its new headquarters. *Recode*. Available at: https://www.recode.net/2017/10/23/16521500/ama zon-hq2-new-second-headquarters-rfp-proposals-bids. Accessed 26 October 2018.

Evans, D.W., Blitstein, J., Hershey, J.C. and Renaud, J. (2008) Systematic review of public health branding. *Journal of Health Communication*, 13: 721–741.

Fournier, S. and Avery, J. (2011) The uninvited brand. *Business Horizons*, 54 (3): 193–207.

Garfield, L. (2018a) Cities are throwing hundreds of millions at Amazon to land HQ2- here's how they stack up. *Business Insider*. Available at: https://www.businessinsider.com/ama zon-hq2-cities-developers-economic-tax-incentives-2017-10. Accessed 21 November 2018.

Garfield, L. (2018b) The battle for Amazon's $5 billion headquarters has intensified- but these states don't want to be involved. *Business Insider*. Available at: https://www.businessinsider.com/ama zons-headquarters-cities-states-didnt-submit-bids-2017-10. Accessed 21 November 2018.

Gravlund, W. (2011) Dubbla budskap om öppenheten. Helsingborgs Dagblad 2011-2001-16.

Gromark, J. and Melin, F. (2013) From market orientation to brand orientation in the public sector. *Journal of Marketing Management*, 29 (9–10): 1099–1123.

Hatch, M.J. and Schultz, M. (2003) Bringing the corporation into corporate branding. *European Journal of Marketing*, 37 (7/8): 1041–1064.

Identx (2018) Analys varumärkespåverkan – Hur påverkas varumärket Svedala av att det etableras en kriminalvårdsanstalt i kommunen? (Analysis brand impact – How is the Svedala brand affected by the establishment of a prison in the municipality). Identx Kommunikation. Retrieved from: https://www.svedala.se/contentassets/5cb9d5f5d5c441eca5111652453d189c/ana lys-varumarkespaverkan-svedalakommun-komp.pdf.

Karens, R., Eshuis, J. and Klijn, E. (2016) The impact of public branding: An experimental study on the effects of branding policy on citizen trust. *Public Administration Review*, 76 (3): 486–494.

Kornberger, M. (2010) *Brand society: How brands transform management and lifestyle*. Cambridge University Press.

Kärreman, D. and Rylander, A. (2008) Managing meaning through branding: The case of a consulting firm. *Organization Studies*, 29 (1): 103–125.

Loacker, B. and Sullivan, K. R. (2016) The liminality of branding: Interweaving discourses 'making up'a cultural intermediary occupation. *Marketing Theory*, 16 (3): 361–382.

Marland, A. (2016) *Brand command: Canadian politics and democracy in the age of message control*. Vancouver, UBC Press.

Moor, L. (2007) *The rise of brands*. Oxford, Berg Publishers.

Mumby, D.K. (2016) Organizing beyond organization: Branding, discourse, and communicative capitalism. *Organization*, 23 (6): 884–907.

Östberg, H. (2018) Fängelseanalysen försöker jämföra med orter som inte är jämförbara (The prison analysis compares incomparable towns). *Sydsvenskan*, September 6. Retrieved from: https://www.sydsvenskan.se/2018-09-06/fangelseanalysen-forsoker-jamfora-med-orter-som -inte-ar-jamforbara.

Pehrsson, J. and Gravlund, W. (2011) *Kritiken stängs inne på jobbet*. Helsingborgs Dagblad 2011-2001-15.

Rennstam, J. (2013) Branding in the sacrificial mode: A study of the consumptive side of brand value production. *Scandinavian Journal of Management*, 29 (2): 123–134.

Rochette, C. (2015) The public brand between new practices and public values, *International Review of Administrative Sciences*, 81 (2): 326–345.

Sataøen, H.L. and Wæraas, A. (2015) Branding without unique brands: Managing similarity and difference in a public sector context. *Public Management Review*, 17 (3): 443–461.

Shockley-Zalabak, P., Barge, J.K., Lewis, L., and Simpson, J.L. (2017) Engaged scholarship, in C.R. Scott and L. Lewis (eds.), *The International Encyclopedia of Organizational Communication*. New York, NY: John Wiley & Sons: 807–821.

Sydsvenskan (2017) Kräver folkomröstning om fängelse: "Tryggheten i samhället minskar" (Demand for referendum on prison: "The social safety will decrease"). Retrieved from: https://www.syds venskan.se/2017-03-21/kraver-folkomrostning-om-fangelse-tryggheten-i-samhallet-minskar.

Sydsvenskan Web-TV (2009) Retrieved from http://www.sydsvenskan.se/webbtv/webbtv_malmo/a rticle411003/WEBB-TV-Polischefen-ber-om-ursakt.html.

Urde, M. (1999) Brand orientation: A mindset for building brands into strategic resources. *Journal of Marketing Management*, 15 (1–3): 117–133.

Wæraas, A. (2008) Can public sector organizations be coherent corporate brands? *Marketing Theory*, 8 (2): 205–221.

Wæraas, A. and Maor, M. (2015) Understanding organizational reputation in a public sector context, in A. Wæraas and M. Maor (eds.), *Organizational reputation in the public sector*. New York, Routledge: 1–14.

10 Is Lean Management the natural order in public services transformation?

Irvine Lapsley

Introduction

Lean Management has become a movement which has transformed production tech-nologies in manufacturing and has become the most favoured business process improvement methodology worldwide (Samuel et al., 2015). Also, Lean Management has become a widespread, international practice within reforms to transform public services (Lapsley and Miller, 2019). It promises to deliver quality services while using less resources. At a time where budgets are being cut and recruitment freezes are rife, it is vital that the government makes the most of the resources it has. In an era of cash-strapped public services, whether through austerity measures or from the desire to meet taxpayer demands for more value for money, Lean Management is presented as an attractive proposition for managers in public services (Radnor, 2011). Lean Manage-ment, as a service improvement tool, was developed by Toyota Car Manufacturing Company in the 1920s. The Lean principles of streamlining processes and tying service improvement to the strategies of the organization is the latest approach to public management which is being supported by the government. The attraction of Lean for public sector modernisers can also be found in the premise that "private is better" and the desire on the part of key policy makers to encourage the adoption of private sector practice with the expectation of improving efficiency in the public sector. The present widespread use of Lean in public services has been the outcome of the concerted pro-motion of Lean, particularly by management consultants who seek opportunities to implement Lean policies.

The Lean Management approach

The Lean Management approach has been widely attributed to Womack et al. (1990) with the publication of their book: *The Machine That Changed the World*. However, it is more precise to attribute the introduction of the term Lean to John Krafcik, a fellow colleague of Womack et al. on the Massachusetts Institute of Technology`s Interna-tional Motor Vehicle Programme (IMVP). Indeed, the emergence of what was called the Toyota Production System (TPS), known as Lean in much management literature can be attributed to early work on mass production by Frank Woollard in 1925 and 1945 and to Toyota`s appointment of the engineer, Taicchi Ohno, who was preoccupied with the elimination of waste (*buda*) – see Samuel et al. (2015). *The Machine That Changed the World*, by Womack et al. (1990, p.13), defines Lean Management and its key principles as follows:

DOI: 10.4324/9781003154389-14

compared to mass production it uses less of everything – half the human effort in the factory, half the manufacturing space, half the investment in tools, half the engineering hours to develop a new product in half the time.

This is achieved by the adoption of five principles:

1 Specify the value desired by the customer.
2 Identify the value stream for each product/service providing that value, and challenge all of the wasted steps.
3 Make the product flow continuously. Standardise processes around best practice allowing them to run more smoothly, freeing up time for creativity and innovation.
4 Introduce "pull" between all the steps where continuous flow is impossible. Focus upon the demand from the customer and trigger events backwards through the value chain.
5 Manage towards perfection so that non value-adding activity will be removed from the value chain so that the number of steps, amount of time and information needed to serve the customer continually falls.

The above definition and principles may have appeal. But they have also been contested by critics. Next these criticisms are elaborated upon and guidance is offered on how to make sense of the differing claims.

Critiques of Lean Management

There are numerous critiques of Lean. These stem from the strengths of Toyota's claim to an efficient production system, the applicability of management systems developed in manufacturing to other sectors and the lack of rigour in Lean – specifically the absence of a robust theorisation of Lean process improvement. These critiques are considered next:

1 The efficiency of TPS and Lean

There have been reservations about the efficacy of Lean Management at Toyota (Arnaboldi et al., 2015). The article by Arnaboldi et al. gives an account of a serious concern with the TPS system. Specifically, concerns have been expressed that the constant focus on cost reduction has affected the safety of their vehicles. On February 3, 2010, Chris Lastrella, an off-duty Highway Policeman in California was driving his Toyota Lexus with his family on board when the accelerator pedal jammed. All of the car occupants were killed in the ensuing crash. There were a further 30 reported deaths in the U.S. from sudden unintended acceleration on Toyota vehicles at this time. At a subsequent hearing of the U.S. Congressional Oversight and Government Reform Committee, Roy LaHood, the U.S. Transport Secretary said Toyota was "safety deaf" and Akio Toyoda, the grandson of the Toyota company founder apologised for the accidents. However, a senior US executive challenged Toyota's handling of safety issues as it expanded its operations. These outcomes undermine the application of Lean Thinking as a relentless driver for cost reduction without due consideration for other important issues such as safety.

2 Portability of Japanese car manufacturer operating systems to public services

While Lean was developed in car manufacture, it has been modified for use in service industries (Abdi et al., 2006). But service industries are significantly different from public services. In the first instance, Lean has a major focus on the customer. This implies purchasers of Lean products exercise choice in the selection of which product they prefer at a price which they are willing to pay. The aggregate of all prices paid by consumers for a company's products creates a measure of value: a crucial concept in the enabling of Lean Management – see the five principles outlined above. By contrast, users of public services are citizens who express preferences as political choices at the ballot box in elections. This is a markedly different concept from the customer. Advocates of Lean in public services have introduced the concept of the "end user" (Radnor and Osborne, 2013). The "end user" concept falls short of the "customer" in numerous ways. For example, the end user may be confronted with a local or national monopoly with no opportunity to exercise choice. Also, the end user may be unable to act independently – they may be frail, vulnerable or elderly. Unlike the purchase of a motor vehicle, they may be in an entirely novel setting with little or no reference points to guide them. An example of this, in extremis, is patients receiving palliative care. Furthermore, the kind of options confronting them may be complex in terms of procedures and outcomes. In these cases, the 'end user' is usually assisted by a surrogate or proxy who acts on his or her behalf. The proxy is most likely to be a professional from health, social care, education, or whatever service is under discussion. But this is a long way from the customer and makes the idea of the end user as a significant influence on service delivery rather tenuous. It is also in direct contrast with the Lean approach which prioritises customer needs over producers' perceptions of what customers' needs are.

Furthermore, the Lean Management approach presumes a specific form of organization, with strong top-down management (Golledge and Sommer, 2002; Radnor and Osborne, 2013). This fits the organization of the typical industrial organization but not the typical public sector organization. Within public sector organizations there have been reforms to management structures, but there remain many voices from a variety of sources (elected politicians, articulate professionals from health care such as doctors and nurses, educationalists, social care workers, engineers and more). The idea of top-down management is anathema to these various voices. The opposition of these groups raises the possibility of significant internal opposition to the introduction of Lean Management.

Finally, while Lean Management is recognised as a particularly efficient variant of mass production systems, it nevertheless has the characteristics of classic production lines – the linear progression of products at different stages of production until completion, in a process of increasing automation and use of robot tools. This contrasts markedly with many public services which exhibit less linear patterns of service delivery with considerable joint costs in multi-service delivery systems, in which front line service deliverers have significant discretion over the nature of services. This is the phenomenon of "street level bureaucrats" in public services (Lipsky, 2010). These influences undermine the potential for the standardised approach used in Lean Management.

In short, there are significant barriers to the simple transfer of Lean Management to public services. This chapter highlights how and where the Lean Approach might be applied successfully.

3 Lean Management as a failed theory

Radnor and Osborne (2013) have suggested that Lean Management is a failed theory. In their view, the pursuit of Lean has resulted in the use of the tools and techniques of Lean without the approach being located in a rigorous theoretical framework. These authors elaborate their own preferred theory: a public-services-dominant theory of Lean. The authors have particular concerns about the portability of Lean Management to public services (see discussion above). This approach would entail a value-creation process through the recognition of the coproduction of services by both end users and providers of services. This framework has the potential to elevate Lean Management from being described as a set of tools to a rigorous theory of Lean for public services. While most managers will be more concerned with how Lean is implemented rather than why this approach is adopted, the Radnor and Osborne initiative offers a more enduring prospect for Lean Management.

Issues and challenges for Lean Management implementation

There are three specific issues which are addressed here to enhance our understanding of Lean implementation: (1) short- v long-term perspectives, (2) the turbulence of political initiatives and (3) tests of readiness for Lean adoption.

Short- v long-term perspectives

There are numerous cases of Lean adoptions which fail. These failures may be due to many reasons: inadequate resources devoted to the project, inexperienced staff handling complex issues, poor design of the proposed project or unrealistic expectations of Lean. However, it is suggested here that many failures may be attributed a lack of recognition of what Lean is. Specifically, Lean Management is a management philosophy. The initial work on Lean commenced in the 1920s and 1930s. The TPS system reached maturity in the 1960s and 1970s. It was transferred to Western companies in the 1980s and1990s. This management system took almost 50 years to fully develop. The use of Lean as a quick fix to address budget deficits is entirely inappropriate. This quick fix mentality is a counter to the Lean approach. An elaboration of the Lean approach is shown in Table 10.1.

Casual observers will immediately connect with the Process dimension of Lean: Just in time stock supply, continuous production flow with standardisation, the quality fixation to get it right, first time. But this concept of Lean is too narrow. As Table 10.1 shows, Lean is fundamentally about people. It is a long-term approach in which senior managers and operational colleagues adhere to and live by the desire for continuous improvement. The idea of relentless reflection in the pursuit of continuous improvement reflects a distinct culture. This has raised questions over whether the transmission of Japanese culture to Western organizations can be achieved effectively. This issue is addressed further below.

The turbulence of political initiatives

As noted above, in the 21st century, the Lean Management approach to achieving efficient processes within organizations is being applied to the UK public sector and,

Table 10.1 An overarching perspective on Lean implementation

Lean as a long-term philosophy

- Take the long-term perspective over the short term

Get the process right

- Standardise tasks – the foundation of continuous improvement
- Identify problems from the continuous process flow
- Use a visual control so all problems can be seen
- Level out the workload
- Stop to fix problems: get the quality right, first time
- Use 'Just in Time' replacement of stock as it is used to avoid overproduction

The value of people

- Leaders must understand, live and teach the Lean philosophy
- Teams and people must follow the Lean philosophy
- Respect but help your Supply Chain to improve

Organisational learning

- Inspect and understand difficult situations
- Make decisions slowly (by consensus) but implement quickly
- *Kaizen* (relentless reflection and continuous improvement)

Source: Adapted from Liker (2004).

specifically, the National Health Service. These initiatives underline the importance of central government in the endorsement, encouragement and facilitation of new approaches to management. But just as central government may support such initiatives, it may also turn off its support. In 2006, the Scottish Government commissioned a study of Lean Management to evaluate its usefulness in the public sector in Scotland (Radnor et al., 2006). While that 2006 government initiative gave an impetus to the adoption of Lean Management, changes in the political administration of this Government diluted the Lean effort. While traces of Lean can be seen in some form over the entire Scottish health care system, the variation between stages of implementation is vast and no part of the Scottish health care system has achieved a fully systemic implementation of Lean in which Lean thinking has been embedded in the culture of the organization. This underlines the importance of coercive mimicry in the adoption of new practices and the vulnerability of such initiatives to changes in political direction.

Tests of readiness

The UKs National Audit Office (NAO) investigated the adoption of Lean practices in government to improve process management (NAO, 2010). This study was a systems approach with a more pragmatic determination of success than the purist approach depicted in Table 10.1. The NAO assessed the maturity of a government department's ability to operate efficiently by focussing on five dimensions of process management:

- Using Strategy to define and drive process activity
- Using Continuous Improvement to target areas of greatest benefit
- Using Information to manage and improve process performance
- Helping People to manage and improve process performance
- Ensuring the end-to-end process has the capacity and capability to meet demand.

Overall, this study found that none of the departments investigated had a sufficiently mature system of process management in place. This underlines the challenge of adopting this route to improved efficiency and the need to handle unrealistic expectations carefully. This study identified three specific gaps in process management in UK central government. First, there was limited understanding of the level and type of customer demand and of the implementation of a planned response to changes in demand. Second, the organizations studied did not have an environment where staff felt obliged to improve business process – or even had the necessary training, skills and support to do so. Third, there was a failure to make the case for change and to identify the benefits. These observations underline the difficulty of the presumption that government departments operate in a market environment and have "customers" for their services. These findings underline the need for "soft" culture change – the need for staff to feel obliged to behave in a specific way. This observation also hints at incurring extra resources and costs to become effective. Their final observation presumes the "do nothing" option is not an option at all, and that the identification of benefits is assured and straightforward. These issues are revisited below.

Finally, this chapter comments on the emergence of Lean and offers guidance to the managers of public services on what they might realistically expect from the adoption of Lean. Specifically, this chapter discusses critical issues or tensions of (1) Tension One – can you afford not to adopt Lean? A crucial element of this tension is the level of resources required for an intensive Lean start up process; (2) Tension 2 – is your organization capable of a complete culture change? What is the relevance of Lean as a "total systems" approach to entire organizations? and (3) Tension 3 – is it possible to mobilise Lean ideas to generate local star optima in operational sections of organizations? Does this approach to Lean add value to the wider organization or not? This chapter is not an exercise in recipe management – its purpose is to inform public managers embarking on, or engaged in, Lean as a major policy initiative. This chapter helps managers to make evaluations of whether Lean may or may not be a viable management tool for their organizations.

Tension 1: Can you afford not to adopt lean?

While governments have initiated Lean Management developments in an effort to make their funds go further, the impetus for Lean in public services is often after the prompting of management consultants. This activity by management consultants is something I have witnessed at conferences and workshops. I have seen and heard management consultants advance the case for improving business processes by the advocacy of Lean. The rubric for adoption of Lean as advanced by the management consultancy community is illustrated in the following collage of advocacy statements (see Figure 10.1) made by management consultants.

The comments made in the above statement are accurate, save for the expression of a view that Lean is the natural and logical approach to more efficiency in public services. This is the nub of the matter. It is easy to see why a public services manager would accept Figure 10.1 as the verbatim and accurate position on Lean in public services. But the fact is not all Lean adoptions have been successful. That fact is glossed over by the statement in Figure 10.1. This chapter offers insights and questions to inform thoughtful managers on the question of if and how they might recommend Lean to their organization. The advocacy statement in Figure 10.1 may be enough to convince public managers of the merits of Lean. The adoption of Lean merits two considerations: (1) an assessment of organizational readiness and capacity for adoption and (2) evidence of the distinct financial benefits to flow to public services which have adopted Lean.

The first matter to address is the question of the identification of benefits. The identification of benefits is very important and the most difficult exercise. As noted above, most public services do not have income streams from their services. They have a variety of lumpy forms of income such as government allocations, specific grants for service provision and perhaps some charging systems which may or may not cover the costs of services provided. This means the most likely financial benefit to accrue to government agencies is through cost savings. However, cost savings may be difficult to compute because of interdependent services and joint costs.

But first it is important for public service organizations contemplating the adoption of Lean to get a firm grip of likely costs – see Table 10.2. The management consultants will not get past their own fee. You need to be more precise. This table prompts public service managers to look carefully at the readiness of their staff to engage with a Lean Management initiative. They need to assess their staffing profile to identify if existing staff have the capacity to take on Lean developments. If they are already hard pressed and this additional duty is given to them, the prospects are not good. If existing staff do have spare capacity this has the advantage of enabling the build-up of expertise within the existing workforce which could be the basis of continuity once consultants have departed the scene. New, dedicated staff may have to be recruited. If they have existing Lean experience this would help to drive the project forward. It is important to note at this stage that your organization is making additional outlays before you have seen any benefits.

"Lean is tried and tested. It has been developed extensively over the past seven decades. It is a product of the management practices of one of the world's most famous companies – Toyota. Toyota is one of the most successful companies in the world. Toyota has an outstanding reputation for excellence in design and engineering and for innovation. The Toyota system has been adopted by many commercial companies in recent decades. This adoption has transformed manufacturing processes in many industries. Toyota's Lean management is now being adopted by many government organisations. This is the natural and logical approach to be adopted by government organisations in which resources are becoming scarcer and scarcer."

Figure 10.1 The management consultant's pitch

When it comes to the estimation of benefits, management consultants may be happy to provide you with an assessment of likely benefits based on previous assignments. Be sceptical of this. Do not take management consultants' offers of typical cost savings as accurate. Do your own. An important issue is the proposed time frame. If your staff have not engaged with Lean before, or have significant project management experience, this may take much longer than planned. See Table 10.2 – the time period here is indicative rather than definite but the likely cost categories are reasonable. This table specifically identifies bottlenecks in processes. This may be limited capacity of a specific category of skilled staff, or physical space or limited equipment which is worked intensely. You and your colleagues may be well aware of such bottlenecks. The Lean approach is to eliminate bottlenecks to improve throughput. This is easier to demonstrate where there is a distinct income stream, but this may prove difficult dependent on the process and you may be looking for cost savings. You may look at significant new investments or simply replacement of like for like to enhance capacity. These are additional outlays before you identify any benefits.

The important issue to be aware of is the need to spend further taxpayers' money before gaining benefits. You need to ensure the expected benefits at least recoup the costs projected over your planning horizon and preferably exceed these additional outlays significantly. The key to unlocking significant cost savings is the identification of complicated, multi-layered procedures and processes which can be stripped down (Lean) to generate savings. This is a useful starting point to address the Tension 1 posed above.

Tension 2: Is your organization capable of a complete culture change of lean thinking?

Lean proponents advocate an organizational culture change to reap the full benefits of Lean Management (see, for example, Radnor and Osborne, 2013). It is evident what a Lean culture change would look like in any organization – see Table 10.1. This may be envisaged as getting work processes operating at the highest level of efficiency. But it is much more than that. The CEO and senior management must understand, practice and teach the Lean philosophy. The workers within the organization must relentlessly reflect on continuous improvement. The management of the organization must take a long-term perspective and not be moved from their path by short-term crises. A study of the management profiles, actions and responsibilities will reveal if an organization

Table 10.2 The costs of Lean Adoption

Time frame	Year 1	Year 2	Year 3
Management Consultancy fee	?	?	?
New dedicated staff	?	?	?
Existing staff: Time commitments	?	?	?
Key services, processes, bottlenecks	?	?	?
• Investment in new facilities • Replacement of existing facilities			
Total cost	x	x	x

has "arrived" or is likely to do so, or how long it might take to have success in terms of culture change.

The route to culture change requires a comprehensive rethink on the management of the organization. As Table 10.3 indicates, there are functional activities which can be reshaped, but much more is required. The indicators in Table 10.3 prompt a "complete organization" approach to Lean Management. While "cultural change" is included as the second most important factor in the successful implementation, there is no real pathway given to achieve this. Implicit in this model is the presumption that all these important points can be initiated successfully, immediately, at the same time. This is highly unlikely. It is more likely to raise unrealistic expectations. Within this framework there are certainly "most important" factors which could be addressed directly, such as linking the adoption of Lean to the organization's strategy, having a corporate communications policy which underpins and supports Lean, having closer links with customers and raising the awareness of the adoption of Lean throughout the organization. But there are also issues amongst the "most important" factors, such as cultural change and leadership style, which could be problematic. Within the Highly Important factors, there are many of these which any competent organization could implement, including project management and prioritisation for Lean, delegating financial accountability and tracking and reviewing projects, plus the more overt Lean policy of working with data on the organization's data to intervene (Plan, Do,

Table 10.3 Critical success factors in implementation

Most important

- Management commitment
- Cultural change
- Links to strategy
- Leadership style
- Communication
- Links to customers
- Awareness

Highly important

- Selection of staff
- Data-based approach (plan, do, check, act)
- Project prioritisation
- Project tracking and review
- Resources for implementation
- Training
- Tools and techniques
- Project management
- Financial accountability

Important

- Organisation infrastructure
- Supply chain issues
- HR rewards

Source: Adapted from Laureani and Antony (2012).

Check, Act). However, the single most contentious item is the resources required for implementation. In organizations considering Lean, this is indicative of limited resources for new projects. This complete organization approach to implementation also necessitates a compatible (flatter) organization structure, the resolution of any supply chains issues and appropriate incentives for staff. All of these are within the "can do" range of most organizations. But let us revisit the issue of cultural change and leadership style.

In the discussion above, the portability of Lean from a car manufacturing company to public services on a different continent was discussed as particularly difficult because of the obstacle of the different professional groups which worked in public services. These professionals may identify with their employer but primarily identify with their profession. An interesting example of this was found in a study of military officers who were expected to absorb management roles into their existing warrior status as part of a major culture change programme (Skaerbaek and Thornbjornsen, 2007). This did not work. There was significant conflict within these professionals as they struggled with these contested roles. More specifically relevant is the study by McCann et al. (2015), in which they studied a major Lean project implementation in a UK National Health Service hospital where a culture change was attempted by management consultants. The investigation by McCann et al. (2015) reveals the complexities of pursuing culture change to embed Lean thinking in an organization.

In this study they found that Lean ideas were initially championed, subsequently diluted and finally eroded. This is not a successful implementation of culture change at this hospital. Initially, the journey to implement Lean at this hospital was optimistic. But a deep problem kept recurring. Specifically, the nature of healthcare necessarily involving living, thinking, complex human beings, rather than pieces of hardware. This was mentioned in the context of patients not following Lean procedures in X-ray. This was attributed to patients being nervous during medical examinations. At training events, facilitators explained "value stream mapping" and "rapid improvement events" and encouraged Lean thinking throughout the hospital. In addition to meetings, the Lean initiative had a dedicated newsletter which was circulated to all staff and PowerPoint presentations from training events were made available on the staff intranet. One such slide said Lean was an important part of its organizational development. It had slogans like "Satisfied Staff", Loyal and Committed Staff, Staff that Support Service Values, Satisfied Patients, Loyal Patients and Membership (McCann et al., 2015, p. 1564).

At one training event, a Lean facilitator observed that Tesco and Morrisons supermarkets left milk cartons on trolleys on the shop floor. This saved time on stacking milk cartons on shelves. This was met with a degree of puzzlement by healthcare professionals. One of them brought up the issue of Accident and Emergency, where workload is unpredictable. At this point, one participant said you could stack the patients up on trolleys and just wheel them in as and when required like Tesco. This whimsical comment reveals a stronger identification with patients than processes. This study reported repeated doubts and misgivings over Lean. Many clinicians and managers expressed reservations about Lean. Some NHS managers suggested Lean was best suited to back-office functions but not to patient care. One manager with a clinical background stated that (McCann et al., 2015, p. 1569):

> There is no way in a million years the NHS is going to be Lean. There is lots of lip service to new ideas, but they can't happen. Soon it will be something else.

Overall, despite repeated training events and workshops on Lean, McCann et al. (2015) reported a sense of doubt and unreality which was exacerbated by proponents of Lean claiming any kind of minor improvement as an example of Lean. The message is clear. The plan of "culture change" is ambitious. It will not be achieved over a short time span. Advisers and management consultants who advocate for "culture change" without clear, effective and realistic pathways to achieve it are unrealistic. This is a recurring finding within Lean projects. The recognition of the time required to develop a culture of change is crucial. In this regard, the work of Emiliani and Emiliani (2013) deserves greater consideration. In their view learning and practising music is directly comparable to learning and practising Lean. Table 10.4 details items from their analysis. The comparisons are remarkably close. Emiliani and Emiliani (2013) also suggest key elements of music have counterparts in Lean thinking. In music there is a Lean counterpart: Music (note), Lean (part); Music (Pitch), Lean (Pitch); Music (harmony), Lean (parts in an assembly); Music (rhythm), Lean (pattern of parts in time); Music (tempo); Lean (speed of the parts). The implication of this observation and connection is important. To encourage the engagement of all employees (including senior management), workers should be encouraged to think of Lean as like learning a musical instrument. This insight could result in greater levels of absorption. This raises the possibility of culture change due to Lean Management.

Tension 3: Is there scope for Lean local star optima in parts of your organization?

The previous discussion of Lean addressed the adoption of this management approach as a total systems or "all or nothing" approach. However, that represents a radical change. An alternative approach is incremental. Specifically, in the context of the organization are there identifiable stages of business processes which could become examples of best practice by using Lean? This refers to the phenomenon of local star

Table 10.4 Music and Lean compared

Music	Lean
Requires development of fine motor skills	Requires development of fine thinking skills
Most people need a teacher	Most people need a teacher
Cannot play a song if you cannot remember the notes	Cannot practice Lean if you cannot remember the principles
Must practice every day	Must practice every day
Cannot just play music: must think and do	Cannot just do Lean: must think and do
Must adhere to standardised work	Must adhere to standardised work
Must know your part and whole song	Must know your part and whole process
Players must play just-in-time	Material and information must be just-in-time

Source: Adapted from Emiliani and Emiliani (2013).

optima. However, the incremental option has been described as the "low hanging fruit" (Radnor and Osborne, 2013). They also say this is a far way short of a full-blown adoption of Lean. This criticism is correct, of course. But there is no advantage in going for a full-blown Lean implementation if its adoption does not work. A major factor here is the overselling of Lean and its virtues with scant regard to the decades of development work in designing Lean and establishing a culture of Lean at Toyota. That degree of commitment is exceptional and not readily available to hard pressed organizations.

The incremental approach is more gradual. It is pragmatic. This may incur the displeasure of both government officials and management consultancy firms who drive forwards apparently cost-saving management practices. But it can work. It may identify benefits. It may lead to wider adoption of Lean. Success breeds success. The handling of expectations is crucial. And the approach of searching for local star optima applications of Lean is a recognition of the difficulties of complex interdependent activities in many public services.

Table 10.5 sets out examples of local star optima. There are three examples from healthcare, one university and one police force. The health care examples reveal significant changes in work processes which result in faster, more efficient service provision while maintaining quality. These are examples of local star optima rather than a total systems approach to Lean adoption. The continuing success of these examples provides credibility and builds a reputation for Lean in these organizations. Of the other two examples, the university library is a straightforward example of Lean with significant reduction in procedures which improved efficiency. This is one of many Lean examples which places a monetary valuation on the benefits flowing from a Lean adoption. However, the sums realised are rather small. The final case of the Bedfordshire Police has a significant impact. This is a response to central government initiatives on alternative policies to the arrest of citizens suspected of criminal activity. This specific application of Lean has very significant financial benefits. So, the description of low hanging fruit does not necessarily apply to incremental applications of Lean.

In terms of pathways to local star optima, the most obvious focus by organizations would be on known bottlenecks or parts of processes where there is evidence of inefficiencies (complaints from other departments or audit reports, for example). This focus helps but the issue of the availability of resources is a crucial question. It is best to be in a situation where the organization has sufficient resources to consider all possible options. But there are many Chief Executives who have experienced cutbacks year after year as part of austerity programmes, until they no longer have development budgets. Major consultancy firms are unlikely to be interested in small scale projects. However, alternative routes to implementation exist. First, many professional associations have networks which share experiences and challenges. This could be a valuable source of information on the identification of suitable projects for Lean. This could also lead to a concerted action on tackling Lean projects. Second, the business schools at neighbouring universities may have valuable expertise. Most contemporary business schools are charged with an engagement policy which involves reaching out to local organizations. They may have talented MBA students looking for projects to work on. This has the bonus of identifying potential new recruits for the organization. This means the incremental approach of identifying local star optima can be a meaningful way forward for organizations considering Lean. A successful project could lead to more Lean activity and build a case for Lean more widely.

Table 10.5 Local Star Optima

Setting	Impact	Source
Medical Laboratories	• Shortened turnaround times • Improved quality (reduced errors) • Improved productivity	Clark et al. (2013)
Integrated Health Care System	New outcomes-based performance system which focusses on: • Preventable mortalities • Frequency of patient Re-admissions	Mannon (2014)
Orthopaedics Supply Unit	• Elimination of excess inventory • Simplified workflows • Simplified supply handling	Hwang et al. (2014)
University Library	• Rationalised scanning process in university library • 28 steps reduced to 1 • Turnaround time improved by 70% • Estimated cost savings of £10k per annum	Antony and Rodgers (2016)
Police (Bedfordshire)	• Review of Alternatives to arrest as part of UK Home Office programme • Cashable savings of £700k per annum and efficiencies of £1.8mill	Barton and Matthews (2017)

Managerial implications

This chapter has discussed the nature and challenges of Lean Management. It has reflected on the international diffusion of Lean Management. It has specifically examined the progress and spread of Lean Management in public services. Two major factors in the widespread adoption of Lean ideas have been the advocacy of Lean by both governments seeking cost savings and management consultants. Yet, despite these concerted actions, the successful adoption of Lean has been uneven.

This chapter has shown how the idea of Lean is to save costs, but its adoption may entail significant costs. The importance of people in public services, whether as recipient or provider of services, is a major obstacle for Lean. Indeed, the complexity of public services with many articulate professionals who focus on their profession rather than business processes can confound Lean implementation. The presumption of Lean is that top management will drive through its adoption. But in many public services, authority and legitimacy is more diffuse. There is also the significant challenge of complex interdependent services with joint costs and multiple services, which can make disaggregation into different processes cause difficulties for cost attribution and the design of Lean processes which do not adversely affect other parts of services in public sector organizations.

There are ways in which Lean can be applied successfully in public services. The adoption of an incremental approach may be dismissed by purists as gathering low hanging fruit. But this avenue affords the opportunity to gain success stories, to build up expertise and credibility and offer a foundation for a more comprehensive implementation. The most challenging task is the idea of culture change, which is frequently discussed too casually. This chapter has suggested the adoption of the ideas of Emiliani and Emiliani (2013), who argue the ideas of music and Lean are closely aligned. In the articulation of expectations by and from participants in Lean Management projects, this perspective is both informative and refreshing as a reference point.

References

Abdi, F., Shavarini, S. and Hoseini, S.M. (2006) Glean Lean: How to use the Lean Approach in service industries. *Journal of Services Research*, July: 191–206.

Antony, J., Rodgers, B. and Gijo, E.V. (2016) Can Lean Six Sigma make UK public sector organisations more efficient and effective? *International Journal of Productivity and Performance Management*, 65 (7): 995–1002. doi:10.1108/IJPPM-03-2016-0069.

Arnaboldi, M., Lapsley, I. and Steccolini, I. (2015) Performance management in the public sector: The ultimate challenge. *Financial Accountability and Management*, 31 (1): 1–22.

Barton, H. and Matthews, R. (2017) An assessment of the impact of Lean interventions within the UK police service. *American Journal of Management*, 17 (2): 9–22.

Clark, D., Silvester, K. and Knowles, S. (2013) Lean Management systems: Creating a culture of continuous improvement. *Journal of Clinical Pathology*, 66: 638–643.

Emiliani, M.L. and Emiliani, M. (2013) Music as a framework to better understand Lean Leadership. *Leadership and Organisation Development Journal*, 31 (5): 407–426.

Golledge, T. and Sommer, R. (2002) Business project management: Public sector implications. *Business Process Management Journal*, 8 (4): 364–376.

Hwang, P., Hwang, D. and Hong, P. (2014) Lean Practices for quality results: A case illustration. *International Journal of Health Care Quality Assurance*, 27 (8): 729–741.

Krafcik, J. (1988) The triumph of the Lean production system. *Sloan Management Review*, 30 (1): 41–52.

Lapsley, I. and Miller, P. (2019) Transforming the public sector: 1998–2018. *Accounting, Auditing & Accountability Journal*, 32 (8): 2211–2252. https://doi.org/10.1108/AAAJ-06-2018-3511.

Liker, J. (2004) *Toyota Way: 14 Management Principles from the World's Greatest Manufacturer*. New York, Chicago, San Francisco, Athens, London, Madrid, Mexico City, Milan, New Delhi, Singapore, Sydney, Toronto, McGraw-Hill Education. https://www.accessengineeringlibrary.com/content/book/9780071392310.

Lipsky, M. (2010) *Street Level Bureaucracy: Dilemmas of the Individual in Public Services*. New York, Russel Sage Foundation.

Laureani, A. and Antony, J. (2012) Critical success factors for the effective implementation of Lean Sigma: Results from an empirical study and agenda for future research. *International Journal of Lean Six Sigma*, 3 (4): 274–283.

Mannon, M. (2014) Lean healthcare and quality management: The experience of Thedacare. *Quality Management Journal*, 21 (1): 7–10.

McCann, L., Hassard, J., Granter, E. and Hyde, P. (2015) Casting the Lean spell: The promotion, dilution and erosion of Lean Management in the NHS. *Human Relations*, 68 (10): 1557–1577.

National Audit Office (NAO) (2010) *Maturity of Process Management in Central Government: Cross Government Findings*. London, NAO.

Radnor, Z., Walley, P., Stephens, A., and Bucci, G. (2006) *Evaluation of the Lean Approach to Business Management and its use in the Public Sector*. Report for the Chief Research Officer, Scottish Executive, Edinburgh.

Radnor, Z. (2011) Debate: How mean is Lean really? *Public Money and Management*, 31 (2): 89–90.

Radnor, Z. and Osborne, S.P. (2013) Lean: A failed theory for public services? *Public Management Review*, 15 (2): 265–287. doi:10.1080/14719037.2012.748820.

Samuel, D., Found, P. and Williams, S. (2015) How did the publication of the book *The Machine That Changed the World* change management thinking? Exploring 25 years of Lean literature. *International Journal of Operations and Production Management*, 35 (10): 1386–1407.

Skaerbaek, P. and S. Thornbjornsen (2007) The commodification of the Danish Defence Forces and the troubled identities of its officer. *Financial Accountability & Management*, 23 (3), August: 243–268.

Womack, J., Jones, D. and Roos, D. (1990) *The Machine That Changed the World*. New York, Rawson Associates.

11 Managing resilience

Hans Knutsson

Organizational resilience and common understanding

The more changes a local government faces, the more managers must increasingly act guided by a crude and changing model of causalities in local government. Managing resilience is based on shared narratives based on active and deliberative performance management which motivates and justifies actions taken in a particular setting. In this framing, the distinction between elected officials and managers as employed public servants is blurred. The chapter does not address this particular distinction. The focus is instead on how resilient organisations seem to be successfully tending to four particular tensions.

Tensions, in this context, may be understood as forces pulling in different and sometimes opposite directions. In a clear public management context, Dunsire (1990) once pointed out the difference between homoeostasis on one hand, and isostasys on the other. The difference between the two is basically about whether there exists a pre-set state of equilibrium (e.g. a speed limit that necessitates a gas pedal, a brake pedal, and a speedometer) or not. Isostasy Dunsire (1990, p. 8) defines as "equilibrium brought about by equal pressures (or suctions, or tensions)". Price is said to be a function of supply and demand, a simple case of isostasy. However, resilience, it is suggested here, is a function of several factors creating a number of different tensions. The chapter proposes that four different tensions underlying the management of resilience need to be reconciled. The four specific tensions treated are derived from theoretical concepts and models, but herein translated into empirical illustrations. The order of the four tensions and their causal relationships are not explicitly addressed, but may well deserve particular attention elsewhere.

Resilience is observed in (1) actions (organisations and people prove themselves resilient or not); (2) understanding actions (resilience may require new thinking); (3) heuristics for expressing understanding (thinking require communicable models of causality); and (4) goal orientation (the aim of an organisation's actions; recovery or transformation), which need to come together in order to balance the fine line between confidence and doubt about what to do next.

The first tension is a matter of the actions of operators. Subject and object interact, although it is a common fallacy to see only the object, normally the organisation, and how it regains its former shape, or a new and adapted shape, after having been under pressure. An object with feelings, however, becomes a subject, which leads to a second tension to deal with, the cognitive disposition of the subject in question.

DOI: 10.4324/9781003154389-15

Second, understanding actions or, more formally, *cognitive disposition* affects resilience. In a person or in an organisation, adversities need to be observed and understood in a way that makes effective action possible. Preconceptions may impede a necessary changing of the conceptualisation of events.

A third tension is about the creation of adequate heuristics. Heuristics concern how assumed cause and effect relationships can be expressed and communicated between people. Heuristics thereby *focus the attention* of people and affect how ingrained assumptions are challenged when the context of the organisation is altered. Established patterns of thinking need to be challenged in order to embrace changes in the environment.

Last and fourth, managing resilience also concerns goal orientation, the *direction of efforts*. There is a strong tension between recovery and transformation – recovery is about going back to a former state, transformation is about entering into a new state. The original reason for an organisation to alter its state is a change in the organisation's environment. Going back to a former state is therefore a problematic objective – will the old, established organisation still be efficient and effective when the world around it has changed?

Managing resilience takes sensemaking

Weick and Sutcliffe (2007) suggest that:

> [resilient] action that enables recovery from setbacks is built out of a broad repertoire of action and experience, the ability to recombine fragments of past experience into novel responses, emotional control, skill at respectful interaction, and knowledge of how the system functions.
>
> (Weick & Sutcliffe, 2007, p. 3)

Managing resilience may be seen as a profound concept with action and reactions at its core. Much of the experiences we are confronted with are reactions to or consequences of our own actions. This is what Weick (1979) calls "double interacts" or "interlocked behaviour". These cycles of interactions constitute organizing, in essence a set of factors amplifying or balancing each other.

The complexity involved in such interlocked behaviour is aggravated in politically run organisations. People hold politicians accountable in general elections. An election may thus turn over any interlocked behaviour that has not proven effective. A deeper analysis of how sense is made in resilient local governments, or any other politically run organisation for that matter, could most likely benefit from such a distinction. In this context, we are interested in showing how leaders and managers need to establish unifying social processes in order to deal effectively with the adversities challenging the local government in power (see Figure 11.1). The tensions occur when something happens that needs to be understood and explained, and that requires a decision about what to do about it (see Figure 11.1). Resilience, thus, is basically dependent on (1) unifying social processes where organisational (2) sensemaking requires (3) tending to four different tensions. The success of that influences how (4) resilient an organisation is in facing up to (5) adversities challenging it. The two-way arrows indicate the presence of Weick's "double interacts".

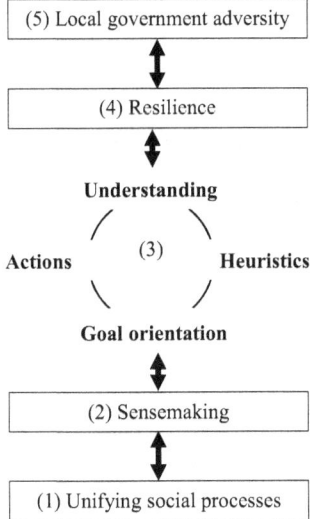

Figure 11.1 The theoretical frame of reference used to illustrate how managing resilience revolves around handling four organisational tensions

The management aspect

Managers manage an organization by making sense of the world. The traditional and systematic view of managing – problems are defined, different solutions are identified and analysed, and ultimately, the best option is chosen – should not be mixed up with sensemaking. According to Weick (1993, p. 636):

> the world of decision making is about strategic rationality. It is built from clear questions and clear answers that attempt to remove ignorance. [The] world of sensemaking is different. Sensemaking is about contextual rationality. It is built out of vague questions, muddy answers, and negotiated agreements that attempt to reduce confusion.

Decisions still need to be made, but managers do not have clear and ready data at their disposal. Decisions are based on what should be considered important, which could be anything other than readily available data. Understanding what is going on requires sensemaking. Henry Mintzberg, renowned for his practical perspective on managing, has shared his view on what it means to take on the apparently mundane task of *managing* an organisation: "You are supposed to figure it out for yourself, like sex, I suppose, usually with equivalently dire initial consequences" (Mintzberg, 2009, p. 3). Managing is no small feat and as a manager, you carry the direct responsibility of how the organisation works. And according to Weick, you need to draw the map as you push forward, navigating in dusky light. Key to this process is that managers "enact" their own world, they create what they try to grasp.

Leaders have a particularly important role in this process. They need to be at the forefront of reflection in order to be able to express to others how the world works. De Pree (1987) states that "the first responsibility of a leader is to define reality".

Managers, in their capacity as leaders for a group, big or small, therefore first of all need to manage things that guide what subordinates pay attention to. Chia suggests that:

> [managing] is firstly and fundamentally the task of becoming aware, attending to, sorting out, and prioritizing an inherently messy, fluxing, chaotic world of competing demands that are placed on a manager's attention. It is creating order out of chaos. It is an art, not a science. Active perceptual organization and the astute allocation of attention is a central feature of the managerial task.
>
> (Chia, 2005, p. 1092)

In the following, you will find an overview of resilience and sensemaking and how those concepts relate to public sector management. The basis for the overview is an introduction to the two main theoretical concepts in the chapter, resilience and sensemaking. Those concepts are briefly illustrated early on by empirical observations from two Swedish local governments. After those initial illustrations, the chapter will present how managing resilience means reconciling the four previously mentioned tensions.

Tension 1. Managing resilience: pay attention to actions

In Sweden, as in other countries with large remote areas such as Canada, general methods for providing equal welfare services are challenged. There are certain basic economic dynamics at work, predominantly economies of scale.

As shown in Table 11.1, the projected share of small-sized Swedish municipalities is increasing. At the same time, the share of larger municipalities is expected to increase too. The share of mid-sized municipalities, then, is expected to decrease. The upshot is that there is an underlying development where densely populated areas will be provided with cost-efficient public welfare services, for many people. In the remote areas, that same level of public welfare services will be increasingly hard to provide. This is what is going on, this is the "action" to pay attention to.

Resilience concerns "an ability to recover from or adjust easily to misfortune or change" (Merriam-Webster, 2019) or, more technically, the "capability of a system to maintain its function and structure in the face of internal and external changes and to degrade gracefully when it must" (Allenby & Fink, 2005, p. 1034). The concept originates from biology. In 1973, Holling, on biological populations, modelled how species stay alive, not primarily as a matter of how steady states of an ecological system are reached but how populations are handling change and are able to find new balance

Table 11.1 Changes in municipality size distribution in Sweden

Share of total number of municipalities			
Size (population)	1974	2013	2040 (projected)
< 8000	15%	16%	19%
8000–49999	73%	67%	61%
> 50000	11%	16%	20%

Source: SOU (2015, p. 101)

points: he introduced a "shifting emphasis from the equilibrium states to the conditions for persistence" (Holling, 1973, p. 2).

Communities, species, and social structures are all objects, occupied by subjects. In the search for resilience in social contexts, the distinction between subjects and objects has become increasingly contested by scholars. Looking closer at the interplay between a subject and an object, it is seen that they affect one another:

> Resilience, in the post-classical framing, is therefore an emergent and adaptive process of subject/object interrelations. Both subject and object are immersed in and are products of complex adaptive processes. Resilience still remains an 'inner' attribute, but an 'inner' or relational attribute of a system or assemblage. In as far as the human subject is part of this system of interconnection, resilience becomes an ongoing process of responding through a self-reflective awareness that the subject is both producer and product of the world. Resilience is thereby both about adapting to the external world and about being aware that in this process of adaptation the world is being reshaped.
>
> (Chandler, 2014, p. 7)

Such reshaping of the world is not always initiated by human beings. Much research has been focused on community resilience in relation to disasters and accidents, but when reviewing tools for assessing community resilience, Sharifi (2016) presents a wide variety of factors to consider from a resilience viewpoint: natural factors (earthquakes, droughts, etc.); social factors (health and diversity); and economic factors (recession). Things change so that people are pushed out of their way of life, i.e. there is an inside and an outside. "Resilience" deals with the capacity to return to an inside equilibrium instead of breaking under outside pressure and stress (Norris et al., 2008). Going back to a pre-existing "inside equilibrium" is a reaction Dunsire (1990) touched upon using the concept of *homoeostasis*.

The preoccupation with emergencies and disasters has led the scholarly interest into studying how organizational structures impact resilience, e.g. Walker and Cooper (2011). Resilience is most likely also a valid concept in relation to public management and local government. According to Thorén and Olsson (2018), resilience is definitely pertinent to local government:

> if we stipulate that having a sufficient number of members in physical proximity to a certain location is what it means for a particular community to exist, then we can in no uncertain terms discuss that community's resilience to various types of disturbances.

There is additional support coming from Rogers, who sees a future for resilience research in the field of organizing and managing, stating that there is "a key research stream for future work in the mapping of organisational resilience with an emphasis on hierarchy, organisational structure, command-and-control, risk and quality management" (Rogers, 2015, p. 58).

The tension between object and subject concerns the fact that an organisation, be it a local government, is not only a product of changing external conditions but very much of its own ability to adapt to them. Past actions as well as current reactions inside a local government influence how resilient a local government will be to outside pressure like a diminishing population. But in this particular example, the prime mover is an amassing of individual acts of moving away that eventually turns into an adversity for the municipality and its incumbent local government.

Tension 2. Managing resilience: understanding and different cognitive dispositions

Since management matters, it is important for managers to know what to do. Herbert Simon, one of the early contributors to the study of administrative behaviour (Simon, 1997 [1945]) has suggested that:

> [the] most important skills required for survival and success in the kind of uncertain, rapidly evolving world in which we live are (1) skill in anticipating the shape of an uncertain future, (2) skill in generating alternatives for operating effectively in changed environments, and (3) skill in implementing new plans rapidly and efficiently.
>
> (Simon, 1993, p. 134)

Now, if we trust Simon, skills that handle future uncertainties, generate different alternative courses of action, and implement the ones chosen, are these not criteria for managing resilience? However, on the face of it, Simon is challenged by Weick (1993), in that Weick bases his argument on the concept of *equivocality* as being central to the need for sensemaking. Sensemaking is contextual since reality may be many things. Simon instead describes a typical process of strategic decision-making where the reality is more clearly discerned from observations than what Weick claims.

So, what about equivocality? Managing resilience means managing in challenging conditions, but what is challenged in local governments? Östh et al. (2018, p. 17) have recently compared resilient local governments in Sweden and the Netherlands and suggest:

> that Swedish municipalities are dependent on either being located in proximity to alternative and resilient labour markets or to be a community where important resilience-building factors including, health, education, industrial mix etc. plays an important role in shaping the local economy.

If municipalities are not located in an active economic region or area, they still need to stay alive by providing apt public services and a varied industry. Managing resilience, Östh et al. (2018) suggest, involves compensating for inferior and deteriorating territorial conditions.

Local governments are the public organizations often responsible for much of a community's basic welfare services such as schools, utilities, and child and elderly care. This varies across countries, of course. In Sweden there are 290 local governments and they face quite different conditions for providing the welfare services above, all depending on where they are located. Throughout the 20th century, the central government has tried various solutions to keeping a fair and equal level of welfare services across local governments. The most renowned system is a progressive tax system, an equalization system, in which local governments with advantageous tax revenues and cost levels pay a fee to the central government, which transfers funds to less advantageous ones.

Then, who is really compensating for deteriorating territorial conditions and how is it done? The central government tax system does not explain why a few waning local governments maintain a healthy operation while others in the same situation fail to do so. It is rare for small shrinking local governments to maintain healthy finances and at the same time provide a high level of local welfare services (Syssner, 2018; Syssner & Olausson, 2015). In 2015, out of the 29 governments with the largest decrease, only seven could account for both welfare quality at or above average standard and a healthy financial situation measured as a combination of solidity and financial result. How can this be?

What we do is a function of what we notice. What we notice is in turn highly influenced by what we already know and how we make sense of the world, our *cognitive disposition*. This idea is at the core of how to manage resiliently. Therefore, there is a basic skill underlying the skills of anticipation, option generation, and implementation á la Simon's (1997 [1945]) idea of decision-making. A manager needs to make sense of what is experienced in order to know what to do and, in doing so, adjust his or her view of the world. Managers face, most likely without thinking about it, an ever-present challenge of conceptualising new situations through the lens of previous experience, their preconceptions.

Sensemaking is a concept that sheds light on the function of "cause maps" or mental models guiding our decision-making. Cause maps are representations of a system of factors and their causal relationships which direct our attention and hence reinforce the way managers act. If you don't understand what is going on, you probably need a new – different – map to guide you. Anyone who begins to see things differently, though, will go unheard if other people fail to see things the same way. Being the only one to break with established preconceptions makes you the odd one out.

Tension 3. Managing resilience: focus of attention

Paying attention to what is going on and the potential ramifications is widely covered by scholars, not least Herbert A. Simon (1997 [1945]) who broke with neoclassical assumptions of human decision-making when he introduced the concept of bounded rationality. People intend to be rational but can never be so due to limited cognitive and perceptual capabilities. Simon's long-standing colleague, James March, elaborated:

> Time and capabilities for attention are limited. Not everything can be attended to at once. Too many signals are received. Too many things are relevant to a decision. Because of those limitations, theories of decision making are often better described as theories of attention or search than as theories of choice. They are concerned with the way in which scarce attention is allocated.
>
> (March, 1994:10)

March's assertion traces back to his own early cooperation with Simon, when they first introduced an idea of organisations being "repertoires of response programs" (March & Simon, 1958, p. 35).

The fact that a few small local governments seem to be resilient in the face of shrinking population is consistent with previous studies of causes of financial results in Swedish local governments. Knutsson et al. (2008), Norrlid (2007), and Hellström et al. (2009) all point at the importance of strategy and management – the progressive tax system can only do so much for securing equal welfare services throughout Sweden. Managers in local governments carry a great responsibility for the decisions made and the actions taken. It matters what management does.

What managers do is done in a particular context, concrete structural conditions as well as cognitive dispositions of local government officials and the population of the municipality. The quality of the interplay between the way things are and how they are perceived determines resilience. Chandler's (2014) description of resilience as an interaction between object and subject resonates well with Weick's ideas of sensemaking (Weick, 1995). In 1969 and in a second edition in 1979, Weick introduced the idea of organizing, a verb, as different from organization, a noun. His conceptual model is an iteration of enactment, selection, and retention, which forms our cause maps or mental models of the world. Later, Weick developed the idea of organizing into the concept of "sensemaking [understood] as a process that is i) grounded in identity construction, ii) retrospective, iii) enactive of sensible environments, iv) social, v) ongoing, vi) focused on and by extracted cues, vii) driven by plausibility rather than accuracy" (Weick, 1995, p. 17). Other scholars have contributed to boiling down the essence of sensemaking in different ways. Maitlis and Christianson (2014, p. 67) frame it as "a process, prompted by violated expectations, that involves attending to and bracketing cues in the environment, creating intersubjective meaning through cycles of interpretation and action, and thereby enacting a more ordered environment from which further cues can be drawn." Brown et al. (2015, p. 267) consolidate much of the research further in suggesting that "[much] current research on how sensemaking occurs is focused on these three sets of interweaving processes: the perception of cues (noticing), making interpretations and engaging in action."

One local government, deep in the north of Sweden, noticed that much of the ageing population also lived outside the main town, scattered over a vast area. Noticing this particular predicament made the managers seize the opportunity when they were approached by a company wanting to establish fibre-based broadband communication in the town. Negotiations rendered the local government with an almost 100% coverage of fibre across the municipality. This has given local government good conditions for providing cheap effective elderly care for all its ageing inhabitants.

When observing successful yet waning local governments, it seems that they shape their own destiny. There is a general preoccupation with numerical "facts" and "data" and structured decision-making is held high. At the same time, pedagogy and storytelling is said to be important, although organized citizen dialogue is not common. What seems to be most important is the time dimension. Local governments which have made the earliest structural changes are the ones with the "best" performance measured in terms of both financial strength (results and solidity) and quality scores in operations. There seems to be systemic relationships reinforced over time. Early decisions have paid off.

However, managing resilience is a social process in which people in the organization interpret their environment as they interact with it: "organizational resilience is a critical component of communities' ability to plan for, respond to, and recover from emergencies and crises" (Lee et al., 2013, p. 29).

Resilience requires anticipation of threats. Looking at the Swedish shrinking municipalities, threats spanned from dissipating economies of scale to lost identity and sense of community. There seems to be lingering antagonism between formerly separate municipalities brought together when the municipality structure was consolidated by merging several small municipalities into a single larger one (Table 11.2), although still containing two or more distinct geographical idiosyncracies less inclined to surrender their "unique" identities.

Table 11.2 The development of the municipality structure in Sweden between 1863 and 2020

Year	1863	1930	1952	1971	2003
Number of municipalities	2500	2532	816	278	290

There are several examples of how challenged local governments have contained threats over time, thereby maintaining both adequate services and healthy finances. They have cleaned up their balance sheets and they have worked hard to control citizen expectations of welfare services provided by the local government. In that way, economic conditions have been kept in check.

What the succeeding municipalities seem to have grasped early on is that there was another – necessary – way of seeing things. They made sense of the environment differently from the less successful. Sensemaking is centre stage and Weick's (1979) sensemaking model of *enactment, selection*, and *retention* captures the essence of resilience. Human beings create the meaning of social interaction in their actions, not in their ideas or intentions. They act upon what they notice, not what is actually done by other people, and remember interactions that have occurred and form their future anticipation and understanding of what different actions mean. All in all, Weick has thoroughly disentangled the ramifications of not paying attention to things outside the prevailing train of thought in organisations.

In Table 11.3, one pattern of "enactment" is visible. The "provision ratio" for the smallest 10% of Swedish municipalities is close to 1, which means that there is only one person to provide tax payments for another person not in the workforce. A ratio of 50% means that there are two persons providing for one. The enactment is about young working people leaving the municipality, whereas their parents are staying put. This creates a vicious cycle, since the demand for private goods and services is reduced, and the supply of labour is also reduced making it even less attractive for any employer to establish operations in the municipality.

An ageing population strains any small, shrinking municipality in that welfare services increase in demand with age. Small-scale elderly care is relatively expensive, compared to scale-efficient operations in more densely populated areas. The higher cost in small municipalities is aggravated by lower tax revenues due to a decreasing share of working inhabitants. Such development seems to be "selected" and "retained" in varying degrees among shrinking Swedish municipalities.

Tension 4. Managing resilience by the direction of effort

Traditional definitions of resilience point out an ability to bounce back to an original state. If organisations bounce back to a previous state that no longer exists, you might ask what direction the efforts had – back to what once was or forward to what now is?

Table 11.3 Development of provision ratio in Swedish municipalities

Cohort	1998	2007	2019
Average, all	79%	78%	88%
Smallest 10%	89%	87%	97%

Source: Kolada (2020)

Note: Ratio=population (0–19, 65+) / (20–64)

In the context of resilient local governments, there is a question whether adaptive capacity relates only to major momentary events of disasters or if it also applies to longer stretches of hardships. There is a movement towards applying resilience to wider social issues:

> More recently, community resilience has begun to be applied across a range of public policy, planning and management discourses as a means of addressing the uneven ability of places to respond to changes wrought by social, economic and political processes. [In this context], community resilience is not so much about surviving a shock and bouncing back quickly to equilibrium. [It] is about the ability to adapt and survive in the face of long-term stress; to respond positively to change and ongoing adversity and risk.
>
> (Platts-Fowler & Robinson, 2016, p. 763)

When applying resilience to social development, there is also a stream of research interested in which direction handling adversities takes you. It can take you back to an original position and state, or forward to a better fit with the environment than before. Shaw (2012) suggests a distinction between resilience as *recovery* and resilience as *transformation*. Resilience as transformation is also termed "bouncing forward" – on the note "what doesn't kill you makes you stronger".

A recurring observation among small shrinking municipalities is a moment in time when the local government realised, or succumbed to, the fact that their municipality would most likely never again grow bigger. Such a realisation changed the focus and called forth the cause map necessary for managing resiliently. The focus of attention was no longer on regaining a former size, but maintaining the quality of public welfare services as far as possible. Resilience was not about quantity but of quality.

Managing resilience: tensions need reconciliation

There is a constant ongoing interaction between the local government organization and its environment. That is why it becomes imperative to make sense of what is happening. Sensemaking creates an understanding from which you act, which again makes it necessary to decipher all that is going on around you. The question, then, is whether your sensemaking takes you back to a consequential state or not and how effective such a state will be to keep the organization alive. Resilience requires adequate sensemaking in order to keep the institutions of a local government alive. Resilience relies on sensemaking and identifies a reliable organisation from an unreliable one.

Weick and Sutcliffe (2007) have later framed resilience as two main activities: anticipating and containing threats. It boils down to sensible sensemaking and mindful attention to critical factors, however small and insignificant. Again, the kinship of resilience and sensemaking is uncovered. In order to deal with all stimuli that an organization is exposed to, a selection of stimuli is required, which creates a limited and simplified version of the world. Selected stimuli then reward certain actions over other actions, creating a connection between what you see and what you should do. Abolafia points at observations that "every organization has a repertoire of plots that it draws from in making sense of its environment", which functions as "a dominant perceptual filter that shapes and biases sensemaking" (Abolafia, 2010, p. 357f).

Although sensemaking is a critical factor to resilience, it is not about a one-time rational strategic plan to be revealed:

> Sensemaking is not about truth and getting it right. Instead, it is about continued redrafting of an emerging story so that it becomes more comprehensive, incorporates more of the observed data, and is more resilient in the face of criticism.
>
> (Weick et al., 2005, p. 415)

"Experience is not what happens to a man. It is what a man does with what happens to him" (Weick, 1979, p. 147). Sensemaking revolves around the concepts of "enactment" and "equivocality". Enactment recognizes that we shape the world with our own actions. Equivocality stresses the fact that one thing may have two or more meanings, equally valid. The meaning of a thing becomes clear when we act according to our understanding of it – was the comment a compliment or a sly insult? The way you react to it helps answer the question.

Enactment materialises in "noticing and bracketing", crude acts of categorization where the resulting data can mean several different things. According to Weick, "interlocked behavior", also called "double interacts", are the building blocks of organisations. Actions or non-actions, both have consequences for future actions or non-actions by others. This adds an important aspect concerned with failing while acting is different from failing to act in the first place (c.f. Ackoff's idea of "errors of omission" and "errors of commission" (Ackoff, 2006)). On top of that, a layer of "chicken race" may be added – instances of local governments demanding central government intervene exemplifies an intricate double interact that may certain early actions void and certain inactions highly valid.

Selection is about dealing with a constant flow of stimuli registered by our senses. The flow requires "bracketing" segments of the past, which are subsequently analyzed in terms of plausible causes and effects. The evaluation associated with such analysis is complicated by equivocality: the flow of experiences is replete with potential meanings. Equivocality should not be confused with ambiguity or uncertainty, which both connote an underlying true and valid meaning; the use of the equivocality concept instead tells us that there is no single, underlying true meaning of what is going on. From several potential meanings of an event or phenomenon, we select one. This is turned into a narrative of causality, albeit tentative and provisional. The selection process creates boundaries through our own imposing of meanings, which explains cause and effect. If you are convinced of a certain causal relationship, this will guide your future action. Then, "sensemaking involves placing stimuli into some kind of framework" (Starbuck & Milliken, 1988).

When a plausible story is retained, it tends to become more substantial because it is related to past experience, connected to significant identities, and used as a source of guidance for further enactment, i.e. formative action. And so it goes – you notice, bracket, and retain the effects of your actions, over and over again. How well this is done tells the story of your resilience.

Managerial implications

The chapter suggests a number of reconciliations underlying the management of resilience.

Tension 1. Actions (and reactions) are key

Subject and object shape one another. Resilience is not necessarily about an organisation regaining its former shape in a changing surrounding. A separation of the organisation from its environment will only deprive us from understanding how adversity changes local governments, whereby the welfare sector is changed too.

Tension 2. Cognitive dispositions of local governments need to be challenged

Preconceptions and conceptualising interact. What you have learnt and how you understand the world will affect how you make sense of adversities. To succeed in altering a certain course of action, preconceptions of certain relationships may need to be tested and, eventually, replaced by other causal explanations.

Tension 3. Heuristics are required to focus the attention of local governments

To take necessary action normally requires a common understanding of what needs to be done. Thus, heuristics, often in the form of stories or "narratives", are needed to translate new causal explanations and mobilise a critical mass of decision-making power.

Tension 4. The direction of efforts will always be forward

Recovery and transformation are two sides of the same coin. Being resilient in a changing environment could never be a simple return to a previous state. Such a recovery would most likely be destined to fail: new adversities with the old existing properties of your organisation that you have managed to maintain will all but produce resilience in the long run.

Reconciliation of the above tensions seems to be necessary in order to balance the fine line between confidence and doubt about what to do next. Managing resilience requires sensitive managers, able to see things that are not yet there to see. Managers must also "be mindful about errors that have already occurred and [ready] to correct them before they worsen and cause more serious harm" (Weick & Sutcliffe, 2007, p. 68). Resilient local governments bounce back to the future; they transform as they struggle to stay alive.

Local government resilience is also about identity. It is about an identification with your village and neighbours being stronger than to an administrative entity. Local government resilience is retrospective and enacting, managers act and are forced to react to the consequences of their own actions. Local government resilience is fostered in social contexts and has to be constantly tended to as population, demography, and revenues and costs change over time. All these "actions" involve hardships that never stop but rather change in character. It is most likely not the same contextual cue that local government managers need to make sense of over the years. Therefore, there is scarce normative advice to give managers, other than they need to act guided by a crude everchanging model of local government causalities. Certainty will not present itself – plausibility will have to do.

References

Abolafia, M.Y. (2010) Narrative Construction as Sensemaking: How a Central Bank Thinks. *Organization Studies*, 31 (3): 349–367.

Ackoff, R.L. (2006) Why Few Organizations Adopt Systems Thinking. *Systems Research and Behavioral Science*, 23: 705–708.

Allenby, B. & Fink, J. (2005) Toward Inherently Secure and Resilient Societies. *Science*, 309 (1034–1036).

Brown, A.D., Colville, I. & Pye, A. (2015) Making Sense of Sensemaking in Organization Studies. *Organization Studies*, 36 (2): 265–277.

Chandler, D. (2014) *Resilience: The Governance of Complexity*. London: Routledge.

Chia, R. (2005) The Aim of Management Education: Reflections on Mintzberg's Managers not MBAs. *Organization Studies*, 26 (7): 1090–1092.

de Pree, M. (1987) *Leadership is an Art*. New York, Doubleday Business.

Dunsire, A. (1990) Holistic Governance. *Public Policy and Administration*, 5 (1): 4–18.

Hellström, M., Knutsson, H. & Ramberg, U. (2009) *Strategier för kommunal hushållning*. Stockholm, Rådet för Kommunala Analyser.

Holling, C.S. (1973) Resilience and Stability of Ecological Systems. *Annual Review of Ecology & Systematics*, 4: 1–23.

Knutsson, H., Mattisson, O., Ramberg, U. & Tagesson, T. (2008) Do Strategy and Management Matter in Municipal Organisations? *Financial Accountability & Management*, 24 (3): 295–319. http://dx.doi.org/10.1111/j.1468-0408.2008.00454.x.

Kolada (2020) Kommun- och landstingsdatabasen. Available online www.kolada.se, accessed 20 May 2020.

Lee, A.V., Vargo, J. & Seville, E. (2013) Developing a Tool to Measure and Compare Organizations' Resilience. *Natural Hazards Review*, 14 (1): 29–41.

Maitlis, S. & Christianson, M. (2014) Sensemaking in Organizations: Taking Stock and Moving Forward. *The Academy of Management Annals*, 8 (1): 57–125.

March, J.G. (1994) *A Primer on Decision Making*. New York, Free Press.

March, J.G. & Simon, H. A. (1958) *Organizations*. New York, John Wiley & Sons.

Merriam-Webster (2020) https://www.merriam-webster.com.

Mintzberg, H. (2009) *Managing*. San Francisco, Berrett-Koehler Publishers.

Norris, F.H., Stevens, S.P., Pfefferbaum, B., Wyche, K.F. & Pfefferbaum, R.L. (2008) Community Resilience as a Metaphor, Theory, Set of Capacities, and Strategy for Disaster Readiness. *American Journal of Community Psychology*, 41 (2): 127–150.

Norrlid, A. (2007) *Var klämmer skon? En modell för analys av ekonomiskt resultat i kommuner*. Retrieved from Stockholm.

Platts-Fowler, D. & Robinson, D. (2016) Community Resilience: A Policy Tool for Local Government? *Local Government Studies*, 42 (5): 762–784.

Rogers, P. (2015) Researching Resilience: An Agenda for Change. *Resilience*, 3 (1): 55–71.

Sharifi, A. (2016) A Critical Review of Selected Tools for Assessing Community Resilience. *Ecological Indicators*, 69: 629–647.

Shaw, K. (2012) The Rise of the Resilient Local Authority? *Local Government Studies*, 38 (3): 281–300.

Simon, H.A. (1993) Strategy and Organizational Evolution. *Strategic Management Journal*, 14 (Special Issue Organizations, Decision Making and Strategy): 131–142.

Simon, H.A. (1997 [1945]) *Administrative Behavior*, 4th ed. New York, The Free Press.

SOU (2015) Demografins regionala utmaning. Bilaga 7 till Långtidsutredningen. Statens offentliga utredningar, 2015:101. Regeringen, Stockholm.

Starbuck, W.H. & Milliken, F.J. (1988) Challenger: Fine-tuning the Odds Until Something Breaks. *Journal of Management Studies*, 25 (4): 319–340.

Syssner, J. (2018) Mindre många: om anpassning och utveckling i krympande kommuner: Dokument Press.

Syssner, J. & Olausson, A. (2015) Att vara en krympande kommun. In SKL (ed.), Urbanisering. Utmaningar för kommuner med växande och minskande befolkning. Stockholm: Sveriges Kommuner och Landsting.

Thorén, H. & Olsson, L. (2018) Is Resilience a Normative Concept? *Resilience*, 6 (2): 112–128.

Walker, J. & Cooper, M. (2011) Genealogies of Resilience: From Systems Ecology to the Political Economy of Crisis Adaptation. *Security Dialogue. Special Issue on The Global Governance of Security and Finance*, 42 (2): 143–160.

Weick, K.E. (1979) *The Social Psychology of Organizing*, 2nd ed. New York, McGraw Hill.

Weick, K.E. (1993) The Collapse of Sensemaking in Organizations: The Mann Gulch Disaster. *Administrative Science Quarterly*, 38 (4): 628–652.

Weick, K.E. (1995) *Sensemaking in Organizations*. Thousand Oaks: SAGE Publications.

Weick, K.E. & Sutcliffe, K.M. (2007) *Managing the Unexpected: Resilient Performance in an Age of Uncertainty*, 2nd ed. San Fransisco, Jossey-Bass.

Weick, K.E., Sutcliffe, K.M. & Obstfeld, D. (2005) Organizing and the Process of Sensemaking. *Organization Science*, 16 (4), 409–421.

Östh, J., Reggiani, A. & Nijkamp, P. (2018) Resilience and Accessibility of Swedish and Dutch Municipalities. *Transportation*. https://doi.org/10.1007/s11116-017-9854-3.

12 The risks of risk management

Irvine Lapsley

Introduction

The theoretical perspective taken in this chapter is the Politics of Attention (Behn, 1998; Jones and Baumgartner, 2005; Johnsen, 2012). From this perspective, the risk of failure has a disproportionate impact in public services. This can make both public administrations and government bodies and agencies focus overly on any instances of failure. This perspective may negate a learning environment and an open transparent approach to public affairs. This is a very timely connection with risk management the subject of this chapter.

The adoption of Risk Management (RM) for organizations remains an apparent solution to the challenges of the "risk society" (Beck, 1992). Beck (1992) identified the individualization of behaviour and global inter-connectivity of bodies, with these elements shaping what he called the "risk society", which means a system where an event occurring in one part of the world affects other parts. Regarding the public sector, while RM has been advocated for public sector organizations, there have not been many investigations of their RM practices. The topic of RM covers an area investigated since the 1960s, when the first two academic books were published by Mehr and Hedges (1963) and Williams and Hems (1964). The early interest in RM gained momentum from financial scandals. The series of financial and business scandals which affected the global market in the mid-1980s and 1990s promoted RM. These scandals were combined with a changing economic environment due to the linkages between globalisation and risk. This was marked by higher complexity of risk in turbulent markets (see Giddens, 2003; Miller, 1998). Risk management was accentuated in the early 2000s after the dot com bubble of major enterprises crashing. However, the failure in the implementation of RM started to be regarded as an issue of integration, which has been confirmed by the second wave of financial scandals beginning in 2000 and resulting in major failures. However, the common response to address this challenge has been over-regulation of RM implementation in every aspect of an organization, leading to what has been defined as "process-obsessed risk management of everything" (Power, 2004). RM ideas have spread and have become an important topic in public sector organizations. Despite criticisms, the spread of this new tool was impressive: the universality of this practice in the public sector was confirmed by Arnaboldi and Lapsley (2014), Arena et al. (2010) and Palermo (2014).

If we examine the challenges the UK government faced from climate change and Covid-19, from the perspective of a contemporary model of risk management, there

DOI: 10.4324/9781003154389-16

Table 12.1 Critical elements of risk management

The fundamentals	Environmental (internal and external) risk horizon scanning unit
Overview	1. Process 2. Integration 3. Culture 4. Infrastructure
Critical Element 1	Identify risk • Impact • Likelihood • Velocity • Persistence
Critical Element 2	Source risk
Critical Element 3	Measure risk
Critical Element 4	Evaluate risk • Avoid • Accept • Reduce • Share
Critical Element 5	Mitigate risk
Critical Element 6	Monitor risk

Source: Adapted from Deloach (2018) as adapted by Lapsley (2020) and this chapter.

may be a case for the government adoption of risk management as a continuing governance tool (see Table 12.1), which is based on the work of Deloach (2018), as adapted by Lapsley (2020, 2021 in this chapter).

The establishment of an effective RM system is complex. The model depicted here includes as its fundamental element, an Environmental Scanning Unit which identifies early risks and determines the status of that risk (immediate, medium or long term). This should shape the position of the entity in its risk exposure. The second element of the RM model is an overall system for your organization. This entails formal processes of risk tracking and management. These processes need to be integrated with the organization's activities. They also need to be imbued in the culture of the organization. To make them effective there must be a supportive infrastructure in the organization.

This article describes the steps in the process – the challenge for public sector reformers is putting them into action. While Deloach (2018) advocates the inclusion of all steps as an overall system, it is suggested here that this approach does not have to be followed as a mechanical process. There is scope for being selective on which dimensions matter most to your organization. This enables you to be both selective as to which elements of this model you use and to develop a timeline of the implementation of the elements which your organization needs.

Critical Element 1: Identify risk

An enterprise risk assessment process identifies and prioritizes an organization's risks, providing quality inputs to decision makers to help them formulate effective risk responses, including information about the current state of capabilities around managing the priority risks. Risk assessment spans the entire organization, including critical business units and functional areas. According to Deloach (2018), the effective appli-cation of business strategy as a context and risk assessment process considers attributes such as: (1) Impact, (2) Likelihood, (3) Velocity and (4) Persistence. This is not to say that these elements are unimportant: they highlight the significance of the risk, how easy it is to manage these risks and how to build profiles for different organizations.

Critical Element 2: Sources of risk

Once priority risks are identified, they are traced to their root causes. If management understands the drivers of risk, it is easier to design risk metrics and proactive risk responses at the source. Will this step present challenges? Almost certainly. Overcoming them is the key to success.

Critical Element 3: Measure risk

It is often said that if you cannot measure something, you can't manage it. Indeed, not all risks are quantifiable and increasing transparency by developing quantitative and qualitative risk measures is common practice. Measurement methodologies may be simple and basic. Here are some examples of how to measure risk, such as sensitivity analysis, stress testing and tracking key variables relating to an identified exposure. More complex methodologies in organizations with more advanced capabilities could differ – and might be more complicated. Other risk management methodologies might include analysing these complex factors.

Critical Element 4: Evaluate risk

Based on the priority risks identified, their drivers or root causes and their suscept-ibility to measurement, this may require management to choose the appropriate risk response. Deloach suggests four key dimensions: (1) Avoid, (2) Accept and (3) Reduce or (4) Share. These responses can be applied to groups of related risks consisting of natural families of risks that share fundamental characteristics (like common drivers, positive or negative correlations) consistent with a portfolio view.

The organization may first decide whether to accept or reject a risk based on an assessment of whether the risk is desirable or undesirable. A desirable risk is one that is inherent in the entity's business model or normal future operations and that the orga-nization believes it can monitor and manage effectively. An undesirable risk is one that does not fit organizational strategy, or which offers unattractive rewards or cannot be monitored or managed effectively.

In managing risk, an organization may choose to accept a risk. There are different ways of enacting this choice. it can accept the risk at its present level, reduce its severity and/or its likelihood of occurrence (typically through internal controls) or share it with a financially capable, independent party (typically through insurance or a hedging arrangement).

Critical Element 5: Mitigate risk

Depending on the risk response selected, management needs to identify any gaps in risk management capabilities. It may then need to improve those capabilities. This may be necessary to implement the risk response. Over time, the effectiveness of risk mitigation activities should be monitored.

Critical Element 6: Monitor risk

Models, risk analytics and web-enabled technologies make it possible to aggregate information about risks using common data elements to support the creation of a risk management dashboard or scorecard for use by risk owners, unit managers and executive management. Deloach (2018) advocated dashboard and scorecard reporting which should be flexible enough to enable the design of reports to address specific needs, including reporting to the board of directors. Examples of dashboard reporting, which often feature "traffic light" indicators, are important elements of monitoring. This could become an internal audit function. The above model may assist organizations in the identification, measurement and evaluation of risks. The next three sections use illustrative examples of three tensions in the application of risk management and test out the model depicted in Table 12.1.

Tension 1: The use of risk management as ceremonial

The adaptation of Enterprise Risk Management to major government entities and indeed, to government itself may seem an obvious course of action, but there are wide-ranging criticisms of the risk management concept and its practice (Lapsley, 2020). After a study of a series of international corporate collapses, Hamilton and Micklethwait (2006) attributed much of these failures to weak corporate governance. They considered risk management as a suitable tool to address weaknesses in corporate governance. However, in a study of corporate failures in Australia, Clarke and Dean (2007) were critical of the potential of risk management, suggesting that it could become a form of legitimation of corporate activity.

Lapsley (2020) noted that this tension over efficacy is increased by the typical public adoption of private sector practices as "best practice" (Hood, 1991, 1995) which had to be followed by public sector organizations, even when the worst excesses of weak governance were entirely private sector in origin. Yet another facet of the public sector is the existence of a blame culture (Hood, 2002; Hood and Rothstein, 2001). In this situation, public sector managers may be receptive to the adoption of risk management as a neutral technology which could operate as a kind of defensive shield against blame attribution by their opponents (Lapsley, 2009). These observations resonate with a public preoccupation with technologies to mitigate reputational risk (Power, 2004; Rika and Jacobs, 2019).

However, as Lapsley (2020) acknowledged, the most powerful critique of risk management was launched by Power in the context of his concept of the Audit Society (Power, 1994, 1997, 2004, 2007). Basically, Power does not regard risk management as an effective management tool, and he identifies many unintended consequences of its use (Merton, 1936). Specifically, Power (2007) attributes the rise in the importance of risk management to the actions of the State as "risk manager", as it seeks to inhibit reputational risks and legitimate its actions and activities. In his view, the importance of risk management to the State's reputation management strategy has resulted in a widespread adoption of risk management throughout the public sector. Indeed, for those who investigate public sector organizations, this phenomenon is evident. More importantly, Power (2004, 2007) argues that this universal adoption of risk management by public sector bodies can "hardwire" defensive thinking in public sector organizations, imprisoning them in a risk averse, defensive position. The significance of risk management and its position in public sector organizations alongside audit gives a prominence to a compliance culture and a "tick box" mentality (Power, 1994, 1997, 2004, 2007). Collectively, the impact of these practices may lead to public sector workers being absorbed by procedures rather than the needs of citizens. This will result in risk management practices assuming a ceremonial rather than an instrumental role. In many organizations, risk management is regarded as a "tick box" exercise. This achieves little and uses considerable resources; an outcome to be avoided.

Tension 2: Contested values in climate change

One of the key risks in climate change policymaking is the contrasting views of important policy makers who are *populists* versus the *scientific community* which endorses climate change policies.

The populists

If we examine the populists first, there are robust ideas of why climate change is a myth. For example, Tony Abbott, former PM of Australia (cited in Mathiesen, 2017) stated:

> Climate change is probably doing good and policies to combat it were like primitive people killing goats to appease the gods. The so-called settled science of climate change is absolute crap.

Other populists in Brazil made similar comments. Brazil's Foreign Minister, Ernesto Araujo, has warned that Climate Change was a plot by "cultural Marxists" and President Bolsonaro made a campaign promise to pull Brazil out of the Paris Climate Accord. Bolsonaro said Brazil was being unfairly criticised over rising deforestation because of commercial interests but provided no evidence. He described Europe as "an environmental sect". After the highest number of Amazon fires since 2010, Bolsonaro falsely accused Leonardo DiCaprio of giving money to set it on fire (Boyle, 2020).

In the US, President Donald Trump has called himself a "great environmentalist", citing successes in conservation, wildlife protection and the banning of some offshore drilling (see Boyle and Anderson, 2020). But the US is one of the most polluting nations in the world – its factories, power plants, homes, cars and farms pump billions of tonnes of carbon dioxide into the atmosphere each year. Donald Trump has also reversed many of Obama's environmental policies, including withdrawing from the Paris Accord on Climate Change. On global warming, Donald Trump has stated (Boyle and Anderson, 2020):

> It'll start getting cooler. You just watch. I don't think science knows, actually.

President Trump has also argued that China's carbon emissions are nearly twice what the US has (Boyle and Anderson, 2020) This is accurate. The US is the world's second largest emitter of carbon dioxide. But per head of population, the US is the worst emitter of carbon dioxide.

The scientists

There has been a huge scientific effort to research the impact of climate change over the past three decades. In this chapter we demonstrate that by looking at most cited contributions to the literature and examining two contemporary pieces of research on climate change. This includes Parmesan and Yohe's (2003) research to establish a global fingerprint to assess the impact of climate change. This also includes innovative approaches to predicting ecological habitat models. For example, there is related research on extinction risks from climate change (Thomas et al., 2004). The effects of global warming on wild animals and plants have also been investigated (Root et al., 2003). Also, an important facet of climate change has examined global analyses of sea surface temperature and ice (Folland et al., 2001). In terms of climate change there have been studies of the past, including gathering evidence on the instability of past climates (Dansgaard et al., 1993). There has, of course, been research on the acceleration of global warming (Cox et al., 2000). Perhaps most importantly, there has been research on the impact of human environmental interventions on climate change (Charlson et al., 1992). These are insights into different kinds of climate change research but represent a glimpse into what this community of scientists have to offer.

We also look at two important parts of more recent research. This includes work on rising sea levels (Kulp and Strauss, 2019) and air pollution (Whittaker-Wood, 2020). The research on rising water levels due to the disappearance of ice caps reveals the loss of land in many Asian countries. This study forecasts the loss of land due to flooding up to 2050. The study identifies six Asian countries which will have the worst outcome in terms of loss of land. This includes China, Bangladesh, Vietnam, India, Vietnam, Indonesia and Thailand. But other low-level areas will lose out too, with risks for famous structures and monuments. For example, the world-famous Forth Railway Bridge built in Scotland in the 1890s would be underwater.

The Whittaker-Wood (2020) study also produces fascinating results. This was a study of city pollution. To find out which city is the most polluted in the world, they analysed data on air, light and noise pollution in 48 cities worldwide. Each city was ranked on measures of air, light and noise pollution. The ranks were then combined to give an overall pollution score out of 100 for each city. The higher the score, the more polluted a city is. The most polluted cities in the world were:

1 Cairo
2 Delhi
3 Beijing
4 Moscow
5 Istanbul
6 Guangzhou
7 Shanghai
8 Buenos Aires
9 Paris
10 Los Angeles.

The least polluted cities were:

1 Zurich
2 Oslo
3 Munich
4 Vienna
5 Cologne
6 Hamburg
7 Dusseldorf
8 Hanover
9 Stuttgart
10 Sydney.

These results give us cause for anxiety: Will the cities with embedded air pollution ever recover and have clean air? On the other hand, there are cities in Europe which offer exciting prospects for clean air, particularly in Germany.

Managing the risks

Table 12.2 highlights a number of contemporary climate change challenges (rising sea levels, bush fires and air pollution) and offers policy options to address these. There is the important issue of whether your political leader is a populist, in which case, there is a risk that no environmental policies will be implemented. The best response is overarching legislation which specifies which policies need to be implemented and community awareness and support. To mitigate risks to your community a purposeful management strategy is necessary: be active, articulate clear policies, enlist community support, celebrate environmental heroes and successes and work with and support "policy influencers" (this might include elected officials or bodies such as state auditors).

Tension 3: Trade-offs in a pandemic

This tension studies the challenges of the UK in tackling the global pandemic. A pandemic is the most severe civil emergency risk to society (Horton, 2020, p. 25).

Table 12.2 The management of climate change phenomena

Phenomenon	Public policy
Rising sea levels	Population retreats
Coastal erosion	Refuges
Flooding	Flood barriers and water management
Phenomenon: bush fires	Investment in professional fire services, including staff and equipment (land and air)
	Planning controls: location of buildings
	Active management of scrubland
Phenomenon: air pollution	Tree plantation policy
	Incentivise electric and hybrid vehicle use
	Control city centre space
	Fines for noncompliance

Regarding trade-offs, there are two conflicting pressures. The first of these relates to the restrictions imposed on citizens to fight the virus such as testing and tracing potential cases, the need to isolate if you test positive for Covid-19, the closure of activities which facilitate the transmission of Covid-19 and complete closures of almost all activities in lockdowns. This alternative replaces the language of the typical government entity from budgeting and accountability to the metrics of medicine – number of new cases, patients admitted to hospital, daily fatalities, total fatalities. These variables do not readily translate to government, with the specific exception of government support mechanisms which detail the governments financial support for specific industries and individuals because of their compliance. The other pressure is the desire to ease restrictions, to open up businesses and to preserve the economy. This group contains the libertarian groups in political parties who disagree with idea of imposing restrictions on citizens. There is a belief that this will lead to a herd immunity in the community, but this is fiercely contested. The main attack lines of this group are the extent of government support for businesses and individuals, the extent of government debt (almost £2 trillion, the highest level of UK debt since 1960) and shortfalls in GDP (the November figure for GDP fell 4.6%), but these economic arguments have been trumped by the desire to save lives from Covid-19.

The readiness for the pandemic

Can we identify serious threats and hazards to everyday life? One study suggested that the UK was the second-best country (after the US) of 193 countries to be ready for a pandemic (NTI, 2019). It is ironic that both these countries have performed so poorly, with record fatalities. However, an earlier UK government report on pandemics (Cygnus) said that the UK was ill-prepared for a pandemic. This report was initiated by May's 2016 government and predicted 200,000 UK deaths from a pandemic. It is evident that little attempt was made to implement the recommendations of Cygnus. The UK was not able to deal with the extreme demands of a pandemic (Horton, 2020, p. 25) and the UK government was criticised for not learning from early studies. For example, the SARS epidemic of 2003 suggested that the risk of a virally induced global humanitarian emergency was identified as a clear and present danger after SARS and the most important requirement was vigilance, however, the only appointees to the UK Cabinet would be Brexiteers whose focus was on Brexit and with no permanent state of awareness for a possible pandemic (Horton, 2020, p. 31). An even more trenchant criticism of the UK's readiness for a pandemic was delivered by (McTague, 2020). He said a senior official he interviewed told him the UK was not prepared for a pandemic – but it thought it was. McTague (2020, p. 30) was critical of UK readiness for a pandemic.

A critical factor in the UK's handling of the risks of Covid-19 rested on the unpredictable behaviour of the dominant figure in UK politics – Prime Minister Johnson. The UK Prime Minister, Boris Johnson, is a complex character. His biographer (Bower, 2020) identifies him as a "bon viveur" with complex character traits. The Bower (2020) character traits of Johnson include: being a serial adulterer (passim); treating appearance as affectation (pp. 132–133), in which he assumes the persona of an untidy person (for example, leaving his shirt tail hanging out) with dishevelled hair; adopting the character of Bertie Wooster, a fictional character in P.G. Wodehouse novels (Bower, pp. 19–20), in his opportunistic behaviour (p. 75; for example, he never supported the Brexiteers in the Conservative Party until the 2016 Brexit referendum, at which he assumed a central role); being narcissistic (p. 57); being a loner (p. 87); being insecure and insensitive (p. 79 and p. 342); not being a team player (p. 76); being self-absorbed and selfish (p. 164 and p. 211); making racist remarks (pp. 67–68); being a needy character with an inflated sense of his own importance (p. 76); possibly becoming depressed if he is not the centre of attention, accentuated by his loner behaviour (p. 142). These observations make for a complex character but there are more.

One issue is the reputation of Boris Johnson as a serial liar (Bower, 2020, p. 88). Now, many people may say all politicians lie all the time. However, the reputation of serial liar precedes Boris Johnson's involvement in politics. There are examples from both his political life and his professional life as follows. Boris Johnson, as a member of the Conservative Party Shadow Cabinet and editor of the *Spectator*, lied to the Leader of the Conservative Party, Michael Howard, and the national press about his affair with the *Spectator*'s deputy Editor (Wyatt) – he was sacked from the Shadow Cabinet for this lie. Johnson responded that he was entitled to lie (Bower, p. 89). He also earned a reputation for the fabrication of stories for the *Times* when working from Brussels as a journalist (p. 46); this was resolved when Boris confessed to the editor that a story in the *Times* contained many quotations which were fabrications – the shocked editor of the *Times* sacked him immediately (p. 43). He then joined the *Daily Telegraph* where his editor, Max Hastings, subsequently sacked him for being a serial liar (p. 58).

Another facet of his complex character is revealed by the way Boris Johnson was heavily influenced by the habits of his father, notably his father's serial adultery and the adoption of a jocular persona to defuse tense situations. These aspects of his father are evident in his own persona. However, his father had the reputation of physically assaulting the mother of Boris, including an instance where she was so badly beaten up that she was hospitalised for her injuries, including a broken nose (Bower, p. 17). While there is no evidence of this behaviour in the private life of Boris Johnson, there are suggestions that his insecurities and loner behaviour may have been an outcome of his witnessing the physical assaults of his mother (p. 342).

To sum up, we turn to the man who worked with Johnson for many years (and subsequently sacked him) – Sir Max Hastings, former editor of the *Telegraph*. Hastings summed up Johnson's character as follows (Bower, 2020, p. 57):

> First, he will say absolutely anything to man, woman or child that will give him pleasure at that moment, heedless of whether he may be obliged to contradict it 10 minutes later. Second, having registered his wild card status as a brand, he exploits it to secure absolution for a procession of follies, gaffes and idiocies, 'scoun-drelisms', such as would destroy the career of any other man or woman in jour-nalism, let alone government.

The above exposition makes it difficult to predict the impact of the UK's most power-ful man with a complex, almost mercurial, character on the management of the risks of Covid-19.

In December 2019, there was a General Election in the UK. The Prime Minister was one of the key advocates of Brexit in 2016. He made 2019 a Brexit Election. Indeed, he informed his party that his Cabinet would consist of Brexiteers who were prepared to go for a hard Brexit without a trade deal with the EU. This was too extreme for experienced former members of the Theresa May government, many of whom chose to leave public office or leave Parliament altogether. So, the UK government formed after the December 2019 General Election was less experienced than its predecessor. Specifically, this weaker government lost a lot of senior politicians who were well versed on Cygnus. This left a government which was strategically weak on Covid-19. The weakened government was less experienced but shared a common identity as Brexiteers. This gave the UK a government that was fixated on Brexit and celebrating Brexit Day on the 31st of January, just as the pandemic started. There was a permanent and heightened awareness of Brexit issues but, as McTague (2020) argued, there was complacency around a pandemic in the UK, even when major countries like Italy and Spain were in difficulties.

Table 12.3 shows the intensity and spread of Covid-19 in the UK as of 18 February 2021. This reveals a very significant number of cases (4,126,150), but a declining number of hospital deaths (178). Nevertheless, at this time, there were significant numbers of hospital admissions, which were greater than at the peak of the First Wave. The total number of fatalities (120,757) made the UK one of the worst performing countries on the pandemic in the world. This is confirmed by the UK having the highest mortality rate of all countries in the world at 1,779 deaths per million of the population.

The relevance of risk management

One of the specific challenges of risk management is the gap between expectations and capability. Specifically, the presumption of many users of risk management is that all risks under consideration are quantifiable, with an expectation that the quantification will include a relative probability of the risk's occurrence. The reason why this expectations gap occurs is the inability to measure many of these issues. In effect, these "non-measurable" issues are major uncertainties which are "unknown unknowns" and not amenable to standard statistical analysis. However, these elements of uncertainty which are pertinent but not quantifiable should be included in risk assessments. To include these items in our analysis, we need complete transparency on how these uncertainties were identified, how their importance was judged and their overall place in the risk assessment. So, we include these, but perform a rigorous assessment of their importance.

Table 12.3 The incidence of Covid-19 in the UK

Total UK cases	4,126,150
Hospital admissions	18,462
Number of new cases in a single day	10,641
Daily Covid-19 death total	178
Total hospital fatalities	120,757
World mortality rate	1,779 deaths per million of population (No.1 in the world)

Sources: Covid statistics, Department of Health (DoH) UK and the Office of National Statistics (ONS), UK.

Notes: 1. All data collected on 18 February 2021. 2. Total fatalities are deaths in hospital after being diagnosed with Covid-19 within the 28 days prior to death. This understates deaths because of Covid-19 in the community. The Office of National Statistics offers a more rigorous definition of fatalities by examining death certificates. They estimated total UK Covid-19 fatalities at 100,000 in mid-January. 3. The number of total daily deaths has fallen from a peak of 1,820 in mid-January.

Nevertheless, Lapsley (2020) examined the challenges the UK government faced from Covid-19 and concluded there is a case for the government adoption of risk management as a continuing governance tool (see Table 12.1, which is based on the work of Deloach (2018), as adapted by Lapsley 2020). This model implies a consistency of approach and a determination to identify risks, assess their success and mitigate these risks. Our risk management model recommends the use of a high-level environmental scanning unit to detect potential risks to entities. The UK government's THRCC (Threats, Hazards, Resilience and Contingency Committee) was established to do this. It consisted of cabinet level ministers, a high-powered cadre to address dangers such as Covid-19. However, on becoming UK Prime Minister, one of Johnson's first acts was the closure of THRCC to get his cabinet more focused on Brexit (Walters, 2020). The existence of THRCC would have helped the government respond more rapidly to the threat of Covid-19 (Telegraph Reporters, 2020). The closure of this committee was a high-risk action by the UK Prime Minister. It looks like it reflects on a fixation on Brexit above all else.

Regarding the first element on our overall approach to risk management (see Table 12.1), we have a context which looks challenged or compromised. For example, on McTague's (2020) comment about complacency, the Prime Minister made the following statement on 2 March 2020 (Calvert et al., 2020):

> This country is very, very, well prepared ... we've got fantastic testing systems, amazing surveillance of the spread of disease. I wish to stress that, at the moment, it's very important that people consider that they should, as far as possible, go about business as usual.

That statement reveals a complacent and over optimistic attitude, particularly in the context of Covid-19 surges across Europe and, indeed, across the world.

This complacency is made worse by the impact of ten years of austerity on the NHS. A crucial part of the UK government effectiveness hinges on the UK's NHS, which is committed to providing universal healthcare, free at the point of entry. Another layer of complexity is the effect of the austerity programmes after the Global Financial Crisis of 2008. The NHS was given a modest increase in its annual funding of circa 1% by the 2010 Coalition government. But, with industry specific inflation closer to 7%, this was effectively real-terms cuts in its annual funding. After a decade of funding reductions was the NHS in good shape for Covid-19?

A further complication is the longstanding difficulty of modernising computerised information systems in the NHS. This challenge is due to the inherent complexity of the NHS with multiple forms of software and hardware which do not connect with each other in many hospitals and health authorities. Furthermore, the NHS is an organization which has been subject to almost continuous reform and change of its structure and processes by modernising reformers (Brunsson, 1992; Brunsson and Olsen, 1993). All these factors make the overall estimation of risks difficult. While the NHS has great expertise, it is not necessarily agile, has had funding difficulties and has had too many government-inspired re-organizations.

Evaluation of the UK approach to risk management

Overall, the UK government's approach to risk management can be described as reactive with slow responses, with the significant exception of the acquisition and use of vaccines. While the UK has the highest number of fatalities from Covid-19 in Europe, it also has the highest rate of vaccinations in Europe. These two factors may be related with mortalities driving the need and desire for vaccination. In this regard, the UK government did use foresight to order vast quantities of vaccines from a variety of producers even before they had been clinically approved. The amount of vaccines ordered by the UK is greater than required for its population. The government took risks on whether these vaccines would be effective, before clinical trials were concluded. This was a gamble which paid off for the UK.

Regarding Element 1 of our model, the identification of the risks from Covid-19 could have been sharper. Initially, the government had a limited sense of the speed of its spread. However, later in the first wave, its persistence was recognised by the government as posing grave concerns for hospital capacity. As the pandemic worsened, the UK government did see the pressure on both ventilators and intensive care capacity. Its initiatives on encouraging British industry to build capacity were successful. It requested British manufacturers to design and make ventilators, which they did. They built Nightingale hospitals in record time for Covid-19 patients. However, much of this capacity was not used. Regarding Elements 2 and 3, there was clarity and measurement of the principal risks. However, in the evaluation of risk, there were issues around avoiding and reducing risk. For example, on testing and tracing for Covid-19 the UK has had struggles to generate sufficient capacity despite the promptings of official government advisers. On hospital capacity, emergency powers were used to shift vulnerable elderly people without Covid-19 testing and many thousands died. The Prime Minister said many care homes had failed to follow correct procedures, but this was contested by care home leaders (Elliott, 2020).

Why did the UK government perform so badly on its management of the pandemic? Well, Covid-19 presented a set of risky situations for the UK government. It had an overarching desire to preserve hospital capacity. This led to the discharge of some 5000 elderly patients from hospitals to care homes. These elderly patients were not tested for Covid-19 before their transfers to care homes. This fuelled an explosion in Covid-19 cases in care homes with thousands of deaths of the most vulnerable people in society.

Most economies which had success in managing the pandemic had effective test and trace programmes. This includes countries such as Taiwan, South Korea and Malaysia. These countries had experience in fighting the virus outbreaks from SARS and MERS. The UK government outsourced the delivery of its test and trace systems to consulting firms with a private sector manager brought in to oversee the project. Despite the Prime Minister's bullish statements that the UK would have a world-beating track and trace system, this has not happened. The UK system has misfired and underperformed.

The most successful countries in managing the pandemic (e.g. Australia, New Zealand and Norway) had strict border controls. The UK did not. It experimented with air corridors for citizens in countries with low Covid-19 infections to allow some international travel. A UK Parliamentary Committee (Home Affairs) argues that weak border controls had facilitated the entry of thousands of visitors who had Covid-19. This was particularly acute after the relaxation of the first lockdown when the UK government had not introduced any quarantine measures. However, both the UK's Health Secretary and Home Secretary (Interior Minister) pleaded with the Prime Minister to close UK borders, but he refused outright. He subsequently made a statement to the effect that the UK had one of the tightest border controls anywhere. The UK had banned citizens from entering the country, but many were able to enter the UK via other

Table 12.4 Risk Assessments: key dimensions

Category of risk	Actions	Comments
1. Relocation of elderly hospital patients to care homes	Transfer of patients without Covid tests – high risk	Risk assessment – poor
2. The development of Test and Trace	Privatisation at high cost and without a dependable system	Risk assessment – poor
3. The control of borders	Open borders throughout with minimal closures for air corridors to and from selected destinations	Risk assessment – poor
4. The management of lockdowns	Complacency. Prevarication. Easing of restrictions too rapidly	Risk assessment – poor
5. The management of personal protection equipment	Under investigation by State Auditor. High Court judgement rules Health Secretary behaved illegally	Risk assessment – poor
6. Financial Risks to Economy	Comprehensive plan for most businesses and citizens except certain categories e.g. the self employed	Risk assessment – very good
7. Vaccination programme	The UK bought millions of pounds worth of vaccines before they were tested by companies and by medical authorities. A massive gamble as the UK lost control of Covid-19. But the gamble paid off	Risk assessment – very good

countries. For example, in the week beginning 1 March, UK Borders Control discovered six passengers from Brazil (subject to a UK travel ban) who had the highly infectious Brazilian variant of Covid-19. They had flown into Aberdeen airport, a small low traffic airport. This is an example of a weakness in UK border controls.

The UK faced significant risks over its supply of Personal Protective Equipment (PPE) for workers in health care and social care. This was not just a case of the quantity of PPE but also its quality, with many supplies regarded as unfit for purpose and returned to their suppliers. There have also been suggestions of defalcations and fraudulent activity with phoney suppliers of PPE receiving significant UK government funding and disappearing. This activity has prompted an investigation by the UK state auditor.

Further risks were the financial risks to the economy and the risk of inadequate supplies of vaccinations; both these risks were handled well by the UK government. These are discussed below. A further risk which was not handled well was the lack of decisive action over lockdowns. Table 12.5 shows the UK lockdowns in 2020 and the start of 2021. The UK government has consistently stated that its approach to managing the epidemic has been to follow the science. However, the evidence on lockdowns suggests that they have not done this. There were delays over the first lockdown, with the UK Cabinet Ministers wandering around in a "business as usual" mode, and there was complete complacency over the dangers of Covid-19. Indeed, at this time, the Prime Minister visited a hospital and, in an interview afterwards, boasted that he had met Covid-19 patients and shook their hands. Similarly, at an international rugby

Table 12.5 Lockdowns and risk

Lockdown 1: Commenced Monday 23 March 2020; concluded Sunday 7 June 2020 (with a variety of easing of restrictions in May).

Comment: As indicated in the narrative in the text, the delay of seven weeks before the first lockdown displays a complacent attitude by the UK government towards the risks of Covid-19. The most successful countries went quickly into lockdown and closed their borders. The UK government sought to present a "business as usual" vision, with millions of passengers from high infection countries such as Italy, France and Spain.

This lockdown was intended to end in early June, but the PM responded to pressures from influential backbenchers to start easing restrictions in May. This led to more infection, particularly in the North of England, where Covid-19 infections were worse than London, and the South of England.

During the post-Lockdown era, the UK government introduced air corridors from the UK to countries which had apparent low rates of infection. During this period, a second variant of Covid-19 emerged in Kent, England. Many commentators considered this variant was brought into the country by holidaymakers returning from overseas holidays.

Lockdown 2: Commenced Thursday 5 November 2020; concluded 2 December 2020.

Comment: On 1 September, the Sage Committee, the government's expert advisors recommended an immediate lockdown from 1 September. The UK government ignored this advice. The Leader of the Opposition Party was made aware of this advice in October. He demanded an immediate lockdown. The PM assumed his Bertie Wooster persona and started strutting about in front of the dispatch box and, repeatedly pointing to the Leader of the Opposition, proclaiming "He wants to cancel Christmas! He wants to cancel Christmas!" This unedifying spectacle was the official government position until the rising level of infections obliged the PM to authorise a second lockdown.

Again, the pressures of influential backbenchers and the PM's desire for citizens to enjoy Christmas led to a relaxation of restrictions over the Christmas period despite the reservations of the government's expert advisors. This policy predictably led to a spike in infections, with tragic Covid-19 fatalities in families who came together to celebrate Christmas.

The government declared there would be an immediate lockdown after Christmas.

Lockdown 3: Commenced Saturday 26 December; initially to be concluded by 31 March 2021 but extended to 21 June 2021 on 22 February 2021.

Comment: The government said that they had to have a third lockdown because it was now apparent that the second strain of Covid-19 was highly infectious, more so than the first variant. The second variant was now of increased significance in the proportion of UK Covid-19 infections. However, the government's expert advisers said that they had been saying this for months and the government had not responded to their advice.

On Monday 22 February, the PM extended the period of lockdown. He published a roadmap for the easing of restrictions subject to certain conditions, particularly the efficacy of the vaccination programme. The suggested end date for this lockdown was end May 2021, with progressive relaxations of restriction for schools, sporting events and the entertainment industry. Given the impact of relaxing restrictions too soon in 2020, the PM said this was a very cautious plan. This implies the government now had a better understanding of Covid-19.

Overview: The UK government was too slow to lockdown and too fast to ease restrictions. Throughout the pandemic, the UK had never taken complete control of its borders – a strategic weakness. It was too rapid in easing restrictions. The third lockdown may end differently. This has yet to be seen.

---

match the Prime Minister was seen shaking hands with and hugging fellow supporters. Subsequently, the Prime Minister contracted Covid-19. He was hospitalised and had a near-death experience. The successful countries reacted promptly to the first cases by having lockdowns within 6/7 days. It was seven weeks before the UK government announced its first lockdown. This delay was in part attributable to the libertarian values of the Prime Minister, who was reluctant to curtail citizens' freedoms. The second lockdown was delayed by the Prime Minister who embraced his Bertie Wooster persona to declare that the Opposition Leader wanted to cancel Christmas in a Prime Minister's Questions segment which was pure pantomime (see Table 12.5). While the Prime Minister ignored the advice of his experts over lockdown 2 the length of this lockdown was another contested issue. Another issue was the desire of the UK's "bon viveur" to have citizens enjoy Christmas. Despite the misgivings of many political leaders, the Prime Minister pressed ahead with his plans for family Christmas celebrations (this led to an inevitable spike in infections and stories of cross infections by family members). At this time, the government's advisers were highly concerned by the highly infectious nature of the second Covid-19 variant in the UK, which was also more deadly than the first virus. At this stage, the seriousness of the situation was accepted by the Prime Minister and a lockdown to 31 March 2021 was agreed by Parliament and subsequently extended to the end of June 2021.

The UK government's first response to the pandemic is shown in Table 12.6. This was an aid package of £193 billion. Where there were lockdowns and business enterprises had to close, a furlough scheme was launched in which where employees were unable to work, they were paid 80% of their salary, up to £2500. This has been extended to cover all lockdowns and beyond up to September 2021. A 20% cut in welfare payments has been paused for the same time as the furlough scheme. Businesses had property tax and value added tax holidays. Self-employed people were able to apply for business grants when they were not allowed to work because of lockdowns. Most citizens were grateful for these measures. But while the financial arrangements of the government may be heralded as the right thing to do in the pandemic, nevertheless, the libertarian wing of the ruling Conservative Party have expressed concern at the length of and frequency of lockdowns and their impact on the economy. So, when the OECD reported that the UK recession is significantly worse than all other G7 countries (Chapman, 2020), this unsettled this group of backbench MPs. Similarly, these MPs were alarmed when the UK national debt reached £2.13 trillion equivalent to 99.4% of GDP – the highest debt to GDP ratio since 1962 (Norwan, 2021a; Aldrick, 2020). Furthermore, the UK's 2019 financial performance was, according to the UK Office of National Statistics, the worst performance of the UK economy in 300 years (Norwan, 2021b, Aldrick, 2021). The 2020 recession of circa 10% wiped out the growth of the past seven years. This contraction of the economy was the worst since records began in

Table 12.6 Lockdown government support

	£billion
Business support	53.21
Employment support	70.61
Green/environment	8.39
Tax measures	3.07
Extra public services	47.75
Welfare spending	9.31
Total	192.33

Source: Office of Budget Responsibility (2020, 14 July).

1954 and was considered the worst since 1709 (Norwan, 2021b; Aldrick, 2021). These signs of financial distress compelled the libertarians to press for the relaxation of restrictions on business and the opening up of the economy. They forced the government to have open Parliamentary debates on any future restrictions. However, in their most recent lockdown the government had the support of the official opposition party and a lockdown to 31 March 2021 (subsequently extended to 21 June) was approved. Saving lives from Covid-19 had trumped the economic case.

The UK vaccination programme has been described as the success of the UK government's management of the pandemic, but it is more complex than that. By mid-August 2021, 75% of the UK population had been double vaccinated for Covid-19.

The UK government's supply of vaccines reveals an extraordinary gamble, not only on the sheer volume of vaccine doses which it ordered, but its willingness to order vaccines which had neither been approved by the manufacturers nor by the authorising medical bodies in their country of origin. This includes (see O'Neill and Whipple, 2021): (1) 100 million doses of Astra-Zeneca vaccine and (2) 40 million of the Biontech-Pfizer vaccine. Both of these vaccines were subsequently approved and are being used in many countries. In addition to this, there is an order for 17 million Modena vaccine doses, which have been approved. The UK orders also include vaccines which await regulatory approval: (1) 60 million Noravax vaccines and (2) 30 million Jonsson's vaccines. The UK orders also include orders for vaccines which are halfway through clinical trials: (1) 60 million Valneva vaccines and (2) 60 million GSK/Sanofi vaccines. The UK has a total of 407 million vaccine doses on order. It is progressing its programme by age group and plans to vaccinate children in Autumn 2021.

While this success story is attributed to the UK government, its origins are with Oxford University (O'Neill, 2021). As Oxford University was developing its vaccine, it was evident that it only had the capacity to develop 10 litres of vaccine. They sought the advice of Netty England, a manufacturing expert at the UK Biological Association. Within days she had organised a consortium of potential manufacturers of vaccines. This group became the internationally acclaimed UK Vaccine Task Force. The task force drew on industry and science experts to build a portfolio of potential vaccines which sped up contracts. This included contracts to both assist with development funding and agreeing to indemnify the manufacturers against unintended vaccine side effects – a provision other countries, including the EU, baulked at. Their activities included reserving the entire capacity of Wockhardt's new factory in Wrexham which had not yet opened. The task force also gave strong advice on which was most likely to be the first effective vaccine. This task force had four government Ministers on its Investment Committee, which agreed to fund the Valneva factory in Livingston to expand its output up to 200 million doses of vaccine, per year. This entity has now been absorbed into the government after its significant success as a task force.

Managing the pandemic was a massive challenge for the UK and many other governments. But would a more systematic approach to risk assessment have made the UK government's management better? It is suggested here that the formal adoption of the model depicted in this chapter would have been an improvement, with a more systematic approach to risk management replacing the reactive style of the UK government. Table 12.7 illustrates this by showing the risk management model against the trajectory of the pandemic in the UK. An important missing element in the UK was the absence of a framework. In particular, the lack of a high-level unit for

Table 12.7 The UK management of Covid-19 risk management

The fundamentals	Environmental (Internal and External) Risk Horizon Scanning Unit	The closure of the UK's THRCC committee created a major risk – the lack of heightened awareness of a possible pandemic
Overview	1 Process 2 Integration 3 Culture 4 Infrastructure	1. Process – unclear, centralised directives versus localised imperatives. 2. Integration – no sense of integration, more disparate views over different services and geographical areas. 3. Culture – a Brexit-focused agenda on libertarian values which conflicted with community needs. 4. Infrastructure. No sophisticated system of testing tracking and tracing Covid-19 infected patients. The government subsequently introduced such a system but with limited success.
Critical Element 1	Identify risk • Impact • Likelihood • Velocity • Persistence	The initial response of the UK government was too complacent, as if the virus would not reach Europe, despite the Italian experiences of that time. This gave the government little idea of potential impact, likelihood, velocity or persistence.
Critical Element 2	Source risk	This virus emerged from China from initial examination of its trajectory and spread.
Critical Element 3	Measure risk	As the pandemic took hold the dominant calculative practice became medical statistics of infection rates (R-scores), numbers infected, numbers of seriously ill patients, as measured by hospital and intensive care admissions and Covid-19 fatalities.
Critical Element 4	Evaluate risk • Avoid • Accept • Reduce • Share	The most successful act of this government in the pandemic has been (1) the ordering of millions of vaccines from a variety of producers – even before they were recognised by the authorities as suitable and (2) an extensive vaccination programme with a priority for older age groups and vulnerable people with the intention of reducing the risks of Covid-19 spreading further in the population.
Critical Element 5	Mitigate risk	Interventions on daily living including lockdowns (all later than advised by scientific advisors).
Critical Element 6	Monitor risk	Daily press briefings mostly.

Adapted from: Deloach (2018) as adapted by Lapsley (2020; and in this chapter by Lapsley, 2021)

environmental scanning left the UK exposed. There are reports of early Covid-19 cases in neighbouring countries to China before the public declaration of this dangerous coronavirus. The benefits of this early warning system would have been the devising of a plan. This would have looked at the likelihood of the virus going global. It would have examined how Asian countries had dealt with previous dangerous viruses like SARS and Mers. This would have identified the need for a sophisticated track and trace system. Instead of devising one on the hoof as they did during the pandemic, there would have been an opportunity to devise a scheme before the pandemic started.

Furthermore, in terms of the fundamentals of management, this oversight committee would have addressed (1) processes, (2) integration, (3) culture and (4) infrastructure. It is a reasonable expectation that the manner and mechanisms by which this would be addressed would be made explicit processes. This differs from the muddling through approach of the government. There was also scope to consider the relationship of central government to devolved institutions. It may have a step too far for a Brexit-focused government to think more broadly but this is exactly what the environmental scanners should have done. And at the very least there should have been consideration of state of readiness and action plans. For example, the discharge of 5,000 elderly citizens from hospitals to care homes without Covid-19 testing should have been a redline. Also, if these fundamentals had been addressed and debated this would have led naturally into the consideration of the evaluation of risks and procedures for mitigating risk instead of the government reeling from one crisis after another. These could be answered on a "what if?" basis. This may not have led to definitive templates for action, but this preliminary analysis could have helped to inform a more coherent basis for action than simple reactive behaviour.

Managerial implications

Risk management has been with us for some time, from its introduction as a highly effective means of preventing financial scandals in the 1990s to its present status as a taken-for-granted modern management practice which is in play in many large private and public corporations. Given that this is so, how can we describe risk management as new? The newness of risk management is the use of the structured approach to Risk Management discussed in this chapter to major projects. In our considered view, the status quo resembles our first tension of ceremonial use. The first assessment of how an organization's risk management is undertaken should be the construction of a Risk Map, which identifies how members of the organization use this management technique. This entails identifying all meetings on a particular day (or a longer period) and the inspection of both agendas and minutes. If the risk assessment is accepted without comment, in all cases, your organization is either superb at its risk management, or you have found a tick box ceremonial activity. If you find challenges to the risks identified or debates and discussions over the appropriateness of identified risks, you have a meaningful risk management system. However, if there is a complete absence of debates and discussion your risk management needs renewal and in a way which motivates staff.

However, this chapter has suggested a more structured approach to risk management. This is an explicit recognition that robust systems of risk management can be mobilised to enhance the management of any organization. It is also suggested in this chapter that risk management is an appropriate means of addressing big policy projects. When confronted with very large, significant projects, there is a temptation for organizations to muddle through. It is argued here that a structured approach to the identification of how best to identify and deal with risks, as depicted in this chapter, may reduce friction and enable organizations to be agile and effective in confronting the biggest of policy risks confronting them. The two big policy areas addressed in this chapter are climate change and the Covid-19 pandemic. In this chapter, key actors are identified as risk factors, as are the complexity of the challenge and the state of readiness to act. Within modern societies there are forward looking citizens, policy makers and public managers. But one of their biggest challenges is convincing their organization on the identification and management of risks which may threaten the effectiveness or even the future of their mission. This open, transparent approach to public management is a counterweight to the persistent focusing on failures in the politics of attention.

References

Aldrick, P. (2020) National debt swings to its highest level since 1960. *The Times*, 22 October: 36.

Aldrick, P. (2021) The Great Lockdown slump earns its place in the history books. *The Times*, 13 February, 51.

Arena, M., Arnaboldi, M. and Azzone, G. (2010). The organizational dynamics of enterprise risk management. *Accounting, Organizations and Society*, 35: 659–675.

Arnaboldi, M. and Lapsley, I. (2014) Enterprise-wide risk management and organizational fit: a comparative study. *Journal of Organizational Effectiveness: People and Performance*, 1(4): 365–377, http://dx.doi.org/10.1108/JOEPP-09-2014-0056.

Beck, U. (1992). *Risk Society: Towards a New Modernity*. London, Sage Publications.

Behn, R. (1998) The new public management paradigm and the search for democratic accountability. *International Public Management Journal*, 1(2).

Boyle, L. (2020). Brazil is not the environmental villain, Bolsonaro tells UN. *The Independent*, 23 September.

Boyle, L. and Anderson, K. (2020) What would Trump's re-election mean for the climate crisis? *The Independent*, 28 August.

Bower, T. (2020) *Boris Johnson: The Gambler*. London, W.H. Allen.

Brunsson, N. (1992) Reform as routine. *Scandinavian Journal of Management*, 5(3).

Brunsson, N. and Olsen, J.P. (1993) *The Reforming Organization*. London, Routledge.

Calvert, J., Arbuthnott, G., Leake, J. and Gadher, D. (2020) 22 days of dither and delay on coronavirus that cost thousands of British lives. Sunday Times Insight Team, *The Sunday Times*, May 24.

Chapman, B. (2020) UK economy shrunk twice as much as any other G7 nation's during the coronavirus pandemic. *The Independent*, November: 16.

Charlson, R. J., Schwartz, S. E., Hales, J. M., Cess, R. D., Coakley Jr., J. A., Hansen, J. E., and Hofmann, D. J. (1992) Climate forcing by anthropogenic aerosols. *Science*, 255, 423–430.

Clarke, F. and Dean, G. (2007) *Indecent Disclosure: Gilding the Corporate Lily*. Cambridge, Cambridge University Press.

Cox, P., Betts, R. A., Jones, C. D., Spall S. A. and Totterdell, I. J. (2000) Acceleration of global warming due to carbon-cycle feedbacks in a coupled climate model, *Nature*, 408: 184–187.

Dansgaard, W.*et al.* (1993) Evidence for general instability of past climate from a 250-kyr ice-core record, *Nature*, 364, 15 July: 218–220.

Deloach, J. (2018) Key elements of the risk management process, January 10, https://www.corp oratecomplianceinsights.com/key-elements.

Elliott, F. (2020) Stop trying to defect blame home care chiefs tell Johnson, *The Times*, 8 July: 10.

Folland, C., Rayner, N.A., Brown, S.J., Smith, T.M., Shen, S.S.P., Parker, D.E., Macadam, I., Jones, P.D., Jones, R.N., Nicholls, N. and Sexton, D.M.H. (2001) Global temperature change and its uncertainties since 1861, *Geophysical Research Letters*, 28(1): 2485–2669.

Giddens, A. (2003) *Runaway World: How Globalization is Reshaping Our Lives*. London: Routledge.

Hamilton, S. and Micklethwait, A. (2006) *Greed and Corporate Failure: The Lessons from Recent Disasters*. Palgrave Macmillan.

Hood, C. (1991) Public management for all seasons, *Public Administration*, 6 (3).

Hood, C. (1995) The NPM in the 1980s: variations on a theme. *Accounting, Organizations and Society*, 20 (2/3).

Hood, C. (2002) The risk game and the blame game, *Government and Opposition*, 37(1).

Hood, C. and Rothstein, H. (2001) Risk regulation under pressure: problem solving or blame shifting? *Administration and Society*, 33 (1): 21–53. doi:10.1177/00953990122019677

Horton, R. (2020) *The Covid-19 Catastrophe: What's Gone Wrong and How to Stop it Happening Again*. Cambridge, Polity Press.

Johnsen, A. (2012) Why does poor performance get so much attention in public policy? *Financial Accountability & Management*, 28 (2): 121–142.

Jones, B. and Baumgartner, F. (2005) *The Politics of Attention: How Government Prioritizes Problems*. University of Chicago Press.

Kulp, S.A. and Strauss, B.H. (2019) New elevation data triple estimates of global vulnerability to sea-level rise and coastal flooding. *Nature Communications*, 10, Article number: 4844, October.

Lapsley, I. (2009) The NPM agenda: cruellest invention of the human spirit? *Abacus*, 45 (1): 1–21.

Lapsley, I. (2020) An uncertain, erratic story: the pandemic in the UK. *Journal of Accounting and Organisational Change*, 16(4): 549–555.

Mathiesen, K. (2017) Tony Abbott says climate change is 'probably doing good': former Australian PM delivers speech in London comparing global warming action to 'killing goats to appease volcano gods', *The Guardian*, 9 October.

McTague, T. (2020) Covid revealed sickness at the heart of Britain, *The Times*, 15 August: 30–31.

Mehr, R.I. and Hedges, B.A. (1963) *Risk Management in the Business Enterprise*. Homewood, Illinois, Irwin.

Merton, R.K. (1936) The unanticipated consequences of purposive social action. *American Sociological Review*, 1 (6).

Miller, K.D. (1998) Economic exposure and integrated risk management. *Strategic Management Journal*, 19 (5): 497–514.

Narwen, G. (2021a) Borrowing jumps to record levels amid more pandemic restrictions. *The Times*, 23 January: 50.

Narwen, G. (2021b) Economy's 10% fall in 2020 was the worst for three centuries. *The Times*, 23 January: 2.

NTI (2019) Global Health Security Index: building collective action and accountability. USA, National Threat Institute.

Office of Budget Responsibility (2020) Fiscal Sustainability Report, 14 July. London, OBR.

O'Neill, S. (2021) How Britain got it right in the race for a vaccine. *The Times*, 6 February: 10.

O'Neill, S. and Whipple, T. (2021) How Britain placed its bets boldly and reaped rewards. *The Times*, 2 February: 9.

Palermo, T. (2014) Accountability and expertise in public sector risk management: a case study. *Financial Accountability & Management*, 30 (3): 322–341.

Parmesan, C. and Yohe, G. (2003) A globally coherent fingerprint of climate change impacts across natural systems, *Nature*, 421: 37–42.

Power, M. (1994) *The Audit Explosion*. London, Demos.

Power, M. (1997) *The Audit Society: Rituals of Verification*. Oxford, Oxford University Press.

Power, M. (2004) *The Risk Management of Everything*. London, Demos.

Power, M. (2007) *Organized Uncertainty: Designing a World of Risk Management*. Oxford, Oxford University Press.

Power, M. (2009) The risk management of nothing. *Accounting. Organizations and Society*, 34 (6–7): 849–855.

Rika, N. and Jacobs, K. (2019) Reputational risk and environmental performance auditing: a study in the Australian commonwealth public sector. *Financial Accountability & Management*, 35 (2): 182–198.

Root, T., Price, J.T., Hall, K.R., Schneider, S.H., Rosenzweig, C. and Pounds, J.A. (2003) Fingerprints of global warming on wild animals and plants. *Nature*, 421: 57–60.

Telegraph Reporters (2020) Boris Johnson 'scrapped Cabinet pandemic committee six months before coronavirus hit UK'. *Daily Telegraph*, 13 June.https://www.telegraph.co.uk/politics/2020/06/13boris-johnson-scrapped-cabinet-pandemic-committee-six-months/.

Thomas, C.*et al.* (2004) Extinction risk from climate change, *Nature*, 427 (6970): 145–148.

Walters, S. (2020) Revealed: Boris Johnson scrapped Cabinet Ministers' pandemic team six months before coronavirus hit Britain. *Daily Mail*, 12 June.https://www.dailymail.co.uk/news/article-8416075/Boris-Johnson-scrapped-Cabinet-Ministers-pandemic-team-six-months-coronavirus-hit-Britain-.

Whittaker-Wood, F. (2020) The most polluted cities in the world. 25 March. https://www.theecoexperts.co.uk.

Williams, A. and Hems, M.H. (1964) *Risk Management and Insurance*. New York, McGraw Hill.

Section five

The reflective manager in action

13 Concluding comments

The reflective manager in action

Irvine Lapsley, Ola Mattisson and Ulf Ramberg

Introduction

In this concluding chapter of this book, we discuss: (1) the practice and hazards of recipe management, (2) further thoughts on reflective management, (3) a substantive agenda for reflective management and (4) our conclusion on "reflective-management-in action".

Recipe management: a fatal attraction

Managing public services requires public managers that can handle complexities, uncertainties and multifaceted interests from a variety of stakeholders in a context of limited resources, financial as well as physical. This is a demanding challenge for any manager with high ambitions to succeed. Here we explore whether recipe management is the answer to this challenge.

For many years, there have been strands of the literature on public sector organizations which have noted, observed and commented on the phenomenon of "recipe management" (see, for example, Meyer and Rowan, 1977; DiMaggio and Powell, 1983; Brunsson et al., 2012). Recipe management is the imitation, copying, duplication, repetition or mimicry of the management practices and procedures of another entity or entities. In Meyer and Rowan's (1977) version of recipe management, the copying of another organization's management may be interpreted as a signal of excellence – particularly by observers outside the organization. However, this attempt to present themselves as modern and up to date may have no substantive influence on the efficacy and efficiency of the organization – it is purely symbolic. This perspective was further developed by DiMaggio and Powell (1983), who argued that isomorphism was widely used in government entities. Isomorphism is the process by which organizations in similar fields seek to mimic the management and organizational practices of organizations regarded as the leading entities in the relevant field. However, subsequent contributions have challenged this idea of isomorphism. So, the idea of organizations passively accepting the desire to duplicate the actions of other entities has been challenged by the counter argument that organizations may appear to duplicate but may just modify or adapt whichever given practice is apparently a direct copy (Brunsson and Jacobsen, 2000; Rovik, 2002; Lounsbury, 2008). Nevertheless, there are trends within the public to transfer, by mimicry, private sector management practices, under the label of NPM (Hood, 1991, 1995; Lapsley, 2008). A strand of this literature is the way global actors (such as international management consultancies, oversight bodies

DOI: 10.4324/9781003154389-18

(IMF, World Bank) and networks, such as the G7 countries) became carriers of the latest fads and fashions. These carriers introduce new management techniques and ideas to the market or at least advocate them for adoption (Sahlin-Andersson and Engwall, 2002; Djelic and Sahlin-Andersson, 2006; Lapsley, 2009). However, it is suggested here that such acts of mimicry or recipe management are the antithesis of reflective management. The attractions of an option which appears to be working elsewhere offers an easier path than "rediscovering the wheel".

But the reality is many of these reforms are not reinventing the wheel. A devastating critique of the processes by which these managerial or policy reforms are enacted is offered by Brunsson (2006, p. 229):

> Those who want to convince others to reform will invest in failure and hope. They can be expected to argue that the last reform failed, or, at least, that it did not quite succeed, but that the next reform will. Demonstrating that organizations are still not working rationally seems to be the easiest part of selling rational reforms, but inspiring hope is more complex. A strategy that seems to be common and often successful is connected to the belief in change. Sellers of management concepts and reforms often argue that we live in a turbulent world where most phenomena are new, and where experience is no longer valid. And their concepts and ideas for organizational reform are presented as genuinely new – as very different from previous reform concepts. One cannot learn from experience but should apply whatever new concept is adapted to the new situation. People trying to encourage reform are well served by giving new names to old ideas – even ideas as old as the idea of the rational organization. People who want to avoid their own reforms being seen as impractical, or even as failures, may try to secure a continued interest in idea and talk rather than practice. This mechanism helps to make a reform appear successful prior to implementation, or without it ever being implemented. It is unnecessary to wait for implementation when evaluating the success of the reform. Hence, the classic reform problem of implementation merely evaporates.

There are many examples of recipe management which result in only symbolic management rather any substantive improvements in operational activities – the fatal attraction.

Further thoughts on reflective management

The biggest challenge to making sense of "reflection in action" is the way in which "action" is linked with "reflection" (Gosling and Mintzberg, 2003). In their view, this distinction is complex because action refers to doing things in situ, whereas reflection is an abstract activity. The use of action without thinking is described by Gosling and Mintzberg (2003, p.3) as "thoughtless". At first glance this may seem harsh, but Gosling and Mintzberg are referring to a form of repetitive action which does not require deep thought. On the other hand, they depict reflection without action as essentially passive – as having no impact on the organization.

To address this problem and close the gap between "action" and "reflection", they propose five mindsets which should be adopted by managers who wish it to use "reflection-in-action" (op. cit., p. 4):

1   Managing Self: the reflective mindset
2   Managing Organizations: the analytic mindset
3   Managing Context: the wordly mindset
4   Managing Relationships: the collaborative mindset
5   Managing Change: the action mindset.

The above five dimensions of reflection-in-action are the Gosling and Mintzberg (2003) approach to reflective management. The authors acknowledge that these are not tightly coupled, hard and fast definitions (Gosling and Mintzberg, 2003, p. 59), but these concepts are important in framing reflective management. It is important to note that these are ways of thinking which they recommend which collectively make up reflective management. Each of these strands of reflective management has a distinct target of its own. As the authors (Gosling and Minzberg, 2003, p. 54) explain:

> [The five mindsets] are ways in which managers interpret and deal with the world around them. Each has a dominant subject, or target, of its own. For reflection, the subject is the self: there can be no insight without self-knowledge. Analysis goes a step beyond that, to the organization; organizations depend on the systematic decomposition of activities, and that's what analysis is all about. Beyond the organization lies what we consider the subject of the wordly mindset, namely context- the worlds around the organization. The collaborative mindset takes the subject beyond the self, into the manager's network of relationships. Finally, the fifth dimension, the action mindset, pulls everything together through the process of change – in self, organization, context and collaboration.

These mindsets are frames of reference, attitudes which open managers up to new vistas and new ideas. But these perspectives may create problems if there is over-obsessive use of any one dimension (Gosling and Mintzberg, 2003, p. 55). A major feature of this perspective is the desire to encourage managers to step back from all the prevailing pressures they face and reflect thoughtfully on their experiences. When experiences are considered in this way, they become much more influential. Fundamentally, this may lead to changed perceptions of everyday phenomena and occurrences. Regarding the analytic mindset, this relaxes complex phenomena by decomposing them into constituent parts (Gosling and Mintzberg, 2003, p. 56). For the reflective manager, there is a need to go beyond conventional approaches to analysis to see how analytical frameworks deliver and to be skeptical about recipe management (see earlier discussion). This approach provides a deep analysis which does not seek to simplify complex decisions but to both enhance complexity and the organization's capacity to take action (Gosling and Mintzberg, 2003, p. 57). The exercise of the "worldly mindset" requires experienced managers who are sophisticated and knowledgeable. They need to have awareness of different cultures, different practices and social customs to have an appreciation of how things could be different. Gosling and Mintzberg (2003, p. 58) suggest that managers need to get out of their offices, beyond their towers, to spend time where products are produced, customers served and environments threatened. The collaborative mindset would be described as network management in contemporary literature. This dimension of reflective management is getting inside other manager's minds. This may spread not only the managerial message but also enable a wider set of contributors. For example, the different functional specialists could come together and be involved in the management mission for the organization.

Finally, we reflect further on the action mindset. This not a narrative about a driven horseman. Instead, it is necessary to acquire a sensitive awareness of the organizational terrain and the capacity of the management team. This dimension is framed in the context of change – but reflective management may entail minor change or even a steady state, both of which have their own challenges. In the review of this mindset, Gosling and Mintzberg (2003) observed that contemporary management has an overwhelming emphasis on action at the expense of reflection. So, they recommend an awareness of what needs to change in organizations and what does not. In the latter case, careful nurturing would pay greater dividends than making changes which key actors do not understand and which may undermine the organization's effectiveness. It is possible to observe changes which are action-oriented but not reflective. As Gosling and Mintzberg (2003, p. 62) express it:

> Action results from deliberate strategies, carefully planned, that unfold as systematically managed sequences of decisions. This is the analytical mindset not the Action one.

Successful change is not a mechanical process of following itemized steps. Action and reflection have to blend together. Managers need to be alert but also curious and willing to improvise and even experiment.

These observations are on the importance of expertise, knowledge of the organization, maturity in understanding, networks in management culmination in reflective action.

The reflective mindset is a mindset where the manager, in line with the thinking of Nonaka et al. (2014) and Schön (1983), embraces the possibility to create meaning in a situational practice and by that be able to execute informed managerial judgements. To apply a more reflective mindset may also strengthen formative learning and may also attenuate the traditional focus on summative feedback learning, such as weekly or monthly reports.

Thus, in his seminal work on reflective practice Schön (1983) describes this way of "managing a problem" when the manager by artistic and intuitive processes engages "in reflective conversations with the situation" at hand. According to Schön, this approach to problem-solving is used by professionals when they try to understand and solve problems where technically rationality, with fixed and clear ends, are not in place. As many chapters in this book have shown day to day work for managers in public services, to a great extent can be characterized by value conflicts between stakeholders, uncertainty, weak cause and effect relationships, and instability. To have the time and possibilities to reflect-in-action at the precise point of a managerial intervention may not be easy – we comment on this further below.

Both Schön (1987) and Yanow and Tsoukas (2009) introduce the concept of surprise as a trigger for reflection-in-action. They envisage surprise as taking different forms: a "malfunction", a "temporary breakdown" or a "total breakdown" (Yanow and Tsoukas, 2009, p. 1342). However, the introduction of surprise, while interesting, is what we would conventionally regard as uncertainty, although most likely of the Rumsfeldian "unknown unknowns" variety. Here we use the notion of surprise but regard it as interchangeable with uncertainty.

The identification of reflective managers is aided by the attributes set out by Yanow and Tsoukas (2009, p. 1359):

1 Reflective practice is intended to encourage decision-makers to explore "other ways" of considering what is before them.
2 The reflective practitioners are "permeable" – they have an attitude of inquiry rather than one derived from the authority of their position.
3 This approach requires openness and transparency as the decision maker may not have all required knowledge to resolve the issue being addressed.
4 The reflective manager is cognizant of unfolding events which may include surprises.

These processes will challenge existing frames of reference, taken-for-granted assumptions and typical mindsets. But this is most likely to occur as practical reflexivity after the moment of action or improvisation and in the form of retrospective self-questioning (Yanow and Tsoukas, 2009). In their view, this identification process may be more of a reflection after than during interventions. This may make it easier to identify breaks in routines and consequent improvisations by decision makers.

The above observations, plus those of Schön (1983, pp. 26–29), that "reflection-in-action" has experimental characteristics, which often take a sequential twist from routinized action, the encountering of surprise, reflections and then action. This sequence is regarded by Schön (1983) as taking place during flows, interactions and actions in which current activities are carried out, with the possibility of improvisations in action. This framing resonates with the context of firefighting, with the need for managers to think on their feet. So, a pressing need for problems to be addressed and in situations where time is short.

However, Nonaka et al. (2014) argue that history is full of management breakdowns, where you cannot blame a lack of knowledge as a reason. If you want to blame management breakdowns it may be more obvious to blame them on the lack of wise judgement, because when acting wisely you act by:

> acknowledging the limits and limitations of formal knowledge and its sometimes undesired effects, how it twists and turns the world, folding it into shadows as much as it opens up novel possibilities for consideration.
>
> (Nonaka et al., 2014, p. 367)

Reflection, fantasy and the ability to improvise, but also knowledge about what you know and what you don't know and may ignore, is needed if you strive for wisdom. But to act wisely as a manager for public services you also need an in-depth understanding of your service and to constantly, over time, be sensitive and open to learning in different situation-specific issues related to the management problem at hand (Nonaka et al., 2014).

Reflective management: a substantive agenda

Managing public services is nothing to be performed, executed or solved as a task or decision at a single point in time. Instead, it is a continuously ongoing process with trade-offs and priorities where pieces are to be brought together to balance a variety of demands in relation to the capacity to resolve these tensions. Therefore, there is a need and wish for tools and solutions to help managers in these struggles. There is a flood of models and tools for managers claiming to contribute and solve major managerial problems. By introducing new concepts and installing systems to support them there are great hopes of overcoming both daily obstacles and imperfections in practice. However, despite a steady flow of novel implementation ideas, managers still face recurring problems with no quick fixes in evidence. There are no off-the-shelf solutions to resolve fundamental management problems regarding organizational structures, delivery mechanisms or outcomes.

This message is clear and consistent on managerial implications of this book, throughout all chapters, although from different perspectives. There is a shift, or transition, to something else, or something different, compared to how it "always has been" to manage public services. The chapters in this book, in various ways, suggest a need for a more reflective approach when dealing with the management challenges in public sector services.

1. Strategic positioning

For public services there are a plethora of normative models and approaches advising on strategic positioning of the organization. Section two contains examples of areas where normative models and concepts benefit from a more balanced view on implementation and expected results. In Chapter 2 it is shown that a vision can make explicit values and priorities in an organization. The complex setting of public services brings a need for a clear vision to become powerful. However, the formulation of the vision is not a task for an executive committee. Instead, it takes a continuous process of communication within the organization, with active participation to define and articulate an inclusive vision to strive for collectively. Starting from the vision, organizations also need strategizing, which is discussed in Chapter 3. There is a need to find ways to strategically manage public services in more complex contexts, as addressing the unique conditions of public services brings dilemmas and paradoxes. By going beyond an orderly view of the organization and applying a more inclusive, dialogue-based approach to strategizing, we find new ways to understand how democratic, political and managerial requirements can meet. The case studies on change management offered a reflective, nuanced way to deploy management consultants in change programs. This reveals a need for managers to step back and reflect not only on what they aim to achieve, but how they will enable their aspirations. There are issues over the availability of internal expertise and the level of resources needed to seek external management consultants. There are also issues about how best to engage with external management consultants which offer the prospect of both learning and implementation effectiveness.

All in all, the chapters in section two question the fundamental issue of how to strategically position the provision of public services. The complexity inherent in these activities in relation to the variety of circumstances of government entities bring a need for a process of continuous search for the effective means to develop. There is not a single approach or tool to set the structure and solve problems. Instead, it takes a gradual approach of searching and defining the elements of the organizational capacity to deliver public services.

2. Renewal of core practices

In section three, four chapters discuss the renewal of core practices, addressing the importance of reflection and learning. Chapter 5 elaborates on the use of strategic cost management and how it can be used, not solely but in connection with other more qualitative data. Cost data is a representation of the organization that can be used for benchmarking as a base for discussing the future strategic orientation of the organization in a positive manner. However, at the same time it is a demanding task to discuss controversies with other levels. A manager has in these practices an opportunity to initiate reflections and learning for development of the services. Learning also appears to be central in Chapter 6 when discussing performance management. Changes in governance structures imply a new use of performance management. Instead of being a tool for central control, the purpose turns to supporting learning and improvements. And the crucial factor is the use. A reflective manager will not take measures and indicators literally. Rather than "final answers", measures and indicators will be the starting point of a development process that includes qualitative and experience-based data, supporting incremental changes rather than radical shifts.

Dimensions of development and learning are also evident in the discussion of public procurement. From a situation emphasizing legal expertise to avoid mistakes, public procurement can be turned into a tool that supports development in public service provision and delivery. Supporting this type of initiative requires knowledge from multiple areas as well as an organization which supports combining them in a reflective way. Ambitions to use procurement as a tool for development requires support from policy makers and alignment with visions and strategic goals at the organizational level. This calls for an ongoing dialogue and a vital process where visions and goals are related to the specific service supply, not only when signing the contract but during the period of delivery. There are great expectations for what can be achieved from public procurement but reflective capacity will be of use for the task as in reflective management; learning from experiences is vital.

High expectations are also connected to digitalization as a tool. Chapter 8 elaborates on challenges related to the implementation of ICT (information and communications technology) solutions. Even though digitalization has several obvious merits, effective implementation of new solutions requires careful consideration and extensive changes to organizational processes. This development should not be seen as a quick fix. Its implementation needs a comprehensive analysis of the far-reaching implications in different fields. This approach to ICT should create awareness of the known effects as well as learning to understand the unknown effects of new systems. The challenge for policy makers and managers is to implement these kinds of systems with very limited knowledge about the effects. This calls for a reflective approach and ongoing learning to facilitate future adjustments and developments.

The renewal of core practices all strikes a chord of established tools in a new setting used in novel ways to handle uncertainties in the public service supply. Due to the complex challenges, strategic decisions and actions need to be taken based on incomplete information about the conditions and potential effects. Instead of bringing normative algorithms on what to do, attention could be directed to the opportunities for learning in the process. Managers need to act, but with a reflective mindset there will be openings for adjusting and re-adjusting as the strategies put into effect using the management concepts at hand.

3. Innovations in management practices

There are repeated, raised concerns within public services about the uncritical adoption of tools developed for other contexts or purposes. This is a challenge in which reflective management has much to offer and the obvious examples of recipe management in the selection of new tools may result in short-term fixes and long-term damage to the organization. Within this section we discuss the topics of corporate branding, Lean Management, resilience and risk management. The selection of any of these tools by management needs a very careful review of specific settings before proceeding to implementation.

In Chapter 9, the authors raise concerns about uncritically introducing branding concepts from the private sector into public services. For managers, the public context requires them to balance public values and market values and be sensitive to when it is necessary to prioritize one over the other. An increased use of branding in public settings brings implications for managers as branding orientation can impact transparency, inclusion and reflexivity, or critical thinking. Experimenting and development demands a reflexive to safeguard these values when applying new concepts.

One innovation which is spreading widely across public services is the adoption of Lean Management. The chapter on Lean Management questions whether a tool devised by and for a major vehicle manufacturer is also applicable to public services. Organizations adopting a Lean Management initiative for their organization have ample opportunity for standing back from this approach to public service delivery and reflecting on how and where it might work. There is a real danger of public service managers being seduced by the idea of a model which guarantees "more with less". The "more with less" mantra has considerable appeal to managers who have been hit with decades of austerity which severely constrains the kinds of services which they can provide. There are multiple interpretations of what "lean" means, from short-term cost-cutting to long-term cultural change. This range of possibilities requires a great deal of thought and discussion. This may be presented to public service organizations as a quick fix – but it is not.

The chapter on resilience explains how resilient management may be constituted and understood by discussing resilience and sensemaking. Managing resilience requires sensitive managers. It is about an identification with your village and neighbours, being stronger than an administrative entity. Resilience in local governments is cultivated in social contexts and needs constant attention as structural conditions for the public service supply change over time. This chapter therefore concludes that there is limited normative advice to give to managers about resilience. Instead, they need to act themselves, navigating the landscape of changing conditions, settling with plausibility rather than certainty.

Finally, this section has a chapter on the risks of risk management. Many organizations will already have risk management systems. But this practice may have reverted to a symbolic or ceremonial activity. That is a mechanism which does not make your organization more efficient or effective, but because you can say you have a risk management unit, they will see you as effective. However, probing beneath the surface may reveal no such thing. The need to challenge an ineffective system which you have had for some time is a perfect project for reflective management. This chapter shows how a revitalized risk management can refocus and reenergize organizations with ceremonial risk management.

Conclusion

Managers need to have answers to three fundamental management questions in order to complete their mission. These are: why, how and what. As shown throughout this book, the answers to these questions are sometimes hard to find, especially when the management tools and ideas used in public services are based on technical rationality that rarely exists in the public sector. So, there are dangers in jumping to conclusions about possible solutions to a management problem. This book supports an approach to management that invites a more reflective and informed decision making. A manager in public services may face daily and hourly situations where pressures and expectations of actions to solve problems exist. For sure, sometimes immediate action is needed. But more importantly, there is a need to ask if past experiences or other, more diverse perspectives can give any guidance before rushing to conclusions. However, to be part of this kind of reflective institutional arrangement also puts some demand on the public manager's willingness to adopt a more reflective approach. To fulfil the mission that all managers have, to secure efficiency, legitimacy and renewal, is not easy. A great portion of humility is needed.

There are three elements of public services organizations which might be seen as impediments to the successful implementation of reflective management: (1) the sense that you are on your own with this new idea called reflective management, (2) the way reflective management may be seen as unnecessary because public service organizations have so many reporting systems and information flows that reflective management may be seen as unnecessary and (3) the typical public service organization has a hierarchical structure in a bureaucracy, with well-defined procedures which appear to deliver all public services as required (Weber, 1964). However, these three arguments against reflective management are actually endorsements for the need for reflective management.

1   The idea that you are the sole person interested in reflective management might be off-putting. But first check for kindred spirits. The identifiers above show how the other reflective thinkers may work. Be open and transparent about reflective management thinking. Talk about your ideas. Engage with people in your department. Look for boundary spanners in your organization. Create discussion groups where managers can explore possible reflective management tasks. Reach out beyond your organization to other organizations in the same field. Reach out internationally to establish broader networks. The creation of a network of people with the same interests is a rewarding experience – particularly in the field of reflective management.

2   Regarding the strength of existing information flows to public service managers, we could find a lot – budgets, cost analyses, benchmarking exercises, value for money studies. Therefore, it is possible to argue that contemporary possibilities to successfully manage public services in a knowledgeable way is good, given the massive amount of management literature. Especially if you add what advanced business and information systems are able to do regarding collecting and analyzing data to support decision-making. At first sight, being informed does not seem to be an issue for managers in the public sector. On the principle that more knowledge about management techniques and ideas and more data about the public services output and stakeholders should be able to create conditions for better management decision-making. However, these information flows from existing information systems represent what Gosling and Mintzberg (2003) refer to as the analytic mindset. But this is not reflective management. Managers may be tempted to try recipe management in this scenario. To be reflective, managers need to stand back and consider and re-evaluate the available information and its assumptions and implications to realize the active mindset of Gosling and Mintzberg (2003). The

existence of elaborate systems of information may indicate an organization which is too absorbed by current practices to think about how things could change: an ideal location for a reflective thinker.

3   Further, where public managers work the organizations have many of the characteristics of a bureaucracy; a hierarchical, top-down structure which prioritizes procedures and rules, a place where the formal organization's structure, in its "nature", often prioritizes values such as stability and predictability. A more reflective approach to organize the work would be, in Schön's (1983, p. 338) words, to have an institutional arrangement that:

> places a high priority on flexible procedures, differentiated responses, qualitative appreciation of complex processes and decentralized responsibility for judgement and action.

These comments resonate with the reforms observed by Hood (1991, 1995) in which private sector styles of management were adopted by public sector institutions. However, many bureaucratic structures remain. While this may be seen as an impediment to an innovation like reflective management, we should note that there is evidence that bureaucracies have the capacity to innovate and be creative (Thompson, 1965; Hlavacek and Thompson, 1973; Landry and Caust, 2017). Thompson (1965) supported increased professionalization and looser and untidy structures to promote innovative bureaucracy, while suggesting boundary spanning within bureaucracies could lead to innovation. It has always been suggested that projectification can lead to innovation within bureaucracies (Hlavacek and Thompson, 1973). This idea of the project and project teams as a means of innovation has been used successfully in practice (Fred and Hall, 2017). Furthermore, Landry and Caust (2017, p.41) argue that talented, risk-taking and action-oriented people are highly regarded by the world's most successful cities, which are often bureaucratic structures. Indeed, Bichard (2008) has identified a series of important innovations from government and government agencies, including DNA, the world wide web, penicillin, radar, the moon landing and fibre optics. These comments are supportive of the idea of creative bureaucracy as a site where reflective management can flourish.

References

Bichard, M. (2008) Can we deliver better public services for less money? *Design Council Magazine*, A Virtual Discussion, 4, Summer: 16–21.

Brunsson, N. (2006) *Mechanisms of Hope: Maintaining the Dream of the Rational Organization*, Copenhagen Business School Press.

Brunsson, N., Rasche, A. and Seidl, D. (2012) The dynamics of standardization: Three perspectives on standards in organization studies. *Organization Studies*, 33: 613–632.

DiMaggio, P.J. and Powell, W.W. (1983) The iron cage revisited: Institutional isomorphism and collective rationality in organizational fields. *American Sociological Review*, 48 (2): 147–160.

Djelic, M.-L. and Sahlin-Andersson, K. (Eds.), (2009) *Transnational Governance: Institutional Dynamics of Regulation*. Cambridge/New York, Cambridge University Press.

Fred, M. and Hall, P. (2017) A projectified public administration: How projects in Swedish local governments become instruments for political and managerial concerns. Statsvetenskaplig tidskrift. Årgång, 119 (1).

Gosling, J. and Mintzberg, H. (2003) The five minds of a manager. *Harvard Business Review*, 81 (11): 54–63.

Hlavacek, J. and Thompson, V.A. (1973) Bureaucracy and new product innovation. *Academy of Management Journal*, 16 (3): 361–372.

Hood, C. (1991) A public management for all seasons. *Public Administration*, 6 (3): 3–19.

Hood, C. (1995) The NPM in the 1980s: Variations on a theme. *Accounting, Organizations and Society*, 20 (2/3): 93–109.

Landry, C. and Caust, M. (2017) *The Creative Bureaucracy and its Radical Common Sense.* Stroud, UK, Comedia.

Lapsley, I. (2008) The NPM agenda: Back to the future. *Financial Accountability & Management*, 24 (1): 77–96.

Lapsley, I. (2009) New public management: The cruellest invention of the human spirit? *Abacus*, 45 (1): 1–21.

Lounsbury, M. (2008) Institutional rationality and practice variation: New directions in the institutional analysis of practice. *Accounting, Organizations and Society*, 33 (4–5): 349–361.

Meyer, J.W. and Rowan, B. (1977) Institutionalized organizations: Formal structure as myth and ceremony. *American Journal of Sociology*, 83 (2): 340–363.

Nannaka, I., Chia, R., Holt, R. and Peltokorpi, V. (2014) Wisdom, management and organization. *Management Learning*, 54 (4): 365–376.

Røvik, K.A. (2002) The secret of the winners: Managements ideas that flow, in K. Sahlin-Andersson and L. Engwall (Eds.) *The Expansion of Management Knowledge: Carriers, Flows and Sources.* Stanford, CA: Stanford University Press: 113–144.

Sahlin-Andersson, K. and Engwall, L. (Eds.) (2002) *The Expansion of Management Knowledge: Carriers, Flows and Sources.* Stanford, CA: Stanford University Press.

Schön, D. (1983) *The Reflective Practitioner: How Professionals Think in Action.* Basic Books.

Thompson, V.A. (1965) Bureaucracy and innovation. *Administrative Science Quarterly*, 10 (1): 1–20.

Weber, M. (1964) *The Theory of Social and Economic Organization.* Oxford/New York, Oxford University Press.

Yanow, D. and Tsoukas, H. (2009) What is reflection-in-action? A phenomenological account. *Journal of Management Studies*, 46 (8): 1339–1364.

Index

Locators in **bold** refer to tables and those in *italics* to figures.

public relations: brand orientation 119, 120, 126–127; politics of attention 163; strategic landscapes 32
public sector information (PSI) 107–108, **108**
purpose of an organisation *see* corporate vision

Rational reasoning perspective (strategic thinking) 34, 35
rational strategic environment 33–34, 41, **42**
recipe management 187–188, 194
reflection-in-action 7–8, 188–191
reflective approach 6–8, 9; brand orientation 119–120, 121, 126–127, **129–130**, 130–131; implementation 195–196; mindset 188–191; need for 10; performance management 90; strategic cost management 78; a substantive agenda 191–194
reflective mindset 189, 193
Remedies Directive 97–98
renewal of core practices 9
reputation management 166–167; *see also* public relations
resilience *see* organizational resilience
resource programming configuration 73–76
resources: brand orientation 120–121, 122–123; cost accounting *68–69*, 68–70, 74–76; Covid-19 pandemic public funding support **177**, 177–178; Lean Management 139–141, **141**, 143, 146; strategic landscapes 31
risk assessment 164–165, **175**, 178–179
risk management 10, 163–164, 194; as ceremonial 166–167; climate change and air pollution 167–169, **169**; Covid-19 pandemic and trade-offs 169–172, 173–180, **176, 177, 179**; critical elements **164**, 164–166, **179**; managerial implications 180–181; relevance of 170–171
risk society 163

Schön, D. 190, 191, 196
schools, brand orientation case study 122–123, 128, **129–130**
Science, Technology and Innovation (STI) 87–88
scientific research, climate change 168–169
self-knowledge 178
sensemaking, organizational resilience 150, 152, 154–155, 156–157, 158–159
service balance (strategic cost management) 70–73, 76
Simon, Herbert 154, 155
social development 158
social media: health care information case study 112; political context 109–110
Spotify, mission statement 18, 22

strategic cost management 61; Italian higher education case study 61–67; managerial implications 76–78; organizational reshaping configuration 67–70, 76; renewal of core practices 192–193; resource programming configuration 73–76; service balance case study 70–73
strategic landscapes: acting strategically 36–40; awareness of the fundamental conditions 31–32; context and concept of strategy 32–34; cost accounting 61; managerial implications 41–42; thinking strategically 34–36
strategic planning 36–37
strategic positioning 8–9, 192
strategizing 9; acting strategically 36–40; awareness of the fundamental conditions 31–32; context and concept of strategy 32–34; cost 61, 62–65; managerial implications 41–42; positioning 192; thinking strategically 34–36
summative learning 190
sustainability: brand orientation 131; procurement 98–99; public organizations 6; risk management 167–169
Svedala prison case study 124–125
Swedish Transport Agency 24–25
Swedish welfare case study **152**, 152–157, **157**, 160
Systemic school (strategic thinking) 35
systemic strategic environment 33, 34, 41, **42**

targets *see* goal congruence; objectives
technical rationality 195
tender process 100
Thévenot, Laurent 127–128, 131
top-down management 136
Toyota Production System (TPS) 134–135, 137, 140; *see also* Lean Management
transparency: brand orientation 121–123, **129–130**; digitalization in the public sector 107, 109, **110, 114**; performance management 79, 81; public procurement 94, 95
Trump, Donald 167
Tsoukas, H. 190–191

UK government: climate change 167–169; Covid-19 approach and trade-offs 173–180, **176, 177, 179**; risk management 163–164
universities: Alpha University case study **45**, 45–48; Italian higher education cost management 61–67; Lean Management 145, **146**; resource programming configuration 74–76; service balance case study 70–73

values: brand orientation 127–128, **129–130**; Lean Management 135, 137; managers' role

Printed in the United States
by Baker & Taylor Publisher Services